AF684677

Source Selection Answer Book

Second Edition

Source Selection Answer Book

Second Edition

Vernon J. Edwards

MANAGEMENTCONCEPTS
Vienna, Virginia

MANAGEMENTCONCEPTS
8230 Leesburg Pike, Suite 800
Vienna, Virginia 22182
Phone: (703) 790-9595
Fax: (703) 790-1371
www.managementconcepts.com

Copyright © 2006 by Management Concepts, Inc.

All rights reserved. No part of this book may be reproduced in any form or media without the written permission of the publisher, except for brief quotations in review articles.

Printed in the United States of America

Library of Congress Cataloging-in-Publication Data

Edwards, Vernon J., 1947–
Source selection answer book / Vernon J. Edwards.—2nd ed.
p. cm.
Includes index.
ISBN 1-56726-172-8
1. Government purchasing—Law and legislation—United States—Miscellanea. 2. Letting of contracts—United States—Miscellanea. 3. Government purchasing—Miscellanea. I. Title.

KF850.E39 2006
346.7302'3—dc22

2005054431

About the Author

Vernon J. Edwards provides government contracts training to federal agencies, contractors, and subcontractors. He has more than 30 years of experience in the field of government contracts. He has been a contract negotiator and contracting officer for the U.S. Air Force and worked in that capacity in several weapon system program offices. He was assigned to Headquarters, Air Force Systems Command, where he was a tri-services contracting officer, chief of plans, assistant command competition advocate, and member of the contract review committee. He was a contract negotiator for the U.S. Small Business Administration and the Director of Construction Contracting for the Bonneville Power Administration. From 1987 until 1997, he was a member of the faculty of The George Washington University government contracts programs in both the School of Business and Public Management and the Law School, where he developed and taught courses about source selection, evaluation of past performance, oral presentations, statement of work preparation, proposal preparation, cost realism evaluation, and other topics. His email address is: vernedwards@mac.com.

To Carol

Table of Contents

Figures

Foreword to the Second Edition

The second edition of Vern Edwards' *Source Selection Answer Book* is a welcome arrival. The first edition proved to be a useful and popular handbook, and the second edition has been updated and expanded to provide even more useful guidance.

The information in this book sheds light not only on source selection under FAR Part 15, but on all kinds of competitive processes, including contractor selection under the General Services Administration's Federal Supply Schedule contracts. Vern gets to the root of key concepts and explains them in depth—concepts such as *evaluation factors for award, relative importance, cost realism analysis,* and *tradeoffs.* A significant addition to the book is the essays in the appendices, some of which appeared as guest articles in *The Nash & Cibinic Report,* for which Vern now writes as a regular contributing author, and others that were published at Bob Antonio's *Where In Federal Contracting?* website, www.wifcon.com.

The Source Selection Answer Book, Second Edition, is a valuable contribution to the literature of acquisition, and an essential text for every acquisition professional's library.

Ralph C. Nash, Jr.
Professor Emeritus of Law
The George Washington University
Washington, D.C.

Preface to the Second Edition

The first edition of the *Source Selection Answer Book* was written in 2000, three years after the publication of the Federal Acquisition Regulation (FAR) Part 15 Rewrite in September 1997. It has now been nearly eight years since the Rewrite, and it is time for some changes. In this second edition I have updated all FAR citations and quotations and revised the answers to questions based on new regulations and case law. I have also revised answers when appropriate to make them clearer. Because the FAR changes so frequently, I have removed the appendix containing FAR Part 15, which will likely become outdated, and I have replaced it with appendices containing articles that address certain aspects of the source selection process in greater detail, such as using a Level of Confidence Assessment Rating (LOCAR) for risk assessments. My goal continues to be to provide succinct answers to specific questions in a handbook format.

The FAR Part 15 Rewrite, which took effect on January 1, 1998, did not revolutionize the source selection process and does not appear to have prompted agencies to streamline the process as much as had been hoped. There is still a lot of confusion about the distinction between offers and other information in proposals, as well as about the legal status of "technical" and "management" proposals. Agencies still use too many evaluation factors for award, and too many of the wrong kinds of factors. Proposal preparation instructions are still poorly written and hard to understand, and agencies still ask for too much of the wrong kind of information. There is still a great deal of confusion about what must be done during proposal evaluation and how decisions must be documented.

I hope that this second edition of the *Source Selection Answer Book* will help government and contractor personnel by explaining the rules about source selection and providing guidance for simplifying the process.

Vernon J. Edwards
Portland, Oregon

PART I

Introduction to Source Selection

The questions in this part address the definitions of key terms, such as *best value,* and other preliminary matters, such as the differences between source selection and other government contract formation procedures.

1. What is *source selection*?

Source selection is one of several contract formation procedures that the federal government uses to choose contractors and award contracts. It is also called *competitive proposals contracting* and *competitive negotiated acquisition.* The general rules for source selection are delineated in Federal Acquisition Regulation (FAR) Part 15, with specific rules presented in FAR Subpart 15.3 and in agency FAR supplements, policy letters, manuals, and handbooks. The two methods of source selection are: (1) the tradeoff process, in which the government reserves the right to consider tradeoffs among the evaluation factors; and (2) the lowest priced technically acceptable process, in which the government does not consider such tradeoffs. FAR 15.101 says that agencies may combine these two methods.

In general, source selection entails the following steps: (1) preparation of a request for proposals (RFP); (2) solicitation of proposals; (3) receipt and evaluation of proposals; (4) award on the basis of initial proposals without discussions (which would end the process), or establishment of a competitive range followed by discussions with offerors in the competitive range and solicitation of final proposal revisions; (5) receipt and evaluation of final proposal revisions; (6) source selection and contract award; and (7) notification and debriefing of the offerors.

The government's other contract formation procedures include simplified acquisition (FAR Part 13), the test program for commercial items (FAR Subpart 13.5), sealed bidding (FAR Part 14), two-step sealed bidding (FAR Subpart 14.5), sole source acquisition (FAR Part 15, except Subpart 15.3), broad agency announcements (FAR 35.016), two-phase design-build selection (FAR Subpart 36.3), and architect-engineer selection (FAR Subpart 36.6).

2. What is *contract formation*?

Contract formation is the process of making contracts. It is also called the process of *offer and acceptance*. In the U.S. legal system, contracts are formed when individuals or firms bargain for an exchange of promises or acts. Simply put, one party makes an offer of terms and the other party accepts it. The parties may or may not negotiate with each other in the process.

In most cases, an offer is a promise or set of promises, and an acceptance is an expression or other manifestation of assent to the terms of the promise. The acceptance is what creates the contract. The offer and acceptance must reflect mutual assent—a meeting of minds about the terms of the agreement between the parties. For the agreement to be binding, there must be consideration—that is, the parties must have exchanged something with one another, either promises or acts. Source selection, simplified acquisition, and sealed bidding are all processes of contract formation.

3. What is *negotiation*?

The term *negotiation* is used in three ways in government procurement. First, it is used in the ordinary dictionary sense of bargaining, i.e., offer/counteroffer. Second, it is used as a special term that includes any process of contract formation that is not sealed bidding (see FAR 15.000). Thus, simplified acquisitions, broad agency announcements, and architect-engineer selections are all negotiated acquisitions. Third, it is used as a synonym for the term *discussions*, as in FAR 15.306(d), a process in which the government asks or allows offerors to revise their proposals.

4. What is *best value*?

FAR 2.101 defines *best value* as follows:

> Best value means the expected outcome of an acquisition that, in the Government's estimation, provides the greatest overall benefit in response to the requirement.

In simple terms, the best value is the best deal offered by any of the offerors in a competitive acquisition. In sealed bidding, the best value is the lowest *responsive* bid price offered by any *responsible* bidder. In source selection, it is either the proposal that represents the best combination of evaluation factors or the lowest priced technically acceptable proposal.

Prior to October 1997, the term *best value* (or *greatest value*) was the unofficial name for what is now called the *tradeoff process* method of source selection (see FAR 15.101-1). It became popular during the late 1980s as a way of distinguishing that method of source selection from the lowest priced technically acceptable method (see FAR 15.101-2). However, the term *best value* did not appear in the FAR until the current definition was inserted in FAR 2.101 on September 30, 1997, as part of the FAR Part 15 Rewrite.

5. What is the *best value continuum*?

This strange term, *best value continuum*, appears in FAR 15.101, which says:

> An agency can obtain best value in negotiated acquisitions by using any one or a combination of source selection approaches. In different types of acquisitions, the relative importance of cost or price may vary. For example, in acquisitions where the requirement is clearly definable and the risk of unsuccessful contract performance is minimal, cost or price may play a dominant role in source selection. The less definitive the requirement, the more development work required, or the greater the performance risk, the more technical or past performance considerations may play a dominant role in source selection.

In short, the government can use a variety of methods in choosing a contractor. Any one of those methods can enable the government to obtain a best value, with the emphasis on price or cost varying from one procurement to the next.

6. What laws and regulations apply to source selection?

A number of federal laws and regulations govern source selection. Laws (statutes) are enacted by Congress and approved by the President. Federal laws are collected and codified in the United States Code (U.S.C.) and organized in sets called *titles*. Two titles include most of the laws governing federal procurement: Titles 10 and 41. Title 10 includes laws that govern acquisitions by the Department of Defense, the Coast Guard, and the National Aeronautics and Space Administration (NASA). Title 41 includes laws that govern the civilian agencies, but also includes laws of more general applicability.

The Administrator of General Services, the Secretary of Defense, and the Administrator of NASA jointly issue the FAR to implement the laws in the U.S. Code. The FAR appears in Chapter 1 of Title 48 of the Code of Federal Regulations (C.F.R.). The heads of the various federal agencies issue supplements to the FAR, which appear in other chapters of Title 48. For example, the Defense FAR Supplement appears in Chapter 2 of Title 48; the Environmental Protection Agency FAR Supplement appears in Chapter 15. The FAR and the agency supplements are collectively called the Federal Acquisition Regulations (FAR) System. (See Table I-1.)

TABLE I-1

THE FEDERAL ACQUISITION REGULATIONS SYSTEM

Title 48 of the Code of Federal Regulations—
The Federal Acquisition Regulations System (as of October 1998)
(Note: The chapters are not numbered consecutively.)

Chapter 1	The Federal Acquisition Regulation
2	Department of Defense
3	Department of Health and Human Services
4	Department of Agriculture
5	General Services Administration
6	Department of State
8	Department of Veterans Affairs
9	Department of Energy
10	Department of the Treasury
12	Department of Transportation
13	Department of Commerce
14	Department of the Interior
15	Environmental Protection Agency
16	Office of Personnel Management—Federal Employees Health Benefits

continues

TABLE I-1 continued

17	Office of Personnel Management
18	National Aeronautics and Space Administration
19	United States Information Agency
20	Nuclear Regulatory Commission
21	Office of Personnel Management—Federal Employees Group Life Insurance
23	Social Security Administration
24	Department of Housing and Urban Development
25	National Science Foundation
28	Department of Justice
29	Department of Labor
34	Department of Education
35	Panama Canal Commission
44	Federal Emergency Management Agency
51	Department of the Army
52	Department of the Navy
53	Department of the Air Force
54	Defense Logistics Agency
57	African Development Foundation
61	General Services Administration—Board of Contract Appeals
63	Department of Transportation—Board of Contract Appeals
99	Cost Accounting Standards Board (Office of Management and Budget, Office of Federal Procurement Policy)

The FAR System applies to all acquisitions made with appropriated funds, except when expressly inapplicable. It regulates the planning, award, and administration of contracts. It does not apply to the planning, award, or administration of grants and cooperative agreements. Regulations such as the FAR that are included in the Code of Federal Regulations are often said to have the "force and effect of law." [See John Cibinic, Jr., and Ralph C. Nash, Jr., *Formation of Government Contracts*, 3rd ed. (Washington, D.C.: The George Washington University Law School, 1998), pp. 59–63).]

The rules for source selection are in FAR Part 15, *Contracting by Negotiation,* particularly Subparts 15.1 through 15.5. Subpart 15.1, *Source Selection Processes and Techniques,* includes general background information. Subpart 15.2, *Solicitation and Receipt of Proposals and Information,* explains how to prepare RFPs and communicate with prospective offerors. Subpart 15.3, *Source Selection,* includes rules for selecting proposal evaluation factors and for proposal evaluation and negotiation. Subpart 15.4, *Contract Pricing,* includes rules for requesting pricing information from contractors and prospective contractors, and for analyzing and negotiating prices and estimated costs and fees. Subpart 15.5, *Preaward, Award, and Postaward Notifications, Protests, and Mistakes,* includes rules for notifications, debriefings, protests, and resolution of mistakes. Individual agencies supplement these rules in their FAR supplements and in policy letters, handbooks, and manuals.

It is impossible to understand the source selection rules in the FAR without a knowledge of the protest decisions of the U.S. General Accounting Office (GAO). The federal courts also decide protests, especially the U.S. Court of Federal Claims, but the GAO is, by far, the most important interpreter of the rules. It is fair to say that the FAR tells you what the rules *say,* but the GAO decisions tell you what they *mean.* The protest decisions issued by GAO and the U.S. Court of Federal Claims are available without charge on the World Wide Web (www.gao.gov; www.law.gwu.edu/fedcl). On rare occasion, a protester will appeal a decision of GAO or the U.S. Court of Federal Claims to the Federal Circuit Court of Appeals (www.fedcir.gov).

Contrary to popular belief, the rules in the FAR for source selection do not prescribe detailed procedures for proposal evaluation or negotiation. Much of the material in the FAR is informative or suggestive rather than directive. (The word *shall* precedes firm directives. See the definition of *shall* in FAR 2.101.)

7. What are the rules about competition?

Two rules about competition apply to the source selection process: the *full and open competition* rule and the *adequate price competition* rule. They apply in very different ways, however. The full and open competition rule appears in FAR 6.101, *Policy*, which provides:

> (a) 10 U.S.C. 2304 and 41 U.S.C. 253 require, with certain limited exceptions (see Subparts 6.2 and 6.3), that contracting officers shall promote and provide for full and open competition in soliciting offers and awarding Government contracts.
>
> (b) Contracting officers shall provide for full and open competition through use of the competitive procedure(s) contained in this subpart that are best suited to the circumstances of the contract action and consistent with the need to fulfill the Government's requirements efficiently (10 U.S.C. 2304 and 41 U.S.C. 253).

The *adequate price competition rule* appears in FAR 15.403-1 and prohibits the government from requiring offerors to submit *cost or pricing data* (as defined in FAR 2.101) when prices are based on adequate price competition. The *full and open competition rule* has to do with the opportunity to compete under the law called the Competition in Contracting Act (CICA). The adequate price competition rule has to do with the extent to which firms have actually competed for a contract and how that competition affects application of the law called the Truth in Negotiations Act (TINA).

FULL AND OPEN COMPETITION

The Competition in Contracting Act, enacted in 1984 (codified at 10 U.S.C. 2304 and 41 U.S.C. 253, and implemented in FAR Part 6, *Competition Requirements*), requires that agencies promote and provide for full and open competition in all procurements to which that law applies. FAR 6.001, *Applicability*, applies this requirement to all acquisitions except the following:

(a) Contracts awarded using the simplified acquisition procedures of Part 13 (but see 13.501 for requirements pertaining to sole source acquisitions of commercial items under Subpart 13.5);

(b) Contracts awarded using contracting procedures (other than those addressed in this part) that are expressly authorized by statute;

(c) Contract modifications, including the exercise of priced options that were evaluated as part of the initial competition (see 17.207(f)), that are within the scope and under the terms of an existing contract;

(d) Orders placed under requirements contracts or definite-quantity contracts;

(e) Orders placed under indefinite-quantity contracts that were entered into pursuant to this part when—

(1) The contract was awarded under Subpart 6.1 or 6.2 and all responsible sources were realistically permitted to compete for the requirements contained in the order; or

(2) The contract was awarded under Subpart 6.3 and the required justification and approval adequately covers the requirements contained in the order; or

(f) Orders placed against task order and delivery order contracts entered into pursuant to Subpart 16.5.

FAR 2.101 defines *full and open competition* as a competition in which all responsible sources are permitted to compete. The government satisfies the requirement to promote and provide for full and open competition when it: (1) does not make its requirements unduly restrictive; (2) notifies the public about its acquisitions so that prospective offerors can decide whether or not to submit a proposal; (3) conducts its procurements in accordance with applicable laws and regulations using a competitive procedure; and (4) treats all offerors fairly and impartially. If the government does these things, then the requirement to promote and provide for full and open competition is met, even if the government actually receives only one proposal. The number of proposals received, in and of itself, has no direct bearing on the question of whether or not the government promoted and provided for full and open competition; however, the receipt of only one or an unexpectedly small number of proposals may indicate that the government's requirements were unduly restrictive.

FAR Subpart 6.2, *Full and Open Competition After Exclusion of Sources*, provides that, under some circumstances, the government may exclude one or more offerors from a competition and then seek full and open competition from the remaining offerors. A small business set-aside is an example of such a procurement.

FAR Subpart 6.3, *Other Than Full and Open Competition*, permits an agency to limit competition even more strictly under some circumstances, such as sole source situations or when there is an unusual and compelling urgency. In these cases, the government must prepare a written justification for its action, obtain approval at an appropriate management level, and announce its intentions to the public.

Although the FAR permits agencies to obtain other than full and open competition under specified circumstances, agencies must try to obtain as much competition as those circumstances will permit. The authority to obtain other than full and open competition does not allow an agency to contract on a sole source basis as it sees fit.

For a legal analysis of some of the case law about competition requirements, see John Cibinic, Jr., and Ralph C. Nash, Jr., *Formation of Government Contracts,* 3rd ed. (Washington, D.C.: The George Washington University Law School, 1998), pp. 276–311 and 358–361.

ADEQUATE PRICE COMPETITION

If a procurement does not generate adequate price competition, the government may have to request the submission and certification of cost or pricing data. This rule applies to procurements that are expected to exceed the dollar threshold for requiring cost or pricing data. That dollar threshold is stated in FAR 15.403-4(a)(1) (at the time of this edition, the threshold was $550,000, including the value of contract options). FAR 15.403-1(c)(1) establishes the following three standards for adequate price competition:

> A price is based on adequate price competition if—
>
> (i) Two or more responsible offerors, competing independently, submit priced offers that satisfy the Government's expressed requirement and if—
>
> (A) Award will be made to the offeror whose proposal represents the best value (see 2.101) where price is a substantial factor in source selection; and
>
> (B) There is no finding that the price of the otherwise successful offeror is unreasonable. Any finding that the price is unreasonable must be supported by a statement

> of the facts and approved at a level above the contracting officer;
>
> (ii) There was a reasonable expectation, based on market research or other assessment, that two or more responsible offerors, competing independently, would submit priced offers in response to the solicitation's expressed requirement, even though only one offer is received from a responsible offeror and if—
>
> (A) Based on the offer received, the contracting officer can reasonably conclude that the offer was submitted with the expectation of competition, e.g., circumstances indicate that—
>
> (1) The offeror believed that at least one other offeror was capable of submitting a meaningful offer; and
>
> (2) The offeror had no reason to believe that other potential offerors did not intend to submit an offer; and
>
> (B) The determination that the proposed price is based on adequate price competition, is reasonable, and is approved at a level above the contracting officer; or
>
> (iii) Price analysis clearly demonstrates that the proposed price is reasonable in comparison with current or recent prices for the same or similar items, adjusted to reflect changes in market conditions, economic conditions, quantities, or terms and conditions under contracts that resulted from adequate price competition.

The first standard [paragraph (i)] includes five tests. Adequate price competition exists if: (1) the government receives priced proposals from at least two responsible offerors that competed independently; (2) the proposals satisfy the government's expressed requirements; (3) the government plans to award the contract to the offeror that represents the best value; (4) price is a substantial evaluation factor; and (5) there is no finding that the winner's price is unreasonable.

The second standard [paragraph (ii)] includes three tests. Adequate price competition exists, even when the government receives only one proposal, if: (1) the government had expected to receive at least two priced proposals that would satisfy its expressed requirements from responsible offerors competing independently; (2) the government believes that the offeror had expected competition; and (3) the determination that there was adequate price competition is reasonable and approved at a level above the contracting officer.

The third standard [paragraph (iii)] includes only one test. Adequate price competition exists no matter how many proposals are received if the government determines that the proposed price is reasonable based on a comparison with current or recent prices for the same or similar item. In making comparisons, the government may make adjustments to reflect differences in market conditions, economic conditions, quantities, or terms and conditions.

8. What do *responsible* and *responsibility* mean?

The laws and regulations use the term *responsible* with reference to "sources," "offerors," and "prospective contractors." For example, 10 U.S.C. 2305(b)(4)(A) and 41 U.S.C. 253b(d)(1) say that agencies may award contracts "after discussions with the offerors, provided that written or oral discussions have been conducted with all responsible offerors who submit proposals within the competitive range[.]" The definition of *full and open competition* in FAR 6.003 says, "'Full and open competition,' when used with respect to a contract action, means that all responsible sources are permitted to compete."

DEFINITIONS AND STANDARDS

FAR 2.101 defines a *responsible prospective contractor* as "a contractor that meets the standards in 9.104." FAR 9.104 includes general standards of responsibility and allows agencies to establish special standards, as follows:

> **9.104-1 General standards.**
>
> To be determined responsible, a prospective contractor must—
>
> (a) Have adequate financial resources to perform the contract, or the ability to obtain them (see 9.104-3(a));
>
> (b) Be able to comply with the required or proposed delivery or performance schedule, taking into consideration all existing commercial and governmental business commitments;
>
> (c) Have a satisfactory performance record (see 9.104-3(b) and Subpart 42.15). A prospective contractor shall not be determined responsible or nonresponsible solely on the basis of a lack of relevant performance history, except as provided in 9.104-2;
>
> (d) Have a satisfactory record of integrity and business ethics;
>
> (e) Have the necessary organization, experience, accounting and operational controls, and technical skills, or the ability to obtain them (including, as appropriate, such elements as production control procedures, property control systems, quality assurance measures, and safety programs applicable to materials to be produced or services to be performed by the prospective contractor and subcontractors). (See 9.104-3(a).)
>
> (f) Have the necessary production, construction, and technical equipment and facilities, or the ability to obtain them (see 9.104-3(a)); and

(g) Be otherwise qualified and eligible to receive an award under applicable laws and regulations.

9.104-2 Special standards.

(a) When it is necessary for a particular acquisition or class of acquisitions, the contracting officer shall develop, with the assistance of appropriate specialists, special standards of responsibility. Special standards may be particularly desirable when experience has demonstrated that unusual expertise or specialized facilities are needed for adequate contract performance. The special standards shall be set forth in the solicitation (and so identified) and shall apply to all offerors.

(b) Contracting officers shall award contracts for subsistence only to those prospective contractors that meet the general standards in 9.104-1 and are approved in accordance with agency sanitation standards and procedures.

Responsibility is a pass or fail test based on the responsibility standards and does not entail comparisons with other firms.

GAO calls special standards of responsibility *definitive responsibility criteria*. GAO defined such criteria as follows in its decision in *AT&T Corporation* (B-260447, March 4, 1996):

> A definitive responsibility criterion is a specific and objective standard, qualitative or quantitative, that is established by a contracting agency in a solicitation to measure an offeror's ability to perform a contract. In order to be a definitive responsibility criterion, the solicitation provision must reasonably inform offerors that they must demonstrate compliance with the standard as a precondition to receiving award. See generally Data Gen. Corp., B-252239, June 14, 1993, 93-1 CPD ¶ 457.

[See John Cibinic, Jr., and Ralph C. Nash, Jr., *Formation of Government Contracts*, 3rd ed., (Washington, D.C.: The George Washington University Law School, 1998), pp. 422–428.]

Responsibility standards are not *evaluation factors for award* as that term is used in FAR 15.304. However, an agency may use responsibility standards as evaluation factors for award in order to make comparative assessments of competing offerors. Evaluations based on such comparative assessments are not responsibility determinations. In its decision in *Nomura Enterprise, Inc.* (B-277768, November 19, 1997), GAO said:

> An agency may use traditional responsibility factors, such as experience or past performance, as technical evaluation factors, where, as here, a comparative evaluation of those areas is to be made. Dynamic Aviation—Helicopters, B-274122, Nov. 1, 1996, 96-2 CPD ¶ 166 at 3. A comparative evaluation means that competing proposals will be rated on a scale relative to each other, as opposed to a pass/fail basis. Id. The record shows that the award here clearly was based on a comparative assessment of Nomura's and Defense's past performance records. Where a proposal is downgraded or found deficient pursuant to such an evaluation, the matter is one of relative technical merit, not nonresponsibility which would require a referral to the SBA. Id.; see also Smith of Galeton Gloves, Inc., B-271686, July 24, 1996, 96-2 CPD ¶ 36 at 7.

THE RESPONSIBILITY RULE

FAR 9.103 states the *responsibility rule* as follows:

> **9.103 Policy.**
>
> (a) Purchases shall be made from, and contracts shall be awarded to, responsible prospective contractors only.

> (b) No purchase or award shall be made unless the contracting officer makes an affirmative determination of responsibility. In the absence of information clearly indicating that the prospective contractor is responsible, the contracting officer shall make a determination of nonresponsibility. If the prospective contractor is a small business concern, the contracting officer shall comply with Subpart 19.6, Certificates of Competency and Determinations of Responsibility. (If Section 8(a) of the Small Business Act (15 U.S.C. 637) applies, see Subpart 19.8.)
>
> (c) The award of a contract to a supplier based on lowest evaluated price alone can be false economy if there is subsequent default, late deliveries, or other unsatisfactory performance resulting in additional contractual or administrative costs. While it is important that Government purchases be made at the lowest price, this does not require an award to a supplier solely because that supplier submits the lowest offer. A prospective contractor must affirmatively demonstrate its responsibility, including, when necessary, the responsibility of its proposed subcontractors.

An agency must determine the responsibility of a prospective contractor. The prospective contractor must prove its responsibility to the agency, including the responsibility of its prospective subcontractors. In the absence of information that proves that the prospective contractor is responsible, the agency must make a determination of nonresponsibility.

There is a legal question regarding at what point in time a firm must be responsible: Is it at the time at which it submits its proposal, at the time at which the agency evaluates its proposal, or at the time of contract award? The FAR is silent on this matter, but GAO has ruled that an offeror must be responsible as of the time of award, not the time at which it submits its proposal or the time at which the government evaluates its proposal. [See John Cibinic, Jr., and Ralph C. Nash, Jr., *Formation of Government Contracts,* 3rd ed. (Washington, D.C.: The George Washington University Law School, 1998) pp. 405–406.] Thus, when an agency investigates a firm's responsibility, it must decide whether or not the firm is responsible or is likely to be able to become responsible by the anticipated date of award.

If an agency determines that a small business firm is nonresponsible, it must refer the matter to the U.S. Small Business Administration (SBA) for review in accordance with the Certificate of Competency Program described in FAR Subpart 19.6. SBA can effectively overrule the agency's determination of nonresponsibility by issuing a certificate of competency. An agency must withhold contract award for 15 business days after it refers the matter to SBA while SBA decides whether or not to issue a certificate of competency.

PROCEDURE FOR DETERMINING RESPONSIBILITY

FAR 9.105-1(b)(1) says:

> Generally, the contracting officer shall obtain information regarding the responsibility of prospective contractors, including requesting preaward surveys when necessary (9.106), promptly after a bid opening or receipt of offers. However, in negotiated contracting, especially when research and development is involved, the contracting officer may request this information before issuing the request for proposals. Requests for information shall ordinarily be limited to information concerning (i) the low bidder or (ii) those offerors in range for award.

The usual procedure is to solicit and evaluate proposals, choose a prospective contractor, and then investigate its responsibility. Such investigations often include preaward surveys, in which special teams conduct the investigation, perhaps by inspecting the offeror's facilities. (See FAR 9.106.) This procedure was developed for the sealed bidding process, in which it is applied only to the low, responsive bidder.

However, to expedite the source selection process, agencies sometimes determine the responsibility of all offerors concurrently with the evaluations of their proposals and before selecting a winner. In a source selection, it makes little sense to evaluate proposals, select a winner, and *then* determine whether or not the winner is responsible. Instead, the assessment of each offeror's responsibility should be built into the evaluation of proposals, and no offeror should be selected for award unless it has already been determined to be responsible.

DOCUMENTATION

FAR 9.105-2 says that when a contracting officer decides that the prospective contractor is responsible, the contracting officer's signature on the contract is the only documentation required. The agency must place any supporting documentation in its procurement file. However, if a contracting officer determines that a prospective contractor is nonresponsible, he or she must prepare a memorandum that explains the basis for the determination of nonresponsibility and place it in the agency's procurement file along with supporting documentation.

9. What is the Procurement Integrity Act?

The Procurement Integrity Act prohibits the improper disclosure of confidential government procurement information and prohibits certain government procurement officials from accepting employment or other forms of compensation from competing contractors. It is codified at 41 U.S.C. 423 and implemented in FAR 3.104.

The law prohibits government officials from disclosing *contractor bid or proposal information* or government *source selection information* before the award of a federal contract to which that information relates. It prohibits a person from knowingly obtaining such information. It requires government officials to notify their superiors of contacts with competing firms about employment and to disqualify themselves under appropriate circumstances. It prohibits certain former government officials from accepting compensation from a contractor under specified circumstances.

Violations of the Procurement Integrity Act can result in criminal and civil penalties and administrative sanctions. In light of those penalties and sanctions, government personnel should consult with their contracting officer or an agency attorney before providing information about a federal procurement to any prospective offeror or discussing employment opportunities. Industry personnel should consult with an attorney before approaching a government employee to discuss employment opportunities.

10. What is the Federal Acquisition Regulation?

The Federal Acquisition Regulation (FAR) is Chapter 1 of Title 48 of the Code of Federal Regulations (C.F.R.). It is issued by the Secretary of Defense, the Administrator of General Services, and the Administrator of the National Aeronautics and Space Administration. It regulates the acquisition of goods and services with appropriated funds.

The FAR and supplements issued by individual agencies make up the Federal Acquisition Regulations System. Agency supplements appear in other chapters of Title 48. (See Table I-1 on p. 5.) The purpose of the FAR is to codify uniform policies and procedures for acquisitions conducted by agencies of the executive branch of the government. The text of the FAR includes rules, background material, and guidance.

The FAR is maintained by two councils: the Defense Acquisition Regulations Council, which has a representative from NASA; and the Civilian Agency Acquisition Council, which includes representatives from several civilian agencies. These councils develop the language to implement statutes and the other rules and guidance in the FAR. A FAR Secretariat within the General Services Administration arranges for the printing, publishing, and distribution of the FAR.

The FAR is organized into eight subchapters, 53 parts, and numerous subparts, sections, subsections, paragraphs, and subparagraphs. (See Table I-2.) This arrangement and the numbering system for the various components are explained in FAR 1.105-1.

TABLE I-2
THE FEDERAL ACQUISITION REGULATION

The Federal Acquisition Regulation
Subchapter A—General

Part 1	Federal Acquisition Regulations System
Part 2	Definitions of Words and Terms
Part 3	Improper Business Practices and Personal Conflicts of Interest
Part 4	Administrative Matters

Subchapter B—Competition and Acquisition Planning

Part 5	Publicizing Contract Actions
Part 6	Competition Requirements
Part 7	Acquisition Planning
Part 8	Required Sources of Supplies and Services
Part 9	Contractor Qualifications
Part 10	Specifications, Standards, and Other Purchase Descriptions
Part 11	Describing Agency Needs
Part 12	Acquisition of Commercial Items

continues

TABLE I-2 continued

	Subchapter C—Contracting Methods and Contract Types
Part 13	Simplified Acquisition Procedures
Part 14	Sealed Bidding
Part 15	Contracting by Negotiation
Part 16	Types of Contracts
Part 17	Special Contracting Methods
Part 18	Reserved
	Subchapter D—Socioeconomic Programs
Part 19	Small Business Programs
Part 20	Reserved
Part 21	Reserved
Part 22	Application of Labor Laws to Government Acquisitions
Part 23	Environment, Energy and Water Efficiency, Renewable Energy Technologies, Occupational Safety, and Drug-Free Workplace
Part 24	Protection of Privacy and Freedom of Information
Part 25	Foreign Acquisition
Part 26	Other Socioeconomic Programs
	Subchapter E—General Contracting Requirements
Part 27	Patents, Data, and Copyrights
Part 28	Bonds and Insurance
Part 29	Taxes
Part 30	Cost Accounting Standards Administration
Part 31	Contract Cost Principles and Procedures
Part 32	Contract Financing
Part 33	Protests, Disputes, and Appeals
	Subchapter F—Special Categories of Contracting
Part 34	Major System Acquisition
Part 35	Research and Development Contracting
Part 36	Construction and Architect-Engineer Contracts
Part 37	Service Contracting
Part 38	Federal Supply Schedule Contracting
Part 39	Acquisition of Information Technology
Part 40	Reserved
Part 41	Acquisition of Utility Services

continues

TABLE I-2 continued

	Subchapter G—Contract Management
Part 42	Contract Administration and Audit Services
Part 43	Contract Modifications
Part 44	Subcontracting Policies and Procedures
Part 45	Government Property
Part 46	Quality Assurance
Part 47	Transportation
Part 48	Value Engineering
Part 49	Termination of Contracts
Part 50	Extraordinary Contractual Actions
Part 51	Use of Government Sources by Contractors
	Subchapter H—Clauses and Forms
Part 52	Solicitation Provisions and Contract Clauses
Part 53	Forms

Changes to the FAR are published in the *Federal Register* in the form of Federal Acquisition Circulars (FACs). The regulation is available from Management Concepts, Inc. (www.managementconcepts.com/publications), the Government Printing Office (www.gpo.gov), and on the World Wide Web (www.acqnet.gov/far).

The single largest part of the FAR is Part 52, which includes several hundred solicitation provisions and contract clauses—boilerplate terms and conditions to be used in invitations for bids, requests for proposals, requests for information, requests for quotations, contracts, and other instruments. The topic that occupies more of the FAR than any other is contract pricing, which is addressed in one way or another in several parts, including Parts 15, 16, 30, 31, 42, and 52.

The FAR is badly written and some of the rules are vague or ambiguous. This problem hampers efficient acquisition management and leads to needless litigation. Moreover, much of the regulation cannot be understood without a knowledge of the interpretational decisions of the Government Accountability Office (formerly the General Accounting Office), the boards of contract appeals, and the federal courts. Extensive supplementation by the various federal agencies has undermined the goal of uniformity in government acquisition policies and procedures.

Despite these problems, the FAR is not as much of a barrier to good practice and common sense as some claim. FAR 1.102-4(e) summarizes the guiding principles of the FAR as follows:

> The FAR outlines procurement policies and procedures that are used by members of the Acquisition Team. If a policy or procedure, or a particular strategy or practice, is in the best interest of the Government and is not specifically addressed in the FAR, nor prohibited by law (statute or case law), Executive order or other regulation, Government members of the Team should not assume it is prohibited. Rather, absence of direction should be interpreted as permitting the Team to innovate and use sound business judgment that is otherwise consistent with law and within the limits of their authority. Contracting officers should take the lead in encouraging business process innovations and ensuring that business decisions are sound.

Thus, in theory, agency acquisition personnel have considerable discretion in the way that they go about doing the government's business.

11. What was the FAR Part 15 Rewrite?

The FAR Part 15 Rewrite was a project carried out from 1995 through 1997 to improve the source selection process by clarifying and revising the source selection policies and procedures in FAR Part 15. According to an early announcement:

> The intent is to make Part 15 easier to understand and to eliminate policies, procedures, or requirements that impose unnecessary burdens on contractors or contracting officers. Regulatory requirements that are not required by statute, required to ensure adequately standardized government business practices, or required to protect the public interest will be considered for elimination. Innovative means of simplifying the procurement process and enhancing its efficiency will be considered for incorporation in the regulation.

Federal Register, Vol. 60, No. 236, p. 63023, December 8, 1995 (60 Fed. Reg. 63023).

After two drafts (proposed rules) were published in the *Federal Register*, on September 12, 1996 (61 Fed. Reg. 48380), and on May 14, 1997 (62 Fed. Reg. 26640), a final rule was published on September 30, 1997 (62 Fed. Reg. 51224), and went into effect on January 1, 1998.

> The most important changes effected by the FAR Part 15 Rewrite were: (1) the organization and expression of the rules about exchanging information with industry before the release of the request for proposals (FAR 15.201) and of the rules about exchanging information with offerors after the receipt of proposals (FAR 15.306 and 15.307); and (2) the rule allowing agencies to limit the size of the competitive range for purposes of efficiency [FAR 15.306(c)(2)]. The FAR Part 15 Rewrite added coverage about oral presentations (FAR 15.102) and the advisory multistep process (FAR 15.202). It is too early to tell whether these changes will have a major effect on the ways that agencies conduct source selections.

12. What are the steps in the source selection process?

Although the FAR does not prescribe a standard source selection process, one has evolved in practice. However, since the FAR does not prescribe these steps explicitly, many variations are possible, including phased evaluation. (See Appendix A for a discussion of the FAR Part 15 process model.)

STANDARD SOURCE SELECTION

In outline, the steps in the standard source selection process are as shown in Table I-3.

TABLE I-3
THE STANDARD SOURCE SELECTION PROCESS

Step	*Action*
1	The agency identifies a need, researches the market, prepares a description of its requirements, and plans its acquisition (FAR Parts 7, 10, and 11, and FAR 15.304).
2	The agency prepares a request for proposals, publicly announces its intention to conduct a source selection, and develops a list of prospective offerors (FAR Subparts 5.1, 5.2, and 15.2).
3	The agency issues the request for proposals to the prospective offerors (FAR 5.102, 5.203, and 15.205).
4	The prospective offerors decide whether or not to compete, and those that decide to compete prepare and submit proposals.
5	The agency receives the proposals and convenes an evaluation panel [FAR 15.207, 15.303(b)(1), and 52.215-1].
6	The agency panel evaluates the proposals and reports its findings to the source selection authority (FAR 15.305).
7	A. The source selection authority either selects the contractor based on the initial evaluation, and the agency awards the contract without discussions [FAR 15.306(a) and 52.215-1(f)], or B. The agency decides to conduct discussions and establishes a competitive range [FAR 15.306(c) and 52.215-1(f)].

continues

TABLE I-3 continued

8	If the agency establishes a competitive range, it then notifies the offerors that have been eliminated from further consideration and conducts discussions with all the offerors in the competitive range [FAR 15.306(d), 15.307, and 15.503(a)(1)]. The agency may debrief the offerors that were eliminated from the competitive range upon request (FAR 15.505).
9	Upon the conclusion of discussions the agency invites the offerors to submit final proposal revisions (best and final offers) [FAR 15.307(b)].
10	Offerors prepare and submit their final proposal revisions.
11	The agency receives the final proposal revisions and convenes the evaluation panel.
12	The panel evaluates the final proposal revisions and reports its findings to the source selection authority.
13	The source selection authority chooses a contractor and the contracting officer awards the contract [FAR 15.308, 15.504, and 52.215-1(f)].
14	The agency notifies the winner and the losers and makes debriefings upon request (FAR Subpart 15.5).

PHASED EVALUATION

One variation from the standard process is to evaluate proposals in phases, applying different evaluation factors in each phase to reduce the size of the offeror pool progressively and choose the contractor. Phased evaluation has been called *multistep source selection, downselect,* and *phased evaluation.* The objective of phased evaluation is to make the source selection process more efficient when an agency receives a large number of proposals.

One approach to phased evaluation might be to evaluate price first, eliminating those offerors whose prices are too high to be competitive; then to evaluate experience and past performance, eliminating more offerors; and then to obtain written technical proposals or oral presentations from the remaining offerors in order to make a final selection based on price and technical merit. Such an approach would reduce the number of technical proposals or oral presentations the evaluators would have to consider, saving time and money for both the agency and the competitors.

There has been some debate about whether phased evaluation is permissible in light of FAR 15.306(c)(1), which provides:

> Agencies shall evaluate all proposals in accordance with 15.305(a), and, if discussions are to be conducted, establish the competitive range. Based on the ratings of each proposal against *all* evaluation criteria, the contracting officer shall establish a competitive range comprised of all of the most highly rated proposals, unless the range is further reduced for purposes of efficiency pursuant to paragraph (c)(20) of this section. [Italics added.]

Some argue that the word "all" in the second sentence indicates that an agency cannot eliminate any offeror from the competition unless it has been evaluated in light of all the factors described in the solicitation—that is, that agencies cannot apply evaluation factors in phases. They argue further that a decision to eliminate an offeror at the end of a phase of evaluation is tantamount to a competitive range determination, whether the agency intends to conduct discussions or not.

These critics of phased evaluation point to a comment in the "Summary of Changes" that appeared in the *Federal Register* publication of the FAR Part 15 Rewrite, providing that:

> [N]o offeror, otherwise eligible to submit a proposal in response to a Government solicitation, will be excluded from the competitive range without its proposal being initially reviewed and evaluated solely against all the evaluation factors and significant subfactors in the solicitation.

62 Fed. Reg. 51224 (Sept. 30, 1997).

They interpret the phrase *all of the evaluation factors and significant subfactors* to mean that the evaluation factors cannot be applied in phases to reduce the size of the offeror pool progressively. They also point to the fact that earlier drafts of the FAR Part 15 Rewrite had provided for a *multiphase acquisition technique* or *multistep source selection technique* that would have provided for a *mandatory downselect* procedure, but that this provision was not included in the final version of the Rewrite. [61 Fed. Reg. 48380, 48383 (Sept. 12, 1996); 62 Fed. Reg. 26640, 26644 (May 14, 1997).] However, the FAR does not expressly prohibit phased evaluation, and the procedure has been used from time to time for many years.

One warning about phased evaluation: No offeror should be eliminated without consideration of price. Price must be an evaluation factor in each phase of the evaluation. In its decision in *Kathpal Technologies, Inc.; Computer & Hi-Tech Management, Inc.* (B-283137.3; B-283137.4; B-283137.5; B-283137.6, December 30, 1999), GAO stated:

> Cost or price to the government must be included in every RFP as an evaluation factor, and agencies must consider cost or price to the government in evaluating competitive proposals. [Footnote omitted.] 41 U.S.C. § 253a(c)(1)(B) (1994); FAR sect. 15-304(c)(1); S.J. Thomas Co., Inc., B-283192, Oct. 20, 1999, 99-2 CPD ¶ at 3.
>
> This requirement means that an agency cannot eliminate a technically acceptable proposal from consideration for award without taking into account the relative cost of that proposal to the government. SCIENTECH, Inc., B-277805.2, Jan. 20, 1998, 98-1 CPD § 33 at 7.

Agencies that intend to evaluate proposals in phases to reduce the size of the offeror pool progressively must include price or cost to the government as an evaluation factor in each phase.

13. What is the *tradeoff process*?

The *tradeoff process* is one of two approaches to source selection, the other being the *lowest price technically acceptable process*. Its use is authorized by FAR 15.101-1. The tradeoff process allows agencies to select a contractor on the basis of comparisons of the competing offerors' different combinations of quality and price. FAR 15.101-1 reads as follows:

> (a) A tradeoff process is appropriate when it may be in the best interest of the Government to consider award to other than the lowest priced offeror or other than the highest technically rated offeror.
>
> (b) When using a tradeoff process, the following apply:
>
> (1) All evaluation factors and significant subfactors that will affect contract award and their relative importance shall be clearly stated in the solicitation; and
>
> (2) The solicitation shall state whether all evaluation factors other than cost or price, when combined, are significantly more important than, approximately equal to, or significantly less important than cost or price.
>
> (c) This process permits tradeoffs among cost or price and non-cost factors and allows the Government to accept other than the lowest priced proposal. The perceived benefits of the higher priced proposal shall merit the additional cost, and the rationale for tradeoffs must be documented in the file in accordance with 15.406.

Suppose that an agency is evaluating three proposals on the basis of quality and price. Suppose further that the agency is measuring quality on a scale of 0 to 100 points, with 100 being best. Table I-4 shows the results of the evaluation of three fictional proposals.

TABLE I-4
QUALITY/PRICE TRADEOFF

Offeror	*Quality Score*	*Price*
A	95	$990,000
B	85	$950,000
C	75	$915,000

Suppose further that each offeror has proposed an "acceptable" amount of quality. In a tradeoff process, the agency need not award the contract to Offeror C merely because it has the lowest-priced acceptable proposal. Instead, the agency must decide which of the offerors represents the best combination of quality and price. It must do this by identifying the marginal differences among the offerors and comparing them on that basis.

A comparison of Offerors A and B in Table I-4 reveals that A has a 10 point advantage in quality, and B has a $40,000 advantage in price. The agency must decide whether or not the difference in quality represented by the 10 points is worth $40,000. If the agency decides that it is, then Offeror A represents the better value, and the agency will "trade off" the difference in price to get the difference in quality. If the agency decides that it is not, then Offeror B is the better value, and the agency will trade off the difference in quality to save the difference in price. The agency must then compare the winner of the first comparison to Offeror C in the same way.

This procedure is highly adaptable and lets agencies use discretion when evaluating proposals and choosing contractors. This is especially so when the nonprice evaluation factors are not readily susceptible to objective measurement. FAR 15.308 requires agencies to document the rationale for their tradeoff decisions but says that they do not have to quantify their judgments. In its decision in *Madico, Inc.* (Comp. Gen. Dec. B-280003, August 12, 1998), GAO said:

> Agency officials have broad discretion in determining the manner and extent to which they will make use of technical and price evaluation results. Price/technical tradeoffs may be made; the extent to which one may be sacrificed for the other is governed by the test of rationality and consistency with the established evaluation factors.

14. What is the *lowest price technically acceptable process*?

The *lowest price technically acceptable process* authorized by FAR 15.101-2 is one in which the government selects the offeror who both: (1) satisfies the government's minimum technical requirements; and (2) proposes the lowest overall price. The key to understanding this procedure is to recognize that the government will evaluate nonprice considerations on a pass or fail basis and that the award decision will be based on an objective comparison of the offerors' prices. The government does not trade off nonprice differences against differences in price. FAR 15.101-2 reads as follows:

> (a) The lowest price technically acceptable source selection process is appropriate when best value is expected to result from selection of the technically acceptable proposal with the lowest evaluated price.
>
> (b) When using the lowest price technically acceptable process, the following apply:
>
> (1) The evaluation factors and significant subfactors that establish the requirements of acceptability shall be set forth in the solicitation. Solicitations shall specify that award will be made on the basis of the lowest evaluated price of proposals meeting or exceeding the acceptability

standards for non-cost factors. If the contracting officer documents the file pursuant to 15.304(c)(3)(iii), past performance need not be an evaluation factor in lowest price technically acceptable source selections. If the contracting officer elects to consider past performance as an evaluation factor, it shall be evaluated in accordance with 15.305. However, the comparative assessment in 15.305(a)(2)(i) does not apply. If the contracting officer determines that a small business' past performance is not acceptable, the matter shall be referred to the Small Business Administration for a Certificate of Competency determination, in accordance with the procedures contained in Subpart 19.6 and 15 U.S.C. 637(b)(7)).

(2) Tradeoffs are not permitted.

(3) Proposals are evaluated for acceptability but not ranked using the non-cost/price factors.

(4) Exchanges may occur (see 15.306).

The term *technical* refers to all nonprice considerations and is not limited to product or service function, performance, or design. It applies to attributes of the offeror as a business firm as well as to attributes of the proposed product or service. To be acceptable, an offeror and its offer must satisfy all requirements in the request for proposals (RFP):

1. The offer must manifest the offeror's unconditional assent to the material terms of the RFP, including product or service requirements and contract clauses.

2. The offeror must satisfy qualifying criteria, such as requirements for a minimum amount of experience, production capacity, and the education and experience of key personnel.

The lowest price technically acceptable process allows the government's source selection authority to use much less discretion than the tradeoff process does. In fact, the exercise of discretion is limited to the determination of acceptability and offeror responsibility. Once the source selection authority has identified the set of offerors whose proposals are technically acceptable, he or she must make the source selection decision on the basis of an objective comparison of prices.

In theory, when using the lowest price technically acceptable process, the government makes tradeoffs before it solicits and receives proposals, on the basis of information it has obtained through market research. An agency planning to use the lowest price technically acceptable process must: (1) analyze its requirements; (2) choose relevant nonprice evaluation factors; (3) obtain relevant information about as many of the available purchase alternatives as it can find; (4) consider any relevant tradeoffs; and then (5) specify threshold values (minimums and maximums) for the nonprice evaluation factors that will ensure that its needs will be met. Having done this, the only pieces of information that the agency needs from competing offerors are their promises to satisfy the agency's requirements, information about their qualifications, and proposed prices.

For example, suppose that an agency wants to buy desktop computers and that it is interested in the following nonprice evaluation factors: (a) processor speed, (b) hard drive capacity, and (c) random access memory. If the agency can obtain enough information about the ranges of performance available in the market, then it may be able to specify minimums that will satisfy its requirements. If it can do this, and if it is confident that performance greater than the minimums is neither desirable nor necessary, then it can use the lowest price technically acceptable process to chose the contractor. Any offeror who promises to satisfy the minimum requirements will be "technically acceptable," differences among the technically acceptable offerors will not matter, and the offeror whose price is lowest will be the best value.

Based on this analysis, an agency should use the lowest price technically acceptable process when: (1) it can obtain enough information about the available purchase alternatives through market research to specify minimum and maximum values for the evaluation factors; and (2) it does not want or need performance in excess of those thresholds. Such may be the case for certain classes of commercial items and for products or services described in government specifications, such as military specifications. The risk with such a process is that the agency will discover something after the receipt of proposals that changes its mind about what it wants or needs.

An agency should not use the lowest price technically acceptable process when offerors will have to develop purchase alternatives as ad hoc responses to its requirements. In such cases, the agency will not have enough information about alternatives before proposal submission to make sound tradeoffs and specify threshold values in the RFP.

15. How does *source selection* differ from *sealed bidding*?

Source selection differs from *sealed bidding* mainly in three ways (but see below concerning two-step sealed bidding). First, in sealed bidding, agencies must compare bidders to each other on the basis of only price and price-related factors [see FAR 14.101(e), 14.103-2(d), 14.201-8, and 14.408-1(a)], and the agency must award the contract to the low, responsive, responsible bidder. In sealed bidding, tradeoffs are not permitted, and agencies have little discretion when selecting the winning bidder. In source selection, agencies may compare offerors to each other on the basis of almost any evaluation factors and make nonprice/price tradeoffs.

Second, in sealed bidding, an agency may not conduct discussions with offerors and must reject nonresponsive bids without bargaining [FAR 14.101(d), 14.301(a), and 14.404-2]. In source selection, agencies may negotiate with offerors, including offerors who submitted nonresponsive proposals, and let offerors revise their proposals in an effort to eliminate deficiencies.

Third, an agency may use sealed bidding only when contracting on a firm-fixed-price or fixed-price with economic price adjustment basis (FAR 14.104). Agencies may use source selection to contract on the basis of any pricing arrangement or combination of pricing arrangements permitted by the FAR [FAR 16.102(b)].

In addition to these primary differences, sealed bidding procedures differ from source selection procedures in many other ways. For instance, in sealed bidding, bid openings are public, and the public may examine the bids unless they are classified [FAR 14.101(c) and 14.402]; in source selection, agencies must prevent public disclosure of the number and the identities of the offerors and the contents of their proposals [FAR 15.207 and 15.505(f)].

TWO-STEP SEALED BIDDING

Two-step sealed bidding (FAR Subpart 14.5) is similar to lowest price technically acceptable source selection. In Step 1, the competitors submit unpriced technical proposals, which the agency must evaluate on a pass or fail basis. The agency may conduct discussions with bidders whose proposals are unacceptable (but reasonably susceptible of being made acceptable) to let them correct deficiencies (FAR 14.503-1). Step 1 is a qualifying procedure to determine which bidders may participate in step 2. Step 2 is a standard sealed bid procurement, in which the competitors whose technical proposals were judged to be acceptable are invited to submit sealed bids, and the agency awards the contract to the low, responsive, responsible bidder (FAR 14.503-2).

The main differences between lowest price technically acceptable source selection and two-step sealed bidding are that agencies may use two-step sealed bidding only when contracting on a fixed-price basis, while they may use lowest price technically acceptable source selection to contract on the basis of any pricing arrangement, even cost-reimbursement. Also, when using lowest price technically acceptable source selection, an agency does not have to wait until step 2 to solicit prices or issue a separate step 2 solicitation. It can require that offerors submit prices with their technical proposals. Procurements made through two-step sealed bidding are very rare.

16. How does *source selection* differ from *simplified acquisition*?

Agencies may use the *simplified acquisition procedures* described in FAR Part 13 to make acquisitions with a dollar value at or below the *simplified acquisition threshold* (see the definition in FAR 2.101) or with a dollar value of $5 million or less for commercial items. These procedures include the use of the governmentwide commercial purchase card, the issuance of simple purchase orders, the establishment and use of blanket purchase agreements, and the use of imprest (cash) funds and third-party drafts.

Source selection differs from simplified acquisition procedures in several ways. First, when conducting a source selection, agencies must seek full and open competition in compliance with the Competition in Contracting Act and FAR Part 6. However, agencies do not have to seek full and open competition when using simplified acquisition procedures. When making purchases with a dollar value in excess of the *micropurchase threshold* (see the definition in FAR 2.101), but not exceeding the simplified acquisition threshold, agencies need only "promote competition to the maximum extent practicable," soliciting quotations from "at least three sources" (see FAR 13.104).. They do not have to seek any competition at all when making purchases with a dollar value at or below the micropurchase threshold.

Second, when using simplified acquisition procedures, agencies usually (but not always) solicit quotations instead of binding offers. After evaluating quotations, agencies usually issue purchase orders, which are offers to buy. Acceptance of the government's offer by the quoter is what creates the contract (see FAR 13.004). In source selections, agencies solicit offers rather than quotes.

Third, FAR 13.106-1(c) encourages agencies to solicit quotations orally to the maximum extent practicable when using simplified acquisition procedures. FAR 15.203(f) effectively limits the use of oral requests for proposals in source selection to urgent or emergency acquisitions.

Fourth, when using simplified acquisition procedures, agencies do not have to disclose the relative importance of the evaluation factors or describe subfactors [see FAR 13.106-1(a)(2)], but they must do so in source selections [see FAR 15.203(a)(4), 15.204-5(c), and 15.304(e)].

Fifth, the rules in FAR 15.306 about exchanges with offerors after the receipt of proposals do not apply to simplified acquisitions. Thus, agencies may communicate more freely with quoters during a simplified acquisition than they can with offerors during a source selection, as long as they treat all quoters fairly and impartially.

Sixth, FAR 13.106-3(b) encourages agencies to minimize the documentation for simplified acquisitions. The documentation related to a source selection is often voluminous.

Seventh, there is no requirement to debrief offerors after a simplified acquisition [although an agency must provide a "brief explanation" of the award decision if the award was based on factors other than price alone; see FAR 13.106-3(d)]. However, FAR 15.505 and 15.506 require relatively extensive debriefings after a source selection.

Eighth, agencies rarely establish evaluation panels or boards when conducting simplified acquisitions, but such panels or boards are the norm in source selections.

17. What are *broad agency announcements*?

The *broad agency announcement* (BAA)—also called "Program Research and Development Announcement" (PRDA)—described in FAR 35.016, is a procedure for awarding contracts for basic or applied research and for development that is not related to a specific system or hardware procurement. In this procedure, an agency announces its research interests at the Governmentwide Point of Entry (http://www.fedbizopps.gov) and extends an open invitation for organizations to submit research proposals within some period of time. The agency does not issue a request for proposals. A "peer" or scientific panel reviews the proposals and recommends contract awards.

Although the broad agency announcement is considered a competitive procedure [see FAR 6.102(d)], proposals do not have to be evaluated by comparison with one another, and the source selection rules in FAR Part 15 do not apply. Although agencies are supposed to use BAAs only for basic and applied research [see FAR 35.016(a)], a study of such announcements published at http://www.fedbizopps.gov shows that agencies have interpreted the term *basic and applied research* rather broadly.

The following is a short BAA that was issued by NASA:

> PART: U.S. GOVERNMENT PROCUREMENTS
> SUBPART: SERVICES
> CLASSCOD: A—Research and Development
> OFFADD: NASA/Goddard Space Flight Center, NASA Headquarters
> Acquisition Branch, Code 210.H, Greenbelt, MD 20771
> SUBJECT: A—RESEARCH OPPORTUNITIES IN SPACE SCIENCE - 2000
> SOL NRA-00-OSS-01
> DUE 091500
> POC J. David Bohlin, Senior Program Executive,
> Phone (202) 358-0880, Fax (202) 358-3097,
> Email jbohlin@mail.hq.nasa.gov
> DESC: This NASA Research Announcement (NRA) is a broad agency announcement as specified in FAR 6.102 (d) (2). NRA-00-OSS-01, entitled "Research Opportunities in Space Science - 2000," will be available on or about February 9, 2000, by opening "Research Opportunities" from the menu on the NASA Office of Space Science (OSS) homepage at http://spacescience.nasa.gov on the World Wide Web. This NRA solicits proposals for supporting research, analysis, and technology across a broad range of different space science program elements relevant to the four defined OSS science themes, entitled Astronomical Search for Origins, Solar System Exploration, Structure and Evolution of the Universe, and The Sun-Earth Connection. Proposal due dates are staggered from April 28 through September 15, 2000. An electronically submitted Notice of Intent to propose beginning March 10, 2000, is requested for all program elements, and electronic submission of the Cover page is required. Participation through this NRA is open to all categories of U.S. and non-U.S. organizations, including educational institutions, industry, nonprofit institutions, NASA Centers, and other Government agencies. Further information about specific program elements may be obtained from the individual OSS

> Discipline Scientists listed in this NRA, while questions concerning general NRA policy issues may be directed to Dr. J. David Bohlin.

(Most BAAs are considerably longer than this example.)

18. How does *source selection* differ from the *architect-engineer selection process*?

The rules for the selection of firms for architect-engineer contracts are in FAR Subpart 36.6. When agencies select architect-engineer contractors, they negotiate with the *highest qualified firm*. The rules in FAR Parts 13, 14, and 15 do not apply to architect-engineer selections. The main difference between source selection and architect-engineer selection is that agencies do not consider price when choosing an architect-engineer contractor and do not make nonprice/price tradeoffs.

FAR 36.601-4 provides guidance about what kinds of services constitute *architect-engineer* services. An *engineering* service is a service relating to the design or construction of public works, i.e., real property. The term does not include engineering done for systems development and similar work, or for the modification, maintenance, or repair of personal property.

In an architect-engineer selection, an agency announces its requirements by publishing a synopsis at the Governmentwide Point of Entry (http://www.fedbizopps.gov). Interested, qualified firms submit information about their qualifications. To be qualified, a firm must be permitted by state law to practice the profession of architecture or engineering [40 U.S.C. 541 and FAR 36.601-4(b)]. FAR 36.602-1 specifies the selection criteria, which include professional qualifications, specialized experience, capacity, past performance, location of the firm relative to the project site, and other criteria that the agency considers to be important. An agency may conduct a design competition when authorized by the agency head based on guidelines in FAR 36.602-1(b). FAR Subpart 36.6 does not require that agencies announce their evaluation factors or state their relative importance.

Since price is not a factor in the selection of architect-engineer contractors, agencies do not use the tradeoff process (see FAR 15.101-1) or the lowest price technically acceptable process (see FAR 15.101-2) to select a contractor. There is no issue about whether a firm's performance on the nonprice evaluation factors is "worth" its price. However, when ranking the firms based on their relative qualifications, the evaluation board and source selection authority will have to make tradeoffs among the nonprice selection criteria if no firm is best on all the criteria.

Upon receipt of information from qualified firms, the agency convenes an evaluation board. FAR 36.602-2(a) requires that the members of architect-engineer selection boards be "highly qualified professional employees of the agency or other agencies, and if authorized by agency procedure, private practitioners of architecture, engineering, or related professions."

The evaluation board must review the information submitted by the interested firms and information in the agency's files about their qualifications, and rank them. The evaluation must include *discussions* (i.e., interviews) with at least three of the most highly qualified firms concerning service concepts and methods. The evaluation board ranks the firms and submits the names of the top three or four firms to the agency head or designated source selection authority.

The agency head or source selection authority makes the final decision about the order of rank. The source selection authority may not add any firm to the list; if he or she decides to reject the firms recommended by the evaluation board, he or she must return the report to the board without action. The board must then make a new recommendation.

After the final ranking, the contracting officer requests a proposal from the most highly qualified firm and negotiates a contract price and other terms in accordance with FAR Part 15. Since there is no price competition, the contracting officer must request the submission and certification of cost or pricing data if the procurement will exceed $500,000 (see FAR 15.403-4). If the contracting officer cannot reach an agreement on a fair and reasonable price or other terms with the most highly qualified firm, then he or she negotiates with the second most highly qualified firm, and so on until an agreement is reached.

19. What is a *commercial item*?

A *commercial item* is a product or service that meets the definition of commercial item in FAR 2.101, which reads as follows:

> "Commercial item" means—
>
> (1) Any item, other than real property, that is of a type customarily used by the general public or by nongovernmental entities for purposes other than governmental purposes and—
>
> (i) Has been sold, leased, or licensed to the general public; or
>
> (ii) Has been offered for sale, lease, or license to the general public;
>
> (2) Any item that evolved from an item described in paragraph (a) of this definition through advances in

technology or performance and that is not yet available in the commercial marketplace, but will be available in the commercial marketplace in time to satisfy the delivery requirements under a Government solicitation;

(3) Any item that would satisfy a criterion expressed in paragraphs (1) or (2) of this definition, but for—

(i) Modifications of a type customarily available in the commercial marketplace; or

(ii) Minor modifications of a type not customarily available in the commercial marketplace made to meet Federal Government requirements. Minor modifications means modifications that do not significantly alter the nongovernmental function or essential physical characteristics of an item or component, or change the purpose of a process. Factors to be considered in determining whether a modification is minor include the value and size of the modification and the comparative value and size of the final product. Dollar values and percentages may be used as guideposts, but are not conclusive evidence that a modification is minor;

(4) Any combination of items meeting the requirements of paragraphs (1), (2), (3), or (5) of this definition that are of a type customarily combined and sold in combination to the general public;

(5) Installation services, maintenance services, repair services, training services, and other services if—

(i) Such services are procured for support of an item referred to in paragraphs (1), (2), (3), or (4) of this definition, regardless of whether such services are provided by the same source and at the same time as the item; and

(ii) The source of such services provides similar services contemporaneously to the general public under terms and conditions similar to those offered to the Federal Government;

(6) Services of a type offered and sold competitively in substantial quantities in the commercial marketplace based on established catalog or market prices for specific tasks performed or specific outcomes to be achieved and under standard commercial terms and conditions. This does not include services that are sold based on hourly rates without an established catalog or market price for a specific service performed or a specific outcome to be achieved. For purposes of these services

(i) Catalog or market price means a price included in a catalog, price list, schedule, or other form that is regularly maintained by the manufacturer or vendor, is either published or otherwise available for inspection by customers, and states prices at which sales are currently, or were last, made to a significant number of buyers constituting the general public; and

(ii) Market prices means current prices that are established in the course of ordinary trade between buyers and sellers free to bargain and that can be substantiated through competition or from sources independent of the offerors.

(7) Any item, combination of items, or service referred to in paragraphs (1) through (6) of this definition, notwithstanding the fact that the item, combination of items, or service is transferred between or among separate divisions, subsidiaries, or affiliates of a contractor; or

(8) A nondevelopmental item, if the procuring agency determines the item was developed exclusively at private expense and sold in substantial quantities, on a competitive basis, to multiple State and local governments.

Note, first, that the word *item* applies to both products and to services. Paragraphs (1) through (4) and paragraph (8) of the definition apply to products, while paragraphs (5) and (6) apply to services. Paragraph (7) applies to both products and services.

A key to understanding this long definition is to understand what *nongovernmental* means and who is included in *the general public.* The FAR does not now define *general public.* However, an older version of FAR, at FAR 15.804-1(b)(2)(v), defined the term as follows:

> The general public ordinarily consists of buyers other than the U.S. Government or its instrumentalities, e.g., U.S. Government corporations. Sales to the general public do not include sales to affiliates of the offerors or purchases by the U.S. Government on behalf of foreign governments, such as for Foreign Military Sales.

Based on this definition, purchases by state and local governments are for nongovernmental purposes. Paragraph (8) of the definition of *commercial items* says that an item's commerciality is not affected by the fact that it was transferred to or from an affiliate.

As applied to products, the term *commercial item* appears to include almost anything that a firm has sold, has tried to sell, or plans to sell, as long as the government is not its only customer or prospective customer for the item. The term also includes maintenance, repair, training, and other services to "support" a commercial item. However, paragraph (6) says that services must have been "offered and sold competitively in substantial quantities" in the commercial marketplace and that sales must have been based on "catalog or market prices" and "standard commercial terms and conditions." Guidance about what quantities are "substantial" and what prices are "catalog or market prices" was removed from the FAR, so it is not clear what these terms mean as applied to commercial items. It is also unclear what kinds of contract clauses would constitute "standard commercial terms and conditions."

Another peculiar element of the definition of *commercial items*, as applied to services in paragraph (6), is the exclusion of "services that are sold based on hourly rates without an established catalog or market price for a specific service performed." The question raised by this restriction is how "specific" the description of the service has to be. Is *legal services* specific enough, or must the description be of a specific legal task, such as *will preparation*? It is likely that most agencies will shrug off this obscure restriction, but one never knows.

20. How do the rules for source selection apply to the acquisition of commercial items?

When purchasing commercial items, agencies must follow the rules in FAR Part 12 *and* the rules in FAR Parts 13, 14, or 15, depending on which contract formation procedure the agency decides to use. FAR 12.102, *Applicability*, reads as follows:

> (a) This part shall be used for the acquisition of supplies or services that meet the definition of commercial items at 2.101.
>
> (b) Contracting officers shall use the policies in this part in conjunction with the policies and procedures for solicitation, evaluation and award prescribed in Part 13, Simplified Acquisition Procedures; Part 14, Sealed Bidding; or Part 15, Contracting by Negotiation, as appropriate for the particular acquisition.
>
> (c) Contracts for the acquisition of commercial items are subject to the policies in other parts of this chapter. When a policy in another part of this chapter [Title 48 of the Code of Federal Regulations, Chapter 1] is inconsistent with a policy in this part, this Part 12 shall take precedence for the acquisition of commercial items.
>
> (d) The definition of commercial item in section 2.101 uses the phrase "purposes other than governmental pur-

poses." These purposes are those that are not unique to a government.

(e) This part shall not apply to the acquisition of commercial items—

(1) At or below the micro-purchase threshold;

(2) Using the Standard Form 44 (see 13.306);

(3) Using the imprest fund (see 13.305);

(4) Using the Governmentwide commercial purchase card; or

(5) Directly from another Federal agency.

Thus, when using source selection in a procurement of commercial items, the agency must comply with both FAR Part 12 and FAR Part 15, and FAR Part 12 will govern if there is a conflict between the two parts. FAR Part 15 does not apply to procurements of commercial items valued at $5 million or less made under the commercial items test program described in FAR Subpart 13.5.

21. How does source selection differ from the test program for certain commercial items?

The *test program for certain commercial items*, which is described in FAR Subpart 13.5, allows agencies to use the simplified acquisition procedures in FAR Part 13 to purchase commercial items that are expected to cost $5 million or less. The key differences between source selections and purchases under the test program are that, under the test program, agencies do not have to: (1) seek full and open competition; (2) base their evaluations on the factors specified in FAR 15.304; (3) state the relative importance of their evaluation factors; (4) follow the rules in FAR 15.305 for proposal evaluation; or (5) comply with the rules in FAR 15.306 governing exchanges with offerors after receipt of proposals (i.e., the rules about clarification, communication, establishing the competitive range, discussion, or proposal revision).

The test program is authorized by a statute that expires on January 1, 2008. Unless the program is extended or made permanent, agencies will have to use either sealed bidding or the negotiation procedures in FAR Part 15 to make such purchases after that date.

Part II

Source Selection Planning

The questions in this part address critically important planning issues, such as the need to prepare formal *acquisition plans* and *source selection plans* and the contents of such plans, organizational issues such as who selects the contractor, and the nature of and requirements for source selection evaluation factors.

22. What is an *acquisition plan*, and when does an agency have to prepare one?

An *acquisition plan* is a document that describes the objectives of an acquisition and the business strategy that an agency will use to achieve those objectives. Acquisition plans are used to communicate acquisition objectives and strategies to the agency managers who must approve them, and to document their review, coordination, and approval. These plans ultimately go into the files (where, in all likelihood, no one ever sees them again).

The FAR does not say when agencies must prepare an acquisition plan, but FAR 7.103(e) says that agency heads must prescribe procedures for writing acquisition plans. Thus, requirements to prepare acquisition plans vary from agency to agency and should appear in agency FAR supplements. But FAR 7.102(a) says that agencies must perform acquisition planning for "all" acquisitions.

The Department of Defense requires written plans for development procurements estimated at $5 million or more;

procurements for production or services estimated at $30 million or more in total and $15 million or more for any single fiscal year; and for "any other acquisition considered appropriate."

The Department of Justice requires written acquisition plans only for acquisitions of major systems, while the Department of Veterans Affairs requires a written plan for every acquisition in excess of $100,000 and for all acquisitions of automatic data processing hardware and software regardless of dollar value. The National Aeronautics and Space Administration requires a written plan for all acquisitions that require headquarters approval and for certain other acquisitions that will exceed $5 million. The FAR supplements of several agencies say nothing at all about written acquisition plans.

23. What is included in an acquisition plan?

FAR 7.105, *Contents of written acquisition plans,* says that written acquisition plans "must address all the technical, business, management, and other significant considerations that will control the acquisition." It prescribes a two-part organization, as follows:

> (a) *Acquisition background and objectives—*
>
> (1) Statement of need. Introduce the plan by a brief statement of need. Summarize the technical and contractual history of the acquisition. Discuss feasible acquisition alternatives, the impact of prior acquisitions on those alternatives, and any related in-house effort.
>
> (2) *Applicable conditions.* State all significant conditions affecting the acquisition, such as—
>
> (i) Requirements for compatibility with existing or future systems or programs; and

(ii) Any known cost, schedule, and capability or performance constraints.

(3) *Cost.* Set forth the established cost goals for the acquisition and the rationale supporting them, and discuss related cost concepts to be employed, including, as appropriate, the following items:

(i) *Life-cycle cost.* Discuss how life-cycle cost will be considered. If it is not used, explain why. If appropriate, discuss the cost model used to develop life-cycle-cost estimates.

(ii) *Design-to-cost.* Describe the design-to-cost objective(s) and underlying assumptions, including the rationale for quantity, learning-curve, and economic adjustment factors. Describe how objectives are to be applied, tracked, and enforced. Indicate specific related solicitation and contractual requirements to be imposed.

(iii) *Application of should-cost.* Describe the application of should-cost analysis to the acquisition (see 15.407-4).

(4) *Capability or performance.* Specify the required capabilities or performance characteristics of the supplies or the performance standards of the services being acquired and state how they are related to the need.

(5) *Delivery or performance-period requirements.* Describe the basis for establishing delivery or performance-period requirements (see Subpart 11.4). Explain and provide reasons for any urgency if it results in concurrency of development and production or constitutes justification for not providing for full and open competition.

(6) *Trade-offs.* Discuss the expected consequences of trade-offs among the various cost, capability or performance, and schedule goals.

(7) *Risks.* Discuss technical, cost, and schedule risks and describe what efforts are planned or underway to reduce

risk and the consequences of failure to achieve goals. If concurrency of development and production is planned, discuss its effects on cost and schedule risks.

(8) *Acquisition streamlining.* If specifically designated by the requiring agency as a program subject to acquisition streamlining, discuss plans and procedures to—

(i) Encourage industry participation by using draft solicitations, presolicitation conferences, and other means of stimulating industry involvement during design and development in recommending the most appropriate application and tailoring of contract requirements;

(ii) Select and tailor only the necessary and cost-effective requirements; and

(iii) State the timeframe for identifying which of those specifications and standards, originally provided for guidance only, shall become mandatory.

(b) *Plan of action—*

(1) *Sources.* Indicate the prospective sources of supplies and/or services that can meet the need. Consider required sources of supplies or services (see Part 8) and sources identifiable through databases of contracts and other procurement instruments intended for use by multiple agencies available at http://www.contractdirectory.gov. Include consideration of small business, veteran-owned small business, HUBZone small business, small disadvantaged business, and women-owned small business concerns (see Part 19), and the impact of any bundling that might affect their participation in the acquisition (see 7.107) (15 U.S.C. 644(e)). When the proposed acquisition strategy involves bundling, identify the incumbent contractors and contracts affected by the bundling. Address the extent and results of the market research and indicate their impact on the various elements of the plan (see Part 10).

(2) *Competition.*

(i) Describe how competition will be sought, promoted, and sustained throughout the course of the acquisition. If full and open competition is not contemplated, cite the authority in 6.302, discuss the basis for the application of that authority, identify the source(s), and discuss why full and open competition cannot be obtained.

(ii) Identify the major components or subsystems. Discuss component breakout plans relative to these major components or subsystems. Describe how competition will be sought, promoted, and sustained for these components or subsystems.

(iii) Describe how competition will be sought, promoted, and sustained for spares and repair parts. Identify the key logistic milestones, such as technical data delivery schedules and acquisition method coding conferences, that affect competition.

(iv) When effective subcontract competition is both feasible and desirable, describe how such subcontract competition will be sought, promoted, and sustained throughout the course of the acquisition. Identify any known barriers to increasing subcontract competition and address how to overcome them.

(3) *Source-selection procedures.* Discuss the source-selection procedures for the acquisition, including the timing for submission and evaluation of proposals, and the relationship of evaluation factors to the attainment of the acquisition objectives (see Subpart 15.3).

(4) *Acquisition considerations.* (i) Provide rationale if a performance-based contract will not be used or if a performance-based contract for services is contemplated on other than a firm-fixed-price basis (see 37.102(a) and 16.505(a)(3)).

(ii) For each order contemplated, discuss—

(A) For information technology acquisitions, how the capital planning and investment control requirements of 40 U.S.C. 1422 and OMB Circular A-130 will be met (see 7.103(t) and part 39); and

(B) Why this action benefits the Government, such as when—

(1) The agency can accomplish its mission more efficiently and effectively (e.g., take advantage of the servicing agency's specialized expertise; or gain access to contractors with needed expertise); or

(2) Ordering through an indefinite delivery contract facilitates access to small business concerns, including small disadvantaged business concerns, 8(a) contractors, women-owned small business concerns, HUBZone small business concerns, veteran-owned small business concerns, or service-disabled veteran-owned small business concerns.

(5) *Budgeting and funding.* Include budget estimates, explain how they were derived, and discuss the schedule for obtaining adequate funds at the time they are required (see Subpart 32.7).

(6) *Product or service descriptions.* Explain the choice of product or service description types (including performance-based contracting descriptions) to be used in the acquisition.

(7) *Priorities, allocations, and allotments.* When urgency of the requirement dictates a particularly short delivery or performance schedule, certain priorities may apply. If so, specify the method for obtaining and using priorities, allocations, and allotments, and the reasons for them (see Subpart 11.6).

(8) *Contractor versus Government performance.* Address the consideration given to OMB Circular No. A-76 (see Subpart 7.3).

(9) *Inherently governmental functions.* Address the consideration given to OFPP Policy Letter 92-1 (see Subpart 7.5).

(10) *Management information requirements.* Discuss, as appropriate, what management system will be used by the Government to monitor the contractor's effort.

(11) *Make or buy.* Discuss any consideration given to make-or-buy programs (see 15.407-2).

(12) *Test and evaluation.* To the extent applicable, describe the test program of the contractor and the Government. Describe the test program for each major phase of a major system acquisition. If concurrency is planned, discuss the extent of testing to be accomplished before production release.

(13) *Logistics considerations.* Describe—

(i) The assumptions determining contractor or agency support, both initially and over the life of the acquisition, including consideration of contractor or agency maintenance and servicing (see Subpart 7.3) and distribution of commercial items;

(ii) The reliability, maintainability, and quality assurance requirements, including any planned use of warranties (see Part 46);

(iii) The requirements for contractor data (including repurchase data) and data rights, their estimated cost, and the use to be made of the data (see Part 27); and

(iv) Standardization concepts, including the necessity to designate, in accordance with agency procedures, technical equipment as "standard" so that future purchases of the equipment can be made from the same manufacturing source.

(14) *Government-furnished property.* Indicate any property to be furnished to contractors, including material and

facilities, and discuss any associated considerations, such as its availability or the schedule for its acquisition (see Part 45).

(15) *Government-furnished information.* Discuss any Government information, such as manuals, drawings, and test data, to be provided to prospective offerors and contractors.

(16) *Environmental and energy conservation objectives.* Discuss all applicable environmental and energy conservation objectives associated with the acquisition (see Part 23), the applicability of an environmental assessment or environmental impact statement (see 40 CFR 1502), the proposed resolution of environmental issues, and any environmentally-related requirements to be included in solicitations and contracts.

(17) *Security considerations.* For acquisitions dealing with classified matters, discuss how adequate security will be established, maintained, and monitored (see Subpart 4.4).

(18) *Contract administration.* Describe how the contract will be administered. In contracts for services, include how inspection and acceptance corresponding to the work statement's performance criteria will be enforced.

(19) *Other considerations.* Discuss, as applicable, standardization concepts, the industrial readiness program, the Defense Production Act, the Occupational Safety and Health Act, foreign sales implications, and any other matters germane to the plan not covered elsewhere.

(20) *Milestones for the acquisition cycle.* Address the following steps and any others appropriate:

- Acquisition plan approval.
- Statement of work.
- Specifications.
- Data requirements.
- Completion of acquisition-package preparation.

- Purchase request.
- Justification and approval for other than full and open competition where applicable and/or any required D&F approval.
- Issuance of synopsis.
- Issuance of solicitation.
- Evaluation of proposals, audits, and field reports.
- Beginning and completion of negotiations.
- Contract preparation, review, and clearance.
- Contract award.

(21) *Identification of participants in acquisition plan preparation.* List the individuals who participated in preparing the acquisition plan, giving contact information for each.

A careful reading of the topics and issues listed in FAR 7.105 (e.g., life-cycle cost, design-to-cost, application of should-cost, tradeoffs, risks, make or buy, test and evaluation, logistics) suggests that policy makers are especially concerned about major system acquisitions.

24. What is a *source selection plan,* and when does an agency have to prepare one?

A *source selection plan* is a document that describes the evaluation factors, evaluation procedures, and organization that an agency will use to select a contractor in accordance with the source selection procedures delineated in FAR Part 15. Agencies use source selection plans to communicate that information to the agency managers who must approve those factors and procedures, and to document their review, coordination, and approval. They ultimately become a part of the files. Source selection plans are usually separate from acquisition plans.

The FAR does not require that agencies prepare written source selection plans. FAR 15.303(b)(2) says that the agency head must "approve the source selection strategy or acquisition plan, if applicable, before solicitation release," but it does not require the preparation of a written plan. An earlier edition of the FAR required a source selection plan for "formal" source selections; however, that requirement was eliminated by the FAR Part 15 Rewrite, which took effect on January 1, 1998.

Some agency FAR supplements require the preparation of source selection plans. For example, the Department of Defense FAR Supplement 215.303(b)(2) requires source selection plans for "high dollar value and other acquisitions."

25. What is included in a source selection plan?

The contents of source selection plans vary from agency to agency. The Department of Defense FAR Supplement 215.303(b)(2)(C) prescribes the following content for source selection plans:

> (1) The organization, membership, and responsibilities of the source selection team;
>
> (2) A statement of the proposed evaluation factors and any significant subfactors and their relative importance;
>
> (3) A description of the evaluation process, including specific procedures and techniques to be used in evaluating proposals; and
>
> (4) A schedule of significant events in the source selection process, including documentation of the source selection decision and announcement of the source selection decision.

Perhaps the most comprehensive requirements for source selection plans are in Air Force Mandatory Procedure MP5315.3,

Source Selection (17 May 2005), Section 4.3.2, which reads as follows:

> 4.3.2. Source Selection Plan. Acquisitions covered under this Mandatory Procedure shall have a Source Selection Plan. The Source Selection Plan shall include the information outlined below. Whenever the contracting officer is the Source Selection Authority, a streamlined Source Selection Plan may be documented in the Simplified Source Selection Report (see 7.11 below). Whenever possible, refer to and attach supporting documents rather than repeating information in the Source Selection Plan.
>
> 4.3.2.1. A brief description of the requirement, including reference to any applicable guidance such as a Program Management Directive (PMD).
>
> 4.3.2.2. A summary of the acquisition strategy, including, when applicable, type(s) of contract(s) anticipated, the incentives contemplated, milestone demonstrations intended, special contract clauses, performance metrics and language supporting it as a performance based services acquisition.
>
> 4.3.2.3. Source selection team. Describe the proposed organizational structure. List recommended members and advisors by name, position title, company affiliation, if applicable, or by functional area. Identify other government organizations that will participate in the source selection.
>
> 4.3.2.4. Presolicitation activities. Describe the activities leading up to the release of the solicitation such as market research, draft solicitations, and synopsis. For the market research, discuss how it was used to achieve competition, including a discussion of screening criteria, if applicable.
>
> 4.3.2.5. Evaluation factors and subfactors. Describe the evaluation factors and subfactors and their relative order of importance by attaching the relevant portions of the

instructions to offerors and evaluation criteria (Sections L and M or equivalent provisions of the solicitation). Describe the evaluation process, including specific procedures and techniques to be used in evaluating proposals.

4.3.2.6. Schedule of events. Identify the schedule for significant source selection activities in sufficient detail to allow the reviewing authorities to assess the practicality of the schedule.

4.3.2.7. Non-government personnel. Address the use of non-government personnel.

4.3.2.8. Identify and explain requested or approved deviations and delegations.

An old edition of the Air Force FAR Supplement contained even more comprehensive requirements in Appendix BB, as follows:

Source Selection Plan (SSP)

(a) The SSP is a key document in conducting the source selection. It should contain the elements described below to ensure timely review and SSA approval. The SSP should be jointly developed by the contracting personnel and personnel responsible for the requirement. See the table in BB-105 for SSP review and approval levels.

(1) The SSP must be submitted sufficiently in advance of the planned acquisition action to facilitate review and approval by the SSA and early establishment of the source selection organization.

(2) When changes in acquisition strategy require a revision to the SSP, personnel responsible for the requirement will send the proposed revision through source selection channels to the SSA.

(b) The SSP will address the issues below and other things that are important or unusual about a given acquisition.

The SSP should contain a concise description of the acquisition situation. If an extended discussion of any issue is required, supporting details may be provided in separate documents attached to the SSP. Ideally, the wording used in much of the SSP should be identical to the wording used in other documents related to this effort, such as the acquisition plan, acquisition strategy panel minutes, or the solicitation.

(c) The plan shall include the following:

(1) INTRODUCTION. Describe briefly what is being acquired.

(2) SOURCE SELECTION ORGANIZATION. Describe the proposed SSA and SSET organizations (including Government and non-Government advisors). List recommended key members by name, by position title, or by functional area. The plan must identify other Government organizations that will be represented on the SSET.

(3) PROPOSED PRESOLICITATION ACTIVITIES. Describe the activities leading up to release of the solicitation, including market survey, draft solicitations, synopsis, and solicitation release meeting. For the market survey, discuss how it was used to achieve competition, including a discussion of screening criteria, if applicable.

(4) EVALUATION PROCEDURES. This section discusses the process that will be used by the SSET to evaluate offerors' proposals and develop a Proposal Analysis Report. In other words, it describes what the SSET will do and how they will document what they did. Describe how the proposals will be evaluated and how they will be rated. Describe how the Government estimate was developed including any cost drivers that have been identified. Describe how those cost drivers will be treated by the pricing team during proposal evaluation. Although the cost (price) criterion will not be given a color or a risk rating during proposal evaluation, the process that will be used to evaluate offerors' proposals must be described

in this section. NOTE: When the plan adopts something verbatim from this regulation, simply cite the regulation instead of quoting verbatim in the plan. This includes the color coding and risk definitions.

(5) EVALUATION CRITERIA. Describe the cost (price) criterion and specific criteria including factors and, when appropriate, subfactors and elements. The information in this section must be exactly duplicated in Section M of the RFP. Describe the assessment criteria and how they apply to the evaluation. The relative importance of the cost (price) criterion, specific criteria, and general considerations will be stated. Assessment criteria must also be ranked in relative order of importance or identified as of equal importance. Describe general considerations and how they relate to the evaluation of the offeror's proposal.

(6) ACQUISITION STRATEGY. The SSP will include a summary of the acquisition strategy, including type of contract(s) proposed, the incentives contemplated, special contract clauses, etc. The SSP acquisition strategy must reflect the strategy developed in the AP/SAMP.

(7) SCHEDULE OF EVENTS. Identify and establish the schedule for significant source selection activities in sufficient detail to allow the reviewing authorities to assess the practicality of the schedule. The schedule of events in Attachment BB-2 may be used as a guide.

(8) NON-GOVERNMENT ADVISORS. The source selection plan shall address the use of non-Government advisors (see FAR 15.305(c) and AFFARS Appendix BB-108).

(d) The SSP shall be approved by the SSA before issuing the solicitation.

(e) Only include tailored information; otherwise, cite the appropriate paragraph of this regulation.

A review of agency FAR supplements shows that many of them do not require source selection plans.

Once a source selection is underway, an agency is not required to stick to its source selection plan, only to the terms of its RFP. GAO has long held that it will not a sustain a protest based on the complaint that an agency failed to follow its source selection plan. In its decision in *Lear Siegler Services, Inc.* (B-280834; B-280834.2, November 25, 1998), GAO noted that:

> [To] the extent LSI argues that the Navy failed to follow the source selection plan, its argument ignores the distinction between an evaluation scheme included in the RFP, and a source selection plan provided to evaluators as a guideline. As between these two documents, it is the RFP—and the evaluation scheme set forth therein—that forms the compact between the agency and the offerors about how proposals will be evaluated. Loral Aeronutronic, B-259857.2, B-259858.2, July 5, 1995, 95-2 CPD ¶ 213 at 9. Source selection plans are internal agency instructions and do not give rights to outside parties. Id. at 9-10.

26. How does the government organize to conduct a source selection?

The FAR does not prescribe the organization of source selections. In most agencies, one official makes the source selection decision based on the findings and recommendations of a proposal evaluation board, team, or panel; that person is called the source selection authority (SSA). FAR 15.303 describes the organizational responsibilities for source selection as follows:

> (a) Agency heads are responsible for source selection. The contracting officer is designated as the source selection au-

> thority, unless the agency head appoints another individual for a particular acquisition or group of acquisitions.
>
> (b) The source selection authority shall—
>
> (1) Establish an evaluation team, tailored for the particular acquisition, that includes appropriate contracting, legal, logistics, technical, and other expertise to ensure a comprehensive evaluation of offers;
>
> (2) Approve the source selection strategy or acquisition plan, if applicable, before solicitation release;
>
> (3) Ensure consistency among the solicitation requirements, notices to offerors, proposal preparation instructions, evaluation factors and subfactors, solicitation provisions or contract clauses, and data requirements;
>
> (4) Ensure that proposals are evaluated based solely on the factors and subfactors contained in the solicitation (10 U.S.C. 2305(b)(1) and 41 U.S.C. 253b(d)(3));
>
> (5) Consider the recommendations of advisory boards or panels (if any); and
>
> (6) Select the source or sources whose proposal is the best value to the Government (10 U.S.C. 2305(b)(4)(B) and 41 U.S.C. 253b(d)(3)).
>
> (c) The contracting officer shall—
>
> (1) After release of a solicitation, serve as the focal point for inquiries from actual or prospective offerors;
>
> (2) After receipt of proposals, control exchanges with offerors in accordance with 15.306; and
>
> (3) Award the contract(s).

Some agencies have published rules that prescribe source selection organization in more detail. For example, the Air

Force prescribes the various organizational components of a "source selection team" in its Mandatory Procedure MP5315.3, Source Selection Team (17 May 2005), Section 4.1, as follows:

> 4.1. Source Selection Team
>
> 4.1.1. The Source Selection Authority [DEF] shall —
>
> 4.1.1.1. Be responsible for the proper and efficient conduct of the source selection process in accordance with this procedure.
>
> 4.1.1.2. Appoint the respective chairpersons for the Source Selection Evaluation Team [DEF] and the Source Selection Advisory Council [DEF] when used.
>
> 4.1.1.3. Establish a source selection team as needed and ensure that the team membership remains consistent for the duration of the selection process.
>
> 4.1.1.4. Ensure all involved in the source selection are knowledgeable of policy and procedures for properly and efficiently conducting the source selection.
>
> 4.1.2. The Source Selection Advisory Council Chairperson. When the Source Selection Authority establishes a Source Selection Advisory Council, the appointed chairperson shall, subject to source selection authority approval, appoint source selection advisory council members and request, when appropriate, additional Secretariat, HQ USAF, and joint service members. The chairperson shall ensure all Source Selection Advisory Council members are knowledgeable of their responsibilities.
>
> 4.1.3. The Source Selection Evaluation Team Chairperson. When the Source Selection Authority establishes a Source Selection Evaluation Team, the appointed chairperson shall —

4.1.3.1. Appoint members to the Source Selection Evaluation Team, including a Performance Confidence Assessment Group [DEF] and its chairperson as required, subject to approval of the Source Selection Authority.

4.1.3.2. Establish a Performance Confidence Assessment Group for all source selections in excess of $100 million.

4.1.3.3. Ensure personnel, resources, and time assigned to the source selection reflect the complexity of the program. Personnel substitutions for the Source Selection Evaluation Team may be approved by the Source Selection Evaluation Team chairperson subsequent to Source Selection Plan approval and documented in an addendum. A formal amendment to the Source Selection Plan is not required.

4.1.3.4. Ensure members of the Source Selection Evaluation Team are knowledgeable of their responsibilities before any proposal is reviewed, including details on how the evaluation is to be conducted.

4.1.4. The contracting officer shall —

4.1.4.1. Ensure that, in accordance with AFFARS 5315.305(c), required approvals are obtained and contract clause requirements are met before non-government personnel are allowed to provide source selection support; and

4.1.4.2. Manage all business aspects of the acquisition.

4.1.5. Advisors. The Source Selection Authority may establish advisors as necessary to assist in the source selection evaluation. Although advisors may assist in and provide input regarding the evaluation, they may not determine ratings or rankings of offerors' proposals.

4.1.6. Primary Responsibility. Government personnel assigned as a source selection team member shall consider

> this duty as their primary responsibility. Their source selection assignment shall take precedence over other work assignments. Supervisors are responsible for ensuring that other work assignments do not adversely impact the source selection process. Key members of the source selection team, such as the Source Selection Evaluation Team Chairperson, the Performance Confidence Assessment Group Chairperson and the contracting officer, shall have source selection experience, if possible, and be designated early in the acquisition process.

The typical source selection board probably includes no more than three to five members. However, the more significant a procurement is to an agency, the larger the board is likely to be. Some agency source selection boards have been very large. The joint Air Force/Navy evaluation board for the Tactical Fighter Experimental (TFX) procurement in the 1960s had "200-plus" members. [See *TFX Contract Investigation, Hearings Before the Permanent Subcommittee on Investigations of the Committee on Government Operations*, Part 1, p. 102, United States Senate, 85th Congress, First Session (1963).] A 1988 protest decision about a procurement for a word processing system described an evaluation board that had 27 or 28 members. [See *Contel Federal Systems, Inc.*, GSBCA No. 9743-P, 89-1 BCA ¶ 21,248, (1988), p. 108,127.] A 1995 GAO report described an Army board for a "streamlined" procurement of a commercial helicopter that included a "core group" of 50 people. (See *Acquisition Reform: Comparison of Army's Commercial Helicopter Buy and Private Sector Buys*, General Accounting Office Report No. GAO/NSIAD-95-54, March 1995, p. 4.) Such large boards are probably rare today.

When the SSA is a high-level agency official, some agencies establish a panel between the evaluation board and the SSA made up of mid-level functional managers. Such mid-level panels are called source selection advisory councils, or SSACs. Their job is to review the evaluation board's work and make recommendations to the SSA.

Agencies have traditionally split evaluation teams into separate technical panels and cost panels. Members of the technical panel evaluate technical proposals and are usually prohibited from seeing the cost or price information in proposals. This is done out of concern for the possibility that exposure to cost or price information would prejudice the technical evaluation. This rule was never in statutes or in the FAR, however, and the FAR Part 15 Rewrite inserted a provision in FAR 15.305(a)(4) that says that cost information may be provided to members of the technical panel in accordance with agency procedures.

Some agencies use government employees from other agencies and even contractor personnel as advisors or consultants to source selection boards. This is permissible. However, FAR 37.203(d) says that agencies may not use contractors to conduct evaluations or analyses of proposals unless: (1) no qualified government personnel are available; (2) the contractor is a federally funded research and development center; or (3) otherwise authorized by law.

FAR 37.204 and 37.205 provide guidelines for determining whether or not qualified government personnel are available, as follows:

> **37.204 Guidelines for determining availability of personnel.**
>
> (a) The head of an agency shall determine, for each evaluation or analysis of proposals, if sufficient personnel with the requisite training and capabilities are available within the agency to perform the evaluation or analysis of proposals submitted for the acquisition.
>
> (b) If, for a specific evaluation or analysis, such personnel are not available within the agency, the head of the agency shall—

(1) Determine which Federal agencies may have personnel with the required training and capabilities; and

(2) Consider the administrative cost and time associated with conducting the search, the dollar value of the procurement, other costs, such as travel costs involved in the use of such personnel, and the needs of the Federal agencies to make management decisions on the best use of available personnel in performing the agency's mission.

(c) If the supporting agency agrees to make the required personnel available, the agencies shall execute an agreement for the detail of the supporting agency's personnel to the requesting agency.

(d) If the requesting agency, after reasonable attempts to obtain personnel with the required training and capabilities, is unable to identify such personnel, the head of the agency may make the determination required by 37.203.

(e) An agency may make a determination regarding the availability of covered personnel for a class of proposals for which evaluation and analysis would require expertise so unique or specialized that it is not reasonable to expect such personnel to be available.

37.205 Contracting officer responsibilities.

The contracting officer shall ensure that the determination required in accordance with the guidelines at 37.204 has been made prior to issuing a solicitation.

If an agency is going to disclose proprietary information in a proposal to a contractor serving as a consultant, it must get permission to do so from the firm that submitted the proposal.

Some agencies have promulgated in-house policies about using contractor personnel to evaluate proposals. For example, the Navy Marine Corps Acquisition Regulation Supplement (NMCARS) 5215.305(90) provides as follows:

> Approval for use of contractor personnel as evaluators is addressed in FAR Subpart 37.2 and 5237.204. Such contractor personnel shall not rank or recommend one proposal over another, assign any ratings or numerical scores, or otherwise act in a decision making capacity. Whenever advisory contractor personnel are to be used, a written release shall be obtained from each offeror.

NMCARS 5237.204 says:

> **Guidelines for determining availability of personnel.**
>
> (a) Approval by the Source Selection Authority of a source selection plan identifying only agency/FFRDC [Federally Funded Research and Development Center] personnel as evaluators may constitute the determination that sufficient personnel are available within the agency to evaluate or analyze proposals. Determinations that sufficient personnel are not readily available within the agency nor within another Federal agency shall be made in accordance with (d) below.
>
> (b) (i) Activities should use common sense and reasonably available information in determining which other Federal agencies or Navy/Marine Corps activities may have personnel with the training and capabilities required to support evaluation of proposals. The nature and extent of efforts an activity should pursue in obtaining information depend on the circumstances of the procurement, taking into consideration such factors as those listed in FAR 37.204(b), the specialized nature of the qualifications and expertise required, and the activity's previous experience in attempting to identify similarly qualified personnel.

(ii) Qualified employees of another agency who could only be available at times other than when needed to conduct a planned evaluation of proposals may be considered "not readily available" if it is not practical to adjust the evaluation schedule to accommodate using them.

(c) If another agency will make personnel available on a reimbursable basis, Subpart 17.5 will generally apply.

(d) (i) HCAs [Heads of Contracting Activities] are delegated authority to determine that personnel with the required training and capabilities needed to conduct evaluations or analyses of any aspect of proposals for an initial contract award are not readily available within the agency or other Federal agencies. The procedures in FAR Subpart 1.7 apply to HCA determinations made under this section.

(ii) Forward one copy of each determination under (d)(1) made prior to 1 October 1997 to ABM [Acquisition and Business Management office] within five days of approval.

27. Who is in charge of the source selection process?

FAR 15.303(a) places the ultimate responsibility for source selection on the agency head. But agency heads usually delegate this responsibility to a lower-level official, who is then called the source selection authority (SSA) or source selection official (SSO). According to FAR 15.303(a), the contracting officer is the SSA unless the agency head appoints someone else. Some agencies have established internal rules about who will serve as the source selection authority. For example, Environmental Protection Agency FAR Supplement 1515.303 provides as follows:

> The Source Selection Authority (SSA) shall be established at the levels specified as follows:
>
> (a) Acquisitions having a potential value exceeding $25,000,000: Service Center Manager (SCM). This authority is not redelegable.
>
> (b) Acquisitions having a potential value exceeding $10,000,000 to $25,000,000: SCM, who has authority to redelegate SSA authority to a warranted 1102 [contract specialist]. If redelegated, review by another warranted 1102 designated by the SCM is also required. A Regional Contracting Officer Supervisor may act as the SSA, as determined on a case-by-case basis, by the Director, Superfund/RCRA Regional Procurement Operations Division (SRRPOD).
>
> (c) Acquisitions having a potential value of $10,000,000 or less: The contracting officer.

Generally, the larger the dollar value of a procurement, the higher the rank of the source selection authority.

FAR 15.303(b) says that the SSA must: (1) establish the evaluation team; (2) approve the acquisition plan and source selection strategy; (3) ensure consistency between the RFP and notices to offerors; (4) ensure that evaluations are conducted in accordance with the laws and regulations and the terms of the RFP; and (5) select the contractor.

An SSA's decision-making authority is not constrained by the findings and recommendations of the evaluation board. In its decision in *EBA Engineering, Inc.* (B-275818, March 31, 1997), GAO found that:

> Source selection officials in negotiated procurements are not bound by the recommendations or evaluation judgments of lower-level evaluators, even though the working level evaluators may normally be expected to

> have the technical expertise required for such evaluations. Grey Advertising, Inc., 55 Comp. Gen. 1111, 1120 (1976), 76-1 CPD ¶325 at p. 11; Calspan Corp., B-258441, Jan. 19, 1995, 95-1 CPD ¶ 28; Benchmark Sec., Inc., B-247655.2, Feb. 4, 1993, 93-1 CPD ¶ 133.

28. What is a *requirement*?

The FAR does not define the term *requirement,* which it uses synonymously with the term *need,* which it also does not define. For example, FAR 10.001(a) says, "Agencies shall (1) Ensure that legitimate needs are identified and trade-offs evaluated to acquire items which meet those needs. . . ." FAR 10.001(a)(3) then says, "Use the results of market research to—(i) Determine if sources capable of satisfying the agency's requirements exist. . . ." FAR 11.002(a) says, "[A]gencies shall—(1) specify needs using market research. . . ." FAR 11.002(a)(2)(i) then says, "State requirements with respect to an acquisition of supplies or services in terms of—(A) Functions to be performed; (B) Performance required; or (C) Essential physical characteristics. . . ."

The meaning of the term *requirement* is important, because GAO says that an offeror's failure to satisfy a requirement makes its proposal unacceptable and makes the offeror ineligible for contract award. For example, in its protest decision in *Plasma-Therm, Inc.* (B-280664.2; December 28, 1998), GAO stated:

> A proposal that fails to meet one or more of a solicitation's material requirements is technically unacceptable and cannot form the basis for the award of a contract. Severn Cos., Inc., B-275717.2, Apr. 28, 1997, 97-1 CPD ¶ 181 at 3-4.

(The protester's micromachining device did not satisfy a specification requirement for a silicon nitrade sensitivity ratio of 500:1.)

However, when GAO uses the term *requirement* it means more than just technical requirements; it includes contract clauses, too. In its decision in *Beckman Coulter* (B-281030; B-281030.2; December 21, 1998), GAO noted:

> In negotiated procurements, any proposal that fails to conform to material terms and conditions of the solicitation should be considered unacceptable and may not form the basis for an award. Barents Group, L.L.C., B-276082, B-276082.2, May 9, 1997, 97-1 CPD ¶ 164 at 10; Martin Marietta Corp., B-233742.4, Jan. 31, 1990, 90-1 CPD ¶ 132 at 7.

In *Beckman Coulter,* the protester had included its own version of a termination clause in its proposal, which was contrary to the RFP requirement to use the clause specified by the FAR.

Thus, a *requirement* is what an agency wants to buy and the terms and conditions to which the agency wants offerors to assent. It is any term or condition of a request for proposals (RFP) to which an offeror must assent in order to be eligible for award. A requirement is "material" when it affects price, quality, quantity, delivery, or performance.

29. What is *market research*, and when does the government have to do it?

Market research is a search for information about products and services that may already be available in the marketplace to meet the government's needs. It is a search for information about specifications, prices, terms and conditions, and business policies and practices.

The FAR does not define the term *market research,* but FAR Parts 10 and 11 state the policy about market research and prescribe market research procedures. FAR 10.001 describes the policy as follows:

> (a) Agencies must—
>
> (1) Ensure that legitimate needs are identified and trade-offs evaluated to acquire items which meet those needs;
>
> (2) Conduct market research appropriate to the circumstances—
>
> (i) Before developing new requirements documents for an acquisition by that agency;
>
> (ii) Before soliciting offers for acquisitions with an estimated value in excess of the simplified acquisition threshold;
>
> (iii) Before soliciting offers for acquisitions with an estimated value less than the simplified acquisition threshold when adequate information is not available and the circumstances justify its cost;
>
> (iv) Before soliciting offers for acquisitions that could lead to a bundled contract (15 U.S.C. 644(e)(2)(A)); and
>
> (v) Agencies shall conduct market research on an ongoing basis, and take advantage to the maximum extent practicable of commercially available market research methods, to identify effectively the capabilities, including the capabilities of small businesses and new entrants into Federal contracting, that are available in the marketplace for meeting the requirements of the agency in furtherance of a contingency operation or defense against or recovery from nuclear, biological, chemical, or radiological attack; and
>
> (3) Use the results of market research to—

(i) Determine if sources capable of satisfying the agency's requirements exist;

(ii) Determine if commercial items or, to the extent commercial items suitable to meet the agency's needs are not available, nondevelopmental items are available that—

(A) Meet the agency's requirements;

(B) Could be modified to meet the agency's requirements; or

(c) Could meet the agency's requirements if those requirements were modified to a reasonable extent;

(iii) Determine the extent to which commercial items or nondevelopmental items could be incorporated at the component level;

(iv) Determine the practices of firms engaged in producing, distributing, and supporting commercial items, such as terms for warranties, buyer financing, maintenance and packaging, and marking;

(v) Ensure maximum practicable use of recovered materials (see Subpart 23.4) and promote energy conservation and efficiency; and

(vi) Determine whether bundling is necessary and justified (see 7.107) (15 U.S.C. 644(e)(2)(A).

(vii) Assess the availability of electronic and information technology that meets all or part of the applicable accessibility standards issued by the Architectural and Transportation Barriers Compliance Board at 36 CFR Part 1194 (see Subpart 39.2).

(b) When conducting market research, agencies should not request potential sources to submit more than the minimum information necessary.

FAR 11.002(a) says, "[A]gencies shall—(1) Specify needs using market research. . . ." Thus, government agencies should undertake some form of market research before every acquisition.

It is too bad that government policymakers have used the term *market research* instead of *purchasing research*, especially given their emphasis on commercial practices. The private sector uses the term *market research* to describe what sellers do to determine what buyers want. This is the way the term is used in college business textbooks. See, for example, Carl McDaniel, Jr., and Roger Gates, *Contemporary Marketing Research*, 2nd ed. (Minneapolis/St. Paul: West Publishing Company, 1993). *Purchasing research* would have been a better term to use in the FAR, since it is the term that the private sector uses to describe what buyers do to determine what they want. See Michiel R. Leenders and Harold E. Fearon, *Purchasing and Materials Management*, 10th ed. (Burr Ridge, Illinois: Richard D. Irwin, Inc., 1993), pp. 448–463; and Donald W. Dobler, et al., *Purchasing and Materials Management: Text and Cases*, 5th ed. (New York: McGraw-Hill Publishing Company, 1990), p. 546.

30. What are the rules about writing specifications and statements of work?

The rules for writing specifications and statements of work are stated in FAR Part 11 and in 37.602-1. The single most important rule is that specifications and statements of work must not unduly restrict competition. Every specification and statement of work is restrictive to some degree, but specifications and statements of work may not restrict competition to a degree that exceeds an agency's bona fide needs.

PROHIBITION AGAINST UNDUE RESTRICTIVENESS

A specification or statement of work is unduly restrictive when it specifies some feature, quality, or characteristic that the agency does not need to do its job and that some companies cannot provide. FAR 11.002, *Policy*, says:

> (a) In fulfilling requirements of 10 U.S.C. 2305(a)(1), 10 U.S.C. 2377, 41 U.S.C. 253a(a), and 41 U.S.C. 264b, agencies shall—
>
> (1) Specify needs using market research in a manner designed to—
>
> (i) Promote full and open competition (see Part 6), or maximum practicable competition when using simplified acquisition procedures, with due regard to the nature of the supplies or services to be acquired; and
>
> (ii) Only include restrictive provisions or conditions to the extent necessary to satisfy the needs of the agency or as authorized by law.

GAO elaborated on this rule in its protest decision in *Container Products Corporation* (B-280603.2; November 4, 1998) as follows:

> Procuring agencies are required to specify their needs in a manner designed to permit full and open competition, and may include restrictive requirements only to the extent they are necessary to satisfy the agencies' legitimate needs (or as otherwise authorized by law). 10 U.S.C. § 2305(a)(1)(B) (1994); see Mossberg Corp., B-274059, Nov. 18, 1996, 96-2 CPD ¶ 189 at 2. Where a protester challenges a specification as unduly restrictive, the agency must establish that the requirement is reasonably necessary to meet its needs; we will examine the adequacy of the agency's position to ensure that it is rational and can withstand logical scrutiny.

REQUIREMENT FOR CLARITY AND PROHIBITION AGAINST BUNDLING

An agency's specification or statement of work must describe requirements clearly and specifically, so that prospective offerors can figure out what the agency wants to buy. Agencies must not unnecessarily combine, or *bundle*, different kinds of work into a single procurement. In letters to the Air Force and the Army (File No. B-277979, dated January 26, 1998), GAO said, in part:

> Statements of work that are too general provide insufficient information for prospective offerors to decide whether to submit a proposal or what to offer to best meet the agency's needs. Also, inclusion of broad categories of work in one statement of work constitutes a form of bundling, since different kinds of work (or tasks in different geographical or technical areas) are combined into one procurement, and an overly broad statement of work can unjustifiably diminish competition just as bundling does, by deterring businesses, particularly small businesses, from competing for a contract, notwithstanding their ability to perform some of the work at issue. See National Customer Eng'g, 72 Comp. Gen. 132 (1993), 93-1 CPD ¶ 225; Airport Markings of Am., Inc., et al., 69 Comp. Gen. 511 (1990), 90-1 CPD ¶ 543. Provisions or conditions that restrict competition (such as bundling) are permitted only to the extent necessary to satisfy the contracting agency's needs. 10 U.S.C. 2305(a)(1)(B)(ii); National Customer Eng'g, supra.

FAR 2.101 contains a lengthy definition of *bundling,* which has become a major concern on the part of Congress, because it limits opportunities for small businesses to participate in government contracts. The FAR now includes extensive rules designed to restrict bundling of requirements. See FAR 7.107.

PERFORMANCE-BASED CONTRACTING

One way to avoid being unduly restrictive is to write specifications and statements of work in terms of required functions or performance, instead of detailed designs or processes. FAR 11.002(a)(2) says:

> To the maximum extent practicable, ensure that acquisition officials—
>
> (i) State requirements with respect to an acquisition of supplies or services in terms of—
>
> (A) Functions to be performed;
>
> (B) Performance required; or
>
> (C) Essential physical characteristics;

This is the so-called "performance-based contracting" or "performance-based acquisition" approach to specification. [See, also, FAR 11.101(a).] Performance-based contracting is an important "acquisition reform" of the 1990s.

Performance-based specification is especially important in service contracting. FAR 37.602-1(b) says:

> When preparing statements of work, agencies shall, to the maximum extent practicable—
>
> (1) Describe the work in terms of "what" is to be the required output rather than either "how" the work is to be accomplished or the number of hours to be provided (see 11.002(a)(2) and 11.101);
>
> (2) Enable assessment of work performance against measurable performance standards;

> (3) Rely on the use of measurable performance standards and financial incentives in a competitive environment to encourage competitors to develop and institute innovative and cost-effective methods of performing the work; and
>
> (4) Avoid combining requirements into a single acquisition that is too broad for the agency or a prospective contractor to manage effectively.

REQUIREMENT TO PROMOTE THE USE OF COMMERCIAL ITEMS

Another important policy is to write specifications and statements of work in ways that allow firms offering commercial items to compete. FAR 2.101 contains a lengthy definition of *commercial item*. FAR 11.002(a)(2)(ii) through (v) provide as follows:

> (ii) Define requirements in terms that enable and encourage offerors to supply commercial items, or, to the extent that commercial items suitable to meet the agency's needs are not available, nondevelopmental items, in response to the agency solicitations;
>
> (iii) Provide offerors of commercial items and nondevelopmental items an opportunity to compete in any acquisition to fill such requirements;
>
> (iv) Require prime contractors and subcontractors at all tiers under the agency contracts to incorporate commercial items or nondevelopmental items as components of items supplied to the agency; and
>
> (v) Modify requirements in appropriate cases to ensure that the requirements can be met by commercial items or, to the extent that commercial items suitable to meet the agency's needs are not available, nondevelopmental items.

31. What is a *statement of objectives?*

A *statement of objectives,* or SOO, is a relatively brief description of service requirements in which an agency specifies what it wants the contractor to accomplish without describing specific tasks or procedures. It replaces the traditional detailed statement of work used in requests for proposals. The idea is that companies competing for the contract will propose a detailed statement of work that is designed to fulfill the objectives described in the SOO. Use of the technique has become popular among both military and civilian agencies.

Department of Defense Handbook (MIL-HDBK) 245D, *Preparation of Statement of Work,* dated April 3, 1996, Section 5, contains an extensive description of the SOO technique.

32. What is an *evaluation factor?*

An *evaluation factor* is an attribute—a feature, quality, property, or characteristic—of an offeror, as a business firm, or of the promises that an offeror makes in its offer. It is something that the government either wants (a positive attribute) or would like to avoid (a negative attribute), and is therefore a basis for determining the value of a proposal. Examples of attributes of business firms include their depth and breadth of experience, the quality of their past performance, the qualifications of their key personnel, the effectiveness of their policies and processes, and the qualities of their facilities. Examples of attributes of offers include the degree to which they conform to the terms of the RFP, the reasonableness of the prices offered, and the features or performance levels of the products or services offered. In order to select evaluation factors, agencies must determine which attributes of offerors and their offers will contribute to the achievement of their acquisition objectives. Such attributes have value. When offerors are likely to be different in terms of such attributes, the attributes are often referred to as "discriminators."

Source selection planners should consider four issues when choosing evaluation factors: (1) whether or not the factor is related to the agency's procurement objectives in a meaningful way; (2) whether or not the offerors are likely to be different in terms of the factor; (3) whether or not the factor is measurable or otherwise subject to clear description; and (4) whether or not the agency will be able to obtain reliable information about each offeror's performance on the factor. (For a discussion of the relative importance of source selection evaluation factors, see Appendix B.)

33. What are the mandatory evaluation factors?

FAR 15.304(a) through (c) prescribe source selection evaluation factors as follows:

> (a) The award decision is based on evaluation factors and significant subfactors that are tailored to the acquisition.
>
> (b) Evaluation factors and significant subfactors must—
>
> (1) Represent the key areas of importance and emphasis to be considered in the source selection decision; and
>
> (2) Support meaningful comparison and discrimination between and among competing proposals.
>
> (c) The evaluation factors and significant subfactors that apply to an acquisition and their relative importance are within the broad discretion of agency acquisition officials, subject to the following requirements:
>
> (1) Price or cost to the Government shall be evaluated in every source selection (10 U.S.C. 2305(a)(3)(A) (ii) and

41 U.S.C. 253a(c)(1)(B)) (also see part 36 for architect-engineer contracts);

(2) The quality of the product or service shall be addressed in every source selection through consideration of one or more non-cost evaluation factors such as past performance, compliance with solicitation requirements, technical excellence, management capability, personnel qualifications, and prior experience (10 U.S.C. 2305(a)(3)(A)(i) and 41 U.S.C. 253a(c)(1)(A)); and

(3)(i) Except as set forth in paragraph (c)(3)(iii) of this section, past performance shall be evaluated in all source selections for negotiated competitive acquisitions expected to exceed $1,000,000.

(ii) Except as set forth in paragraph (c)(3)(iii) of this section, past performance shall be evaluated in all source selections for negotiated competitive acquisitions issued on or after January 1, 1999, for acquisitions expected to exceed $100,000. Agencies should develop phase-in schedules that meet or exceed this schedule.

(iii) Past performance need not be evaluated if the contracting officer documents the reason past performance is not an appropriate evaluation factor for the acquisition (OFPP Policy Letter 92-5).

(4) The extent of participation of small disadvantaged business concerns in performance of the contract shall be evaluated in unrestricted acquisitions expected to exceed $500,000 ($1,000,000 for construction) subject to certain limitations (see 19.201 and 19.1202).

(5) For solicitations involving bundling that offer a significant opportunity for subcontracting, the contracting officer must include proposed small business subcontracting participation in the subcontracting plan as an evaluation factor (15 U.S.C. 637(d)(4)(G)(i)).

> (6) If telecommuting is not prohibited, agencies shall not unfavorably evaluate an offer that includes telecommuting unless the contracting officer executes a written determination in accordance with FAR 7.108.

Thus, there are five "mandatory" evaluation factors: (1) price or cost to the government; (2) quality; (3) past performance; (4) participation in contract performance by small disadvantaged businesses; and (5) small business subcontracting in a bundled procurement. (See FAR 2.101 for the definition of *bundling* and *bundled contract*.) However, a careful analysis of the language in FAR 15.304(c) shows that price or cost and quality are the only factors that agencies must evaluate for every procurement. The requirement to evaluate past performance is not really mandatory, since the contracting officer can decide that it is not an appropriate factor. The small disadvantaged business participation factor applies only when the procurement has not been set aside for small business concerns ("unrestricted") and when it exceeds specified dollar amounts. The proposed small business subcontracting factor applies only in a *bundled* procurement in excess of $500,000. In a procurement of $500,000 or less, price or cost and past performance are the only factors that absolutely have to be evaluated to meet the requirements of the FAR, since past performance doubles as a "quality" factor. (Note that *quality* is broadly defined, and that while "technical excellence" and "compliance with solicitation requirements" can pertain to the product or service being procured, most of the examples of quality factors pertain to the offerors themselves as business entities—e.g., past performance, management capability, personnel qualifications, prior experience.)

In addition to the factors prescribed in FAR 15.304(c), FAR 22.1103 requires agencies to evaluate proposed compensation to "professional employees," as defined at FAR 22.1002, when the dollar value of a service contract is expected to exceed $500,000 and when it will require the services of "meaningful numbers" of such employees. Agencies may adversely evaluate proposals that specify "unrealistically low" compensation.

34. What are the best evaluation factors?

Most contracts can be awarded effectively on the basis of three factors: (1) acceptability of the offer, based on whether or not the offeror assents to the specification or statement of work and the clauses in the RFP, has proposed adequate small disadvantaged business participation, and is eligible for contract award; (2) risk, based on the offeror's experience and past performance; and (3) price or cost and fee. These three factors satisfy all the requirements of FAR 15.304(c) and will allow for an expeditious source selection process. They do not require offerors to prepare *technical* or *management proposals* describing how they will do the work ("proposed approach") or how they will organize to perform, thus saving offerors the time and cost of writing such proposals and saving agencies the time and cost of reading and scoring them. The theory underlying these factors is that if an offeror has done the same type of work before and has a good reputation with its customers, then it has demonstrated that it can do the work, while the ability to write a good plan ("approach") does not, in and of itself, demonstrate the ability to perform.

Agencies should evaluate the acceptability of each offer on a pass or fail basis. They should evaluate risk on the basis of an assessment of each offeror's experience and past performance. The source selection decision should reflect a determination of best value that is based on tradeoffs of risk against price or cost and fee. In many (if not most) cases, award could be made without *discussions*. Questions about experience and past performance should be handled as *clarifications*, rather than *discussions*. [See FAR 15.306(a) and (d).]

Discussions, if necessary, would be limited to giving offerors a chance to withdraw any objections that they may have expressed about the terms of the RFP and/or to improve their prices or estimated costs. The absence of technical or management proposals eliminates the need to discuss and correct the inevitable planning and writing issues that arise when such proposals have to be written under pressure and without free access to the customer.

If agency technical personnel feel uncomfortable about the lack of technical or management proposals, the agency could also evaluate the offerors' relative understanding of the work on the basis of oral interviews (*oral presentations*) with their key personnel. [See FAR 15.102 about oral presentations.] Understanding of the work could be factored into the risk assessment. This approach would be more expeditious and satisfying than having to read pages and pages of text, and would make it harder for offerors to hide behind the work of professional proposal writers.

(For a discussion of streamlining source selection by improving the quality of evaluation factors, see Appendix C.)

35. What do agencies have to tell offerors about their evaluation factors for award?

The rules about the disclosure of evaluation factors are stated in FAR 15.304(d) and (e), as follows:

> (d) All factors and significant subfactors that will affect contract award and their relative importance shall be stated clearly in the solicitation (10 U.S.C. 2305(a)(2)(A)(i) and 41 U.S.C. 253a(b)(1)(A)) (see 15.204-5(c)). The rating method need not be disclosed in the solicitation. The general approach for evaluating past performance information shall be described.

> (e) The solicitation shall also state, at a minimum, whether all evaluation factors other than cost or price, when combined, are—
>
> (1) Significantly more important than cost or price;
>
> (2) Approximately equal to cost or price; or
>
> (3) Significantly less than cost or price. (10 U.S.C. 2305(a)(3)(A)(iii) and 41 U.S.C. 253a(c)(1)(C)).

FAR 15.204-5(c) says:

> *Section M, Evaluation factors for award.* Identify all significant factors and any significant subfactors that will be considered in awarding the contract and their relative importance (see 15.304(d)). The contracting officer shall insert one of the phrases in 15.304(e).

Thus, agencies must: (1) identify the significant evaluation factors; (2) state their relative importance, indicating (a) rank order and (b) intervals of importance; and (3) use one of the phrases in FAR 3.104(e). A factor is significant if it can affect the outcome of the source selection.

A classic formulation of this information in an RFP reads as follows:

> The evaluation factors are listed below in descending order of importance: Technical Approach, Management Plan, Past Performance, and Price. The nonprice factors—Technical Approach, Management Plan, and Past Performance—when combined, are significantly more important than Price. Technical Approach is the most important factor and is approximately twice as important as Management Plan. Management Plan is second in importance, and is approximately three times as important as Past Performance. Past Performance is third in importance, and is approximately twice as important as Price. Price is the least important factor.

What this means in practical terms is anybody's guess!

IDENTIFICATION OF THE FACTORS

Agencies must identify the significant factors, but they do not have to explain them in detail. For example, an agency can say that one of the factors is *soundness of approach* without explaining what *soundness* means or how it will measure soundness. Note, too, that agencies do not have to identify all their evaluation factors and subfactors, only the *significant* ones. GAO has on numerous occasions allowed agencies to consider factors that were not expressly identified in an RFP as long as they were reasonably related to those that were identified. For example, in its decision in *Israel Aircraft Industries, Ltd., MATA Helicopters Division* (B-274389; B-274389.2; B-274389.3; December 6, 1996), GAO stated:

> At a minimum, a solicitation must state all significant evaluation factors and subfactors, and their relative importance. 10 U.S.C. § 2305(a)(2)(A) (1994); Federal Acquisition Regulation § 15.605(d)(1) (FAC 90-31); H.J. Group Ventures, Inc., B-246139, Feb. 19, 1992, 92-1 CPD ¶ 203. However, a solicitation need not identify each element to be considered by the agency during the course of the evaluation where such element is intrinsic to the stated factors or subfactors. Marine Animal Prods. Int'l, Inc., B-247150.2, July 13, 1992, 92-2 CPD ¶ 16.

The FAR Part 15 Rewrite did not change this rule.

STATEMENT OF RELATIVE IMPORTANCE

The statement of relative importance should provide enough information to help offerors make intelligent trade-offs during proposal development, especially with regard to quality versus price or cost. An agency must at least use one of the phrases in FAR 15.304(e). An important rule of GAO's is that if an RFP identifies the evaluation factors but fails to state their relative importance, then the offerors are entitled to assume that the factors are of equal importance, and the agency must evaluate proposals accordingly. In its decision in *Foundation Health Federal Services, Inc.; Humana Military Healthcare Services, Inc.* (B-278189.3; B-278189.4; February 4, 1998), GAO concluded:

> The RFP did not disclose the relative importance of the significant evaluation considerations. Although the solicitation stated that the seven major technical factors were listed in descending order of importance, an offeror could not ascertain from the solicitation the relative weight of each task/subfactor. Thus, for example, one could not tell that Task I/Health Care Providers was nearly twice as important as Task III/Utilization and Quality Management; that Task IV/Enrollment, Marketing and Support Services, a subfactor under the sixth most important major factor, was more important than Task XI/Start-up and Transition, a subfactor under the second most important major factor; or that Task V/Claims Processing was six times more important than Task VI/Program Integrity, another subfactor under the same major factor. The agency maintains that offerors were on notice that the tasks/subfactors were not of equal weight by virtue of the RFP statement that "[t]he subfactors provided under each of the major factors are not listed in any specific order of importance and are only included for purposes of amplification." Where the solicitation is silent as to the relative importance of the subfactors, as was the case here, Serv-Air, Inc., B-194717, Sept. 4, 1979, 79-2 CPD ¶ 176 at 5, 8, offerors can assume that the subfactors are approximately equal. Stone & Webster Eng'g Corp., B-255286.2, Apr. 12, 1994, 94-1 CPD ¶ 306 at 5; Informatics, Inc., B-194734, Aug. 22, 1979, 79-2 CPD ¶ 144 at 6.

GAO sustained the protest.

However, agencies can get away with saying nothing more than "the factors are listed in descending order of importance" as long as the various intervals of importance between the various factors are not disproportionate. In *Optimum Technology, Inc.* (B-266339.2; April 16, 1996), GAO noted:

> The Competition in Contracting Act of 1984 (CICA) requires contracting agencies to set forth in the solicitation all significant evaluation factors that the agency expects to consider and their relative importance. 10 U.S.C. § 2305(a)(2) (1994); H.J. Group Ventures, Inc., B-246139, Feb. 19, 1992, 92-1 CPD ¶ 203. A solicitation which lists evaluation factors in descending order of importance generally meets CICA's requirements unless one factor has a disproportionately high value relative to the others. See, e.g., BDM Servs. Co., B-180245, May 9, 1974, 74-1 CPD ¶ 237. In short, when a solicitation states that evaluation factors are listed in descending order of importance, offerors are on notice that the evaluation criteria listing reflects a reasonable downward progression of relative weights. General Exhibits, Inc., 56 Comp. Gen. 882 (1977), 77-2 CPD ¶ 101.
>
> Here, the evaluation scheme which the agency employed reflects a reasonable downward progression of evaluation weights. No single factor was unusually significant or unusually insignificant. See Raytheon Support Servs. Co., B-219389; B-219389.2, Oct. 31, 1985, 85-2 CPD ¶ 495 (agency's evaluation was proper where solicitation stated listed three factors in descending order of importance and employed a scheme where first factor was worth 75 percent, second factor was worth 15 percent, and third factor was worth 10 percent); cf. BDM Servs. *Co.*, supra (where solicitation listed 5 evaluation factors and most important factor was 6 times the weight of the second factor and 24 times the weight of the fifth factor, predominant value accorded first factor should have been disclosed); Coastal Science and Eng'g, Inc., 69 Comp. Gen. 66 (1989), 89-2 CPD ¶ 436 (where solicitation stated that technical was more important than cost, the fact that technical was 9 times more important than cost should have been disclosed). Accordingly, the agency's evaluation scheme was not unreasonable.

In *Foundation Health Federal Services, Inc.; Humana Military Healthcare Services, Inc.* (B-278189.3; B-278189.4; February 4, 1998), GAO thought that the importance intervals between factors were so disproportionate that *descending order of importance* was a misleading description of relative importance.

Some agencies use language that says that when the proposals are considered to be close on the most important factor, a less important factor will become more important. For example, in *Systems Integration & Development, Inc.* (B-271050; June 7, 1996), GAO described the RFP as follows:

> The RFP stated that the award would be made to the responsible offeror whose proposal was deemed most advantageous to the government, price and technical evaluation factors considered. The technical evaluation factors tracked the RFP requirements and were weighted as follows: (1) technical personnel (40 points); (2) corporate experience and past performance (40 points); and (3) management approach (20 points). The RFP provided that higher scores would be assigned to offerors which demonstrated in their proposals more extensive personnel qualifications and experience in performing the RFP requirements. The RFP also provided that the technical evaluation factors were considered more important than price, and that an offeror's proposed price would only become more important as the technical merit of proposals became more equal.

This has been referred to as *variable, swing,* and *sliding scale* weighting. GAO does not object to this practice.

Relative importance must not be confused with *weight* if by *weight* one means a specific numerical weight, such as a percentage or point distribution. Weighting is one way of expressing relative importance, but agencies need not establish or reveal numerical weights. The FAR was clearer in this regard prior to the FAR Part 15 Rewrite. FAR 15.605(d)(2) used to say, in part:

> Agencies may elect to assign numerical weights to evaluation factors and employ those weights when evaluating proposals. Numerical weights need not be disclosed in solicitations; however, nothing precludes an agency from disclosing the weights on a case-by-case basis.

The FAR Part 15 Rewrite replaced this language with FAR 15.304(d), which says, "The rating method need not be disclosed in the solicitation." Presumably, this has the same meaning as FAR 15.605(d)(2), but no one knows for sure.

Finally, although the FAR does not say so, it should be clear that the concept of relative importance does not apply in the lowest price technically acceptable source selection process, because that process does not entail tradeoffs among any of the factors. *Technical acceptability* is determined on a pass or fail basis, there are no tradeoffs among the technical factors, and price alone determines which of the technically acceptable proposals wins the competition.

36. What does *relative importance* mean?

FAR 15.304(d) says that agencies must disclose the *relative importance* of their evaluation factors. The objective of this rule is to make agencies help offerors determine how to make tradeoffs when developing their proposals by disclosing their preferences among the evaluation factors. However, there is considerable confusion over the meaning of the phrase *relative importance*. What is it that agencies must disclose? Importance of the factors in terms of what? Most individuals would probably say "importance in terms of each other." But that is not a satisfactory answer to the question.

When someone asks which of two things is more important, they are asking with reference to some third thing—some objective, purpose, or end. "Which is more important to you *when it comes to* (fill in the blank)?" Many think that the statement of relative importance in an RFP must disclose which factor will be most important with regard to the source selection decision. They think that agencies must disclose which factor will have the biggest influence on the outcome. That is not correct.

When an agency is preparing an RFP for a tradeoff process source selection, it does not—and *cannot*—know which evaluation factor will have the biggest impact on the decision. That is because the influence that any factor will have on the decision will depend on the differences among the offerors in terms of each of the various factors, which an agency cannot know until the proposals have been evaluated.

If an RFP says that quality is significantly more important than price, and if the offerors are virtually the same with regard to quality, or if the differences in quality are relatively small and the differences in price are relatively large, then price will have a bigger influence on the decision maker than quality. On the other hand, if an RFP says that price is significantly more important than quality, but the differences in price are relatively small and the differences in quality are relatively great, then quality will have a greater impact on the decision than price.

In *BE, Inc.; PAI Corporation* (B-277978; B-277978.2; December 16, 1997), GAO stated:

> As for BEI's challenge to the source selection decision itself, we note that source selection officials in a negotiated procurement have broad discretion in determining the manner and extent to which they will make use of the technical and cost evaluation results; cost/technical tradeoffs may be made, and the extent to which one

> may be sacrificed for the other is governed by the test of rationality and consistency with the established evaluation factors. Family Realty, B-247772, July 6, 1992, 92-2 CPD ¶ 6 at 7-8. Even where cost or price is the least important evaluation factor, an agency may make award to an offeror with a lower-cost, lower-scored proposal if it determines that the cost premium involved in awarding to a higher-rated, higher-priced offeror is not justified. Southern Research, B-266360, Feb. 12, 1996, 96-1 CPD ¶ 65 at 3; Dayton T. Brown, Inc., B-229664, Mar. 30, 1988, 88-1 CPD ¶ 321 at 4-5.

So what does *relative importance* mean? It means the relative importance of the evaluation factors *with regard to the agency's acquisition objectives*. Agencies must describe their preferences among the various factors based on the assumption that they cannot have all that they want of each factor. They must describe which of any two factors they would prefer to have more of—for example, more quality or lower price—if they cannot have more of both. But they cannot state which factor will have the most influence on the decision, because they will not know that until they have compared the proposals and made tradeoffs. This is true not just of the nonprice/price tradeoffs, but also of tradeoffs among the various nonprice factors.

So what does GAO mean when it says that a source selection decision must be consistent with the RFP's statement of relative importance? It means that agencies' decisions must be consistent with their stated evaluation factor preferences. If an RFP says that price is more important than quality, and if the agency chooses a higher-priced, higher-quality offer, then it must explain why the higher quality is worth the higher price. An agency cannot make a source selection decision in a way that indicates that it has, in fact, changed its preferences.

So, in a tradeoff process source selection, what should the statement of relative importance in the RFP say? It should say something like this:

> Offerors: In the course of preparing your proposals, you may have to decide whether to offer us higher quality at a higher price or lower quality at a lower price. If you do, then you should know that quality is significantly more important to us than price. However, when we make our source selection decision we will compare each offer to the others in order to determine which is the best value. When comparing any two offers in order to determine which is better, if one offers higher quality than the other at a lower price, then we will consider it to be the better value. If one offers higher quality than the other at a higher price, then we will decide whether the difference in quality is worth the difference in price. If we think that it is, then we will consider the higher quality–higher priced offer to be the better value. Otherwise, we will consider the lower quality–lower priced offer to be the better value.

Language such as this would help offerors understand how an agency will make a tradeoff process source selection decision.

37. What is the Fast Track/LOCAR source selection procedure?

Fast Track/LOCAR source selection is a streamlined procedure that is designed to reduce the time and administrative effort required to make a source selection for fixed price service contracts. (LOCAR is an acronym for Level of Confidence Assessment Rating.) The key to the procedure is to base the source selection decision on only three evaluation factors for award: (1) offer acceptability; (2) risk, based on offeror experience and past performance; and (3) price. An agency using the Fast Track/LOCAR procedure does not request written *technical* or *management* proposals but assesses each offeror's capability on the basis of its experience and past performance, and perhaps an oral presentation. The objective is to be in a position to make a contract award within 60 working days or less after the public release of the RFP.

The Fast Track/LOCAR procedure (or variations thereof) has been used by a number of agencies, including the Department of Veterans Affairs, the Environmental Protection Agency, the Social Security Administration, the Department of the Navy, and the Department of the Army. The LOCAR technique may also be used in non-Fast Track source selections. (For a detailed explanation of the LOCAR technique, see Appendix D.)

THE EVALUATION FACTORS

In a Fast Track/LOCAR source selection, an agency evaluates proposals based on only three factors. The first evaluation factor is offer acceptability, which is evaluated on a pass or fail (go/no go) basis. To be acceptable, an offer must: (1) manifest the offeror's unconditional assent to the terms of the RFP; (2) propose adequate small disadvantaged business participation in contract performance, if applicable pursuant to FAR Subpart 19.12; and (3) indicate that the offeror is eligible for a government contract based on the offeror's responses to the representations, certifications, and other statements required by the RFP. The second evaluation factor is risk, which is evaluated on the basis of a subjective assessment of the offeror's experience and past performance. The third evaluation factor is price, which is evaluated on the basis of price analysis comparisons of the competing offers. These factors satisfy all the requirements in FAR 15.304, *Evaluation factors and significant subfactors*. The RFP should state that nonprice factors are significantly more important than price and that experience and past performance are equally important.

THE PROCEDURE

To conduct a Fast Track/LOCAR source selection, an agency issues an RFP that instructs offerors to submit an offer and information about their experience and past performance not later than 30 days after the date on which the RFP is released to the public. The RFP says that the offer includes only: (1) a signed offer sheet (e.g., Standard Form 33, *Solicitation, Offer, and Award,* with blocks 12 through 18 completed by the offeror); (2) a schedule of proposed line item price(s); (3) proposed small disadvantaged business participation (if FAR Subpart 19.12 is applicable to the procurement); and (4) the representations, certifications, and other statements that the RFP requires offerors to submit. The RFP tells offerors that the agency plans to award a contract without conducting discussions, that it will entertain no alternate proposals, and that any objection to the terms of the RFP will make an offer unacceptable. Table II-1 provides standard proposal preparation instructions for a Fast Track/LOCAR RFP. Table II-2 provides a standard description of the evaluation factors for award for a Fast Track/LOCAR RFP.

The RFP also instructs offerors to submit information about their experience and past performance. This information consists mainly of descriptions of the work that they have done in the past and customer references. Agencies can obtain information about an offeror's experience and past performance most effectively on forms designed for that purpose. The use of forms increases the likelihood that offerors will provide the information that the agency wants, and the standardized submission format will make it easier for the evaluators to find the information.

After the agency receives the offers, the contracting officer evaluates each offer's acceptability on a pass or fail basis. An offer is acceptable if the offeror submits all the required information and does not object to any of the terms of the RFP. If an offer is acceptable, then the agency gives it a score

TABLE II-1
PROPOSAL PREPARATION INSTRUCTIONS FOR A "FAST TRACK" SOURCE SELECTION

General. If you want to compete for the contract described in this Request for Proposals (RFP), then you must submit a proposal that includes the following: (1) an offer and (2) information about your experience and past performance.

When evaluating your proposal (see RFP Section M) we will consider how well you complied with these instructions. We will consider any significant failure to comply with these instructions to be indicative of what we could expect from you during contract performance. Please contact our contracting officer by telephone, e-mail, or otherwise in writing if you do not understand any part of these instructions.

Offer. Your offer must consist of the following: (1) Standard Form 33, *Solicitation, Offer, and Award*, with blocks 12 through 18 completed by you. (2) RFP Section B, *Supplies or Services and Prices/Costs*, with your proposed prices inserted in the appropriate blank spaces. (3) If you are not a small disadvantaged business (SDB) or if you are an SDB that is not going to take advantage of the SDB price evaluation adjustment, then submit RFP Attachment 1, *Proposed Small Disadvantaged Business Participation Targets*, completed by you.

The completion and submission to us of the above items of information will constitute your offer to perform in accordance with the terms of this RFP. Our acceptance of your offer will create a binding contract between us.

If we select you for award and if you are not a small business as defined in Federal Acquisition Regulation (FAR) Subpart 19.1, then you will have to submit a plan for subcontracting with small, small disadvantaged, and women-owned small businesses, in accordance with FAR Subpart 19.7, within three days of a request by our contracting officer. This plan will be in addition to the small disadvantaged business participation targets mentioned above. If you are required to submit a subcontracting plan, contract award will be contingent upon our ability to reach an agreement with you on the terms of your plan. If we accept your subcontracting plan it will become a part of the contract.

We will not evaluate or otherwise entertain alternate or other proposals that do not assent to the terms of our RFP. If you (1) fail or refuse to assent to any term, (2) propose additional terms, (3) fail to propose reasonable targets for small disadvantaged business participation, or (4) fail to submit

continues

Table II-1 continued

any of the information described in these instructions, then we will consider your offer to be unacceptable, which will make you ineligible for contract award. The only way that an unacceptable offer could be made acceptable would be through discussions (see FAR 15.306(d)). However, we intend to award the contract without discussions, as permitted by FAR 15.306(a) and 52.215-1. Therefore, we warn you to consult with our contracting officer before submitting an alternate proposal or an offer that otherwise does not assent to our terms. We reserve the right to conduct discussions if we consider them to be in our best interests and to permit offerors to revise their offers. **Experience and Past Performance Information.** Prepare and submit one *Offeror Qualifications Statement Form* in the format of RFP Attachment 2. Include the names of references who will verify that you have done the type of work that must be done under the contract described in this RFP and who will provide information about the quality of your performance. In addition, prepare and submit one *Reference Information Sheet,* RFP Attachment 3, for each such reference. Submit as many references as you wish, but we may not contact them all. Make sure that your reference information is up to date and that each reference will cooperate with us. Do not give us the name of a reference unless you have made sure that we can reach that reference at the telephone number, e-mail address, and postal address that you have provided. Failure to comply with these instructions may result in an unfavorable evaluation of your experience or past performance.

of 100 points; if the offer is unacceptable, then the agency gives it a score of 0 points. Since the agency plans to award without discussions, and since the only way to make an unacceptable proposal acceptable is to conduct discussions and allow the offeror to revise its proposal to eliminate any deficiencies, the unacceptable proposals are set aside. (If the agency later changes its mind and decides to conduct discussions after all, it must return to the unacceptable offers and determine whether or not any of them should be included in the competitive range.)

TABLE II-2
EVALUATION FACTORS FOR AWARD FOR A FAST TRACK SOURCE SELECTION

1. General. We will award the contract to the offeror who represents the best value to the Government on the basis of (1) its offer, (2) its experience and past performance, and (3) our level of confidence in the offeror.

2. Offer. We will determine the merits of your offer on the basis of (a) its acceptability and (b) its proposed price.

a. Acceptability. We will determine the acceptability of your offer on a pass or fail basis. We will consider your offer to be acceptable if it (1) manifests your unconditional assent to the terms of this Request for Proposals (RFP) and (2) proposes what we consider to be adequate targets for small disadvantaged business participation in the performance of the contract.

(1) Assent. If you (a) take exception to any term of this RFP, (b) propose additional terms, or (c) omit material information required by this RFP, then we will consider your offer to be unacceptable and you to be ineligible for contract award. We reserve the right to amend the terms of this RFP at any time prior to the source selection decision. If we do, we will give offerors an opportunity to modify their offers.

(2) Small Disadvantaged Business Participation. We will determine the adequacy of proposed small disadvantaged business participation based on market information about the availability of responsible small disadvantaged businesses to perform subcontract work and on the reasonableness of the amount of proposed participation.

b. Price. We will evaluate your price for reasonableness in accordance with FAR 15.305(a)(1) and FAR Subpart 15.4, and as further explained in paragraph 5, below.

c. Discussions. We intend to award a contract without discussions, as permitted by FAR 15.306(a). But if we think that it is in the best interests of the government to do so, we might conduct discussions in accordance with FAR 15.306(d) in order to make an unacceptable offer acceptable.

3. Experience and Past Performance.

a. Experience. Experience is the opportunity to learn by doing similar work under similar conditions. Your experience is relevant to this competition when you have done work that has confronted you with the same kinds of challenges that you would face during performance of the contract described by this RFP. We will assess your relevant experience on the basis of its breadth (how many of the contract tasks you have performed in the past)

continues

Table II-2 continued

and its depth (how many times you have performed each task).

b. Past Performance. Past performance is a measure of the degree to which you have satisfied your customers in the past and complied with federal, state, and local laws and regulations. Our assessment of your past performance will be subjective and based on your reputation with your customers and others, and on our analysis of official and public records.

We will contact some of your customers to ask whether or not they believe: (a) that you were capable, efficient, and effective; (b) that your performance conformed to the terms of your contract; (c) that you were reasonable and cooperative during performance; and (d) that you were committed to customer satisfaction. We may contact other sources of information, including, but not limited to, federal, state, and local government agencies, published media, and electronic databases.

4. Level of Confidence. We will use our assessments of your experience and past performance to develop a level of confidence assessment rating. The rating will reflect our subjective assessment of the likelihood that you will keep the promises in your offer. We will use the assessment when comparing your offer to the offers of your competitors.

5. Relative Importance of the Evaluation Factors and the Source Selection Decision. All evaluation factors other than price, when combined, are significantly more important than price. We consider the various nonprice factors to be equally important. Keep this in mind during preparation of your offer. However, the relative influence that any of the factors will have on the source selection decision will depend on the differences among the competitors.

In order to select the contractor, we will rank the competing offerors from best to worst by making a series of paired comparisons, making tradeoffs between the differences in the nonprice factors and the differences in price.

If one offeror is better in terms of the nonprice factors *and* has the lower price, then we will consider that offeror to be the better value.

If one offeror is better in terms of the nonprice factors but has the higher price, then we will determine whether the differences in the nonprice factors are worth the difference in price. If we consider the differences in the nonprice factors to be worth the difference in price, then we will consider the offeror with the higher price to be the better value. If not, then we will consider the offeror with the lower price to be the better value.

We will continue to make paired comparisons in this way until we have decided which offeror is the best value.

Next, the agency's evaluators assess the risk of doing business with each offeror on the basis of its experience and past performance. The evaluators first assess each offeror's experience based on the number of opportunities it has had in the past to do the kind of work that will be required of it under the terms of the RFP. The more relevant opportunities that an offeror has had in the past to do that kind of work, the better its experience. An opportunity is relevant when it gave the offeror a chance to encounter the kinds of difficulties that it is likely to encounter under the prospective contract.

Next, the evaluators assess each offeror's past performance on the basis of the agency's own experience with the offeror; comments received from the offeror's other customers; information obtained from public organizations such as law enforcement agencies, other government agencies, better business bureaus, and consumer protection agencies; press reports; and any other available information. The evaluators do not assign scores to the offeror's experience and past performance; they simply prepare a short memorandum that summarizes their findings and conclusions. If the evaluators need more information about any offeror's experience or past performance to complete their assessment, the contracting officer can seek clarification from the offeror in accordance with FAR 15.306(a)(2).

Based on the evaluators' assessments of an offeror's experience and past performance, they then develop a risk rating, called a Level of Confidence Assessment Rating (LOCAR). The agency develops a LOCAR for each offeror in two steps. First, the evaluators discuss the information that they have obtained about the offeror's experience and past performance among themselves and develop a consensus about placing the offeror in one of three categories: (1) more likely to succeed than to fail; (2) more likely to fail than to succeed; or (3) equally likely to succeed or to fail (50-50 chance of success). Then, having reached a consensus on the category in which the offeror belongs, the evaluators refine their risk assessment by giving the offeror a specific LOCAR rating on a scale of .1 to .9; they develop this refinement through discussion and consensus. If they believe that the offeror is more likely to succeed than to fail, then they should assign a LOCAR between .6 and .9; if they believe that the offeror is more likely to fail than to succeed, then they should assign a LOCAR of .1 to .4; if they believe that the offeror has a 50-50 chance of success, then they should assign a LOCAR of .5.

Having assigned a LOCAR, the evaluators then adjust the offeror's score for offer acceptability to determine each offeror's expected value. The *offer acceptability score* represents the value of the *promises* that the offeror made; the *expected value score* represents the value of those promises after taking risk into account. To determine expected value, the evaluators multiply the offer acceptability score (100 points) by the LOCAR to develop an expected value score; the expected value score integrates the findings of acceptability and risk. Since the score for an acceptable offer is 100 points, applying a LOCAR of .1 to .9 will produce an expected value score in a range of 10 to 90 points. After this has been done for each offeror, the agency's SSA can make an initial comparison and ranking of the offerors based on their expected values and prices. Table II-3 shows the offer acceptability scores, LOCARs, expected values, and prices for a set of fictional offerors.

TABLE II-3
ILLUSTRATION OF LOCAR TECHNIQUE

Offeror	*Offer*	*LOCAR*	*Expected Value*	*Price*
A	100	.4	40	$1,900,650
B	0	None	None	$1,800,000
C	100	.8	80	$2,100,000
D	100	.5	50	$1,950,075
E	100	.65	65	$1,890,994

The LOCARs are based on the evaluators' assessments of each offeror's experience and past performance. The expected value score represents their integrated assessment of the offer acceptability and risk.

The agency's SSA makes initial tradeoffs and ranks the offerors by comparing them on the basis of their expected values and prices. Offeror B is not eligible for the award because its proposal was unacceptable, so the SSA excludes it from the comparisons. Comparing Offeror A to Offeror C, the SSA knows that Offeror C's higher expected value indicates that it has more experience and/or better past performance than Offeror A and that the evaluators consider Offeror A to be a higher risk. But Offeror C's price is higher, so the SSA must decide whether the lower risk of awarding the contract to Offeror C is worth the higher price.

The answer to this question should depend on the nature of the procurement. If the procurement is for janitorial services, then the answer may be no, since the damages that the agency would suffer from poor performance would be less than the difference in price. But if the procurement is for hazardous waste removal and disposal or some other highly technical service, then the answer may be yes, because poor performance could cost the agency much more than the difference in price.

Assuming that the SSA considers Offeror C to be the better value, he or she now compares Offeror C to Offeror D. The evaluators think that Offeror D has a 50-50 chance of successful performance, while Offeror C represents a very high likelihood of success. But is the lower risk worth the higher price? Again, this will depend on the nature of the procurement. The SSA continues to make comparisons until he or she has ranked the offerors from best to worst. Then he or she confirms the initial rankings by reviewing the memoranda that the evaluators prepared about the offerors' experience and past performance and determining whether or not the LOCARs seem appropriate in light of this information.

Finally, the SSA should consider the difference in price between Offeror B (whose offer was unacceptable) and the highest ranking offeror, and decide whether or not the difference warrants further consideration of Offeror B—and the time and effort associated with establishing a competitive range, conducting discussions, and soliciting and evaluating revised final proposals. This decision, like the risk/price tradeoffs, will depend on the nature of the procurement. It is crucial that the SSA not base his or her source selection decision on a comparison of the offerors' scores, but on careful consideration of the substantive findings of the evaluators about the differences among the offerors. The scores are merely analytical devices.

After the SSA has made the source selection decision, the contracting officer can instruct the selected offeror to submit a small business subcontracting plan, if required pursuant to FAR Subpart 19.7. Alternatively, agencies can instruct offerors to submit small business subcontracting plans with their offers and include the plans in the assessment of offer acceptability.

For a detailed description of the use of the LOCAR technique in a non-Fast Track source selection, see GAO's decision in *Colmek Systems Engineering* (B-291931.2, July 9, 2003).

ORAL PRESENTATIONS

Some agencies may not be willing to assess risk on the basis of experience and past performance alone. In that case, the Fast Track process can be adapted by asking offerors to make oral presentations in which they describe how they will organize to do the work and the performance methods they will use, or in which they describe their own assessment of the risks of performance and the risk mitigation strategies they will use. Agencies should use oral presentations to evaluate offerors' understanding of the work. The conclusions of the evaluators based on oral presentations should then be factored into the LOCAR, along with the evaluations of experience and past performance. The use of oral presentations will enable an agency to deepen its risk assessments without adding the significant time and administrative effort associated with evaluating written technical and management proposals. See FAR 15.102 for the rules about oral presentations.

38. What is the *focused source selection procedure*?

Focused source selection was an experimental source selection procedure tested by the Nuclear Regulatory Commission (NRC) with authorization from the Office of Federal Procurement Policy (OFPP), pursuant to Section 5061 of the Federal Acquisition Streamlining Act of 1994 (Public Law 103-355). OFPP and NRC described the experimental procedure in an announcement in the *Federal Register* on March 22, 1999 (64 Fed. Reg. 13823); it was to be used for procurements of $5 million or less in support of NRC's administrative programs. The test began on December 17, 1999.

Focused source selection was to entail the following seven steps:

- Step 1—NRC notifies the public of the availability of a draft statement of work, which can be accessed via the Internet. The draft statement of work is accompanied by a "summary sheet," which provides information about the procurement such as a project description, standard industrial classification code (SIC code), the dates by which interested firms must submit comments on the draft statement of work and their capability statements, and information about the assessment criteria that NRC will use to evaluate interested firms.

- Step 2—Interested firms submit their comments on the draft statement of work and their capability statements to NRC.

- Step 3—NRC ranks the interested firms on the basis of its assessment criteria.

- Step 4—NRC solicits offers from the top three firms. The solicitation includes a final statement of work, contract terms and conditions, representations and certifications that must be completed by the offerors, and instructions about submitting written technical and cost proposals or oral presentations.

- Step 5—NRC receives and evaluates the technical and cost proposals on the basis of the assessment criteria described in the summary sheet. It then considers its initial evaluations of capability and its evaluations of the offerors' technical and cost proposals in order to rank the offerors.

- Step 6—NRC either makes an award without conducting negotiations or negotiates to final agreement with the most highly ranked offeror. If it is unable to reach agreement with the most highly ranked offeror, then it will negotiate with the second most highly ranked offeror, and then the third, until it reaches an agreement with one of the top three firms.

- Step 7—NRC awards the contract and debriefs the unsuccessful offerors and the other participating firms.

A key feature of focused source selection was use of the Internet to communicate with interested firms and to obtain information from and about them. NRC publishes its draft statements of work, its assessment criteria, and its solicitations electronically, and interested firms are encouraged to submit their comments about the draft statement of work, their capability statements, and their offers electronically.

PART III

Proposal Solicitation

The questions in this part address the preparation, issuance, and amendment of requests for proposals and the submission and receipt of proposals. They include questions about the definitions of key terms such as *offer, proposal, proposal modification,* and *proposal revision.*

39. What is a *solicitation*?

The term *solicitation* refers to invitations for bids (IFB), requests for proposals (RFP), requests for quotations (RFQ), and requests for information (RFI). IFBs and RFPs are requests for offers—that is, requests for promises that will be contractually binding upon acceptance. RFQs and RFIs are both requests for information, such as price quotes, that are not offers (i.e., promises) and that cannot be accepted to create a contract. Some agencies use the term request for offers (RFO); presumably, these are what the name indicates. [See the definition of *offer* in FAR 2.101, and see FAR 13.004, *Legal effect of quotations,* paragraph (a).]

RFPs are the solicitations for offer used in negotiated procurements. FAR 15.203(a) describes the functions of an RFP as follows:

> (a) Requests for proposals (RFPs) are used in negotiated acquisitions to communicate Government requirements to prospective contractors and to solicit proposals. RFPs for competitive acquisitions shall, at a minimum, describe the—

(1) Government's requirement;

(2) Anticipated terms and conditions that will apply to the contract:

(i) The solicitation may authorize offerors to propose alternative terms and conditions, including the contract line item number (CLIN) structure; and

(ii) When alternative CLIN structures are permitted, the evaluation approach should consider the potential impact on other terms and conditions or the requirement (e.g., place of performance or payment and funding requirements) (see 15.206);

(3) Information required to be in the offeror's proposal; and

(4) Factors and significant subfactors that will be used to evaluate the proposal and their relative importance.

Conceptually, RFPs usually consist of two parts a model contract and a set of instructions to offerors. The model contract includes the government's list of the supplies or services that it wants to buy, its specification or statement of work, and the clauses that it wants to include in the contract. The instructions include standard ("boilerplate") solicitation provisions from both the FAR and the agency's FAR supplement, instructions written especially for the procurement in question, and a description of the evaluation factors that the agency will consider when evaluating the proposals it receives.

FAR 15.203 through 15.206, 15.209, and 15.210 prescribe rules for the preparation, issuance, and amendment of RFPs. The government uses a variety of formats for RFPs, but the format used for most large source selections is the Uniform Contract Format described in FAR 15.204 (see Table III-1).

TABLE III-1
THE UNIFORM CONTRACT FORMAT

Section	*Title*
	Part I—The Schedule
A	Solicitation/contract form
B	Supplies or services and prices/costs
C	Description/specification/work statement
D	Packaging and marking
E	Inspection and acceptance
F	Deliveries or performance
G	Contract administration data
H	Special contract requirements
	Part II—Contract Clauses
I	Contract clauses
	Part III—List of Documents, Exhibits, and Other Attachments
J	List of attachments
	Part IV—Representations and Instructions
K	Representations, certifications, and other statements of offerors or respondents
L	Instructions, conditions, and notices to offerors or respondents
M	Evaluation factors for award

In addition to the Uniform Contract Format, the government has formats for commercial items, construction, and other special acquisitions that are prescribed elsewhere in the FAR and in agency FAR supplements. No matter what the format, almost every solicitation includes a list of the supplies or services (the "deliverables"), a specification or statement of work, contract clauses, instructions to offerors, and a description of the evaluation factors.

The FAR provides a number of forms that agencies can use as cover sheets for their RFPs. These forms (which are available at www.managmentconcepts.com/publications and www.arnet.gov/far) include the following:

- Standard Form (SF) 33, *Solicitation, Offer, and Award*
- Standard Form (SF) 1442, *Solicitation, Offer, and Award (Construction, Alteration, or Repair)*
- Standard Form (SF) 1447, *Solicitation/Contract*
- Standard Form (SF) 1449, *Solicitation/Contract/Order for Commercial Items*
- Optional Form (OF) 308, *Solicitation and Offer—Negotiated Contract.*

FAR 15.210 states that agencies do not have to use these forms.

FAR 15.203 allows agencies to request proposals by letter or orally under certain circumstances. FAR 15.203(e) says that an agency may use a *letter RFP* in sole source acquisitions. However, the instructions in that FAR paragraph for preparing letter RFPs indicate that they must contain the same information as other RFPs. FAR 15.203(f) says that an agency may use an *oral RFP* in urgent circumstances, but the need for complex specifications or contract clauses would make the use of oral RFPs impractical.

When an agency wants to change a solicitation, it does so by issuing an amendment (agencies *amend* solicitations and *modify* contracts). Agencies may use Standard Form 30, *Amendment of Solicitation/Modification of Contract* or Optional

Form 309 for this purpose. The rules for amending RFPs are in FAR 15.206, which reads as follows:

> (a) When, either before or after receipt of proposals, the Government changes its requirements or terms and conditions, the contracting officer shall amend the solicitation.
>
> (b) Amendments issued before the established time and date for receipt of proposals shall be issued to all parties receiving the solicitation.
>
> (c) Amendments issued after the established time and date for receipt of proposals shall be issued to all offerors that have not been eliminated from the competition.
>
> (d) If a proposal of interest to the Government involves a departure from the stated requirements, the contracting officer shall amend the solicitation, provided this can be done without revealing to the other offerors the alternate solution proposed or any other information that is entitled to protection (see 15.207(b) and 15.306(e)).
>
> (e) If, in the judgment of the contracting officer, based on market research or otherwise, an amendment proposed for issuance after offers have been received is so substantial as to exceed what prospective offerors reasonably could have anticipated, so that additional sources likely would have submitted offers had the substance of the amendment been known to them, the contracting officer shall cancel the original solicitation and issue a new one, regardless of the stage of the acquisition.
>
> (f) Oral notices may be used when time is of the essence. The contracting officer shall document the contract file and formalize the notice with an amendment (see Subpart 4.5, Electronic Commerce in Contracting).
>
> (g) At a minimum, the following information should be included in each amendment:

(1) Name and address of issuing activity.

(2) Solicitation number and date.

(3) Amendment number and date.

(4) Number of pages.

(5) Description of the change being made.

(6) Government point of contact and phone number (and electronic or facsimile address, if appropriate).

(7) Revision to solicitation closing date, if applicable.

Thus, an agency may amend an RFP at any time, even after it has received and evaluated proposals.

Industry has long complained about the poor quality of government RFPs. Even when agencies prepare their RFPs in strict accordance with the specified formats, they are very complicated documents; but many agencies make matters worse by not following the format specifications and by writing poorly. A solicitation for a contract that is expected to be priced at more than $100,000 can contain more than 75 clauses from the FAR and from the agency's FAR supplement, some of them quite lengthy and complex. It is often the case that at the time of contract award, no one from either party to the contract has read all of the clauses, much less understands what they mean. RFP instructions to offerors are often unclear, bordering at times on being incomprehensible. In many cases, the instructions in RFPs are assembled by cutting and pasting from older solicitations, with the result that agency personnel are not sure what they mean.

40. What information is in a request for proposals?

FAR 15.203 provides, in part, as follows:

> (a) Requests for proposals (RFPs) are used in negotiated acquisitions to communicate Government requirements to prospective contractors and to solicit proposals. RFPs for competitive acquisitions shall, at a minimum, describe the—
>
> (1) Government's requirement;
>
> (2) Anticipated terms and conditions that will apply to the contract:
>
> (i) The solicitation may authorize offerors to propose alternative terms and conditions, including the contract line item number (CLIN) structure; and
>
> (ii) When alternative CLIN structures are permitted, the evaluation approach should consider the potential impact on other terms and conditions or the requirement (e.g., place of performance or payment and funding requirements)(see 15.206);
>
> (3) Information required to be in the offeror's proposal; and
>
> (4) Factors and significant subfactors that will be used to evaluate the proposal and their relative importance.

An RFP includes: (1) a description of the required products and services; (2) a set of contract clauses; (3) instructions for submitting proposals; and (4) information about how the agency will evaluate the proposals and select the contractor. An RFP usually includes blanks to be filled in by offerors to complete the terms of the proposed contract. The part of the RFP that includes the description of the products and services and the contract clauses is sometimes called the *model contract.*

Most RFPs are written in the Uniform Contract Format described in FAR 15.204-1. This format organizes an RFP into four parts and 13 sections. FAR 12.303 prescribes a special format for RFPs for commercial items.

41. What are *contract line items,* and what are the rules about organizing them?

A *contract line item* is a brief description of a product or service that appears in a contract. When a solicitation and contract are prepared in the Uniform Contract Format, contract line items appear in Section B, *Supplies or services and prices/costs*. [See FAR 15.204-2(b).] The organization of contract line items is an important topic, especially with regard to fixed-price contracts, where it can have a significant effect on the rate at which contractors can get paid and can liquidate progress payments.

A contract line item usually includes product or service nomenclature and description, unit of measure, quantities, unit prices, and total price, as appropriate. These may be supplemented by a specification or statement of work. A contract line item usually does not include the date or place of delivery, or packaging or marking requirements, which appear elsewhere in an RFP or contract.

Each contract line item is usually assigned a contract line item number (CLIN). Separate contract line items may be established for products or services that are distinguished by description, national stock number, or manufacturer's part number, for different quantities of a single product or service that must be delivered at different times or places, or that will be paid for with funds from different sources.

The only agency that has established a formal system for organizing the line items in a contract is the Department of Defense (DoD). The DoD system is called the Uniform Contract Line Item Numbering System (UCLINS). This system is described in the DoD FAR Supplement (DFARS), in subpart 204.71, which prescribes criteria and numbering procedures for establishing contract line items and subdivisions called *subline items*, including both *separately identified* and *informational* subline items. UCLINS is an excellent system that provides for a logical and orderly arrangement of contract line items. It is worth studying.

42. What are *solicitation attachments* and *exhibits*?

As defined in DoD FAR Supplement (DFARS) 204.7101, an *attachment* is "any documentation, appended to a contract or incorporated by reference, which does not establish a requirement for deliverables"; an *exhibit* is "a document, referred to in a contract, which is attached and establishes requirements for deliverables." A statement of work may be an attachment to a contract. An exhibit can be used in lieu of a long list of contract line items in the main part of a solicitation or contract document to consolidate descriptions of numerous contract line items conveniently. For example, if a contract will require the contractor to prepare and deliver a large number of separately deliverable reports and other data items, the list of these items can be included in an exhibit rather than in the main body of the contract. Department of Defense form (DD Form) 1423, *Contract Data Requirements List,* is an example of an exhibit. (See DFARS 204.7105.)

43. What information can an agency require offerors to include in a proposal?

An agency can ask for just about any information that it wants about offerors, their promises, their qualifications to perform, and their plans. However, FAR 15.403-1(b) forbids agencies from requiring offerors to submit *cost or pricing data* when prices are based on *adequate price competition, prices are set by law or regulation,* when the acquisition is for a *commercial item,* or when a waiver has been granted. See FAR 2.101 for the definition of *cost or pricing data* and *commercial item.* See FAR 15.403-1 for explanations of adequate price competition, prices set by law or regulation, and waivers.

44. What is a *proposal*?

As used in source selection, the term *proposal* refers to a response to a government agency's RFP. A proposal includes an offer, which is a set of promises, and information about the firm submitting the proposal (see Figure III-1).

A proposal is usually a document or a set of documents, but proposals can include oral presentations and videotapes,

FIGURE III-1
INFORMATIONAL STRUCTURE OF A PROPOSAL

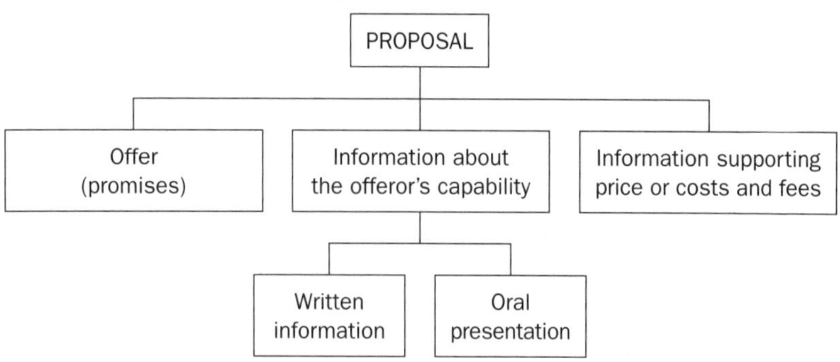

and an RFP may allow or require offerors to submit proposals on electronic media, via facsimile transmission, or via the Internet. Government agencies are currently expressing growing interest in paperless proposals—i.e., electronic submission of proposals via the Internet. However, at present, FAR 15.102(b) says that "certifications, representations, and a signed offer sheet (including any exceptions to the Government's terms and conditions) shall be submitted in writing," and FAR 15.102(f) says, "When an oral presentation includes information that the parties intend to include in the contract as material terms or conditions, the information shall be put in writing." See FAR 2.101 for the definition of *in writing*.

Proposals are the bases for both source selection and contract formation, so it is important to understand the nature of their contents. The source selection process produces executory contracts (i.e., exchanges of promises). But while contracts are promises, not all the statements in proposals are promises, and confusion about the meaning of the word *proposal* can lead to confusion about the content of the contract that results from a source selection. This is especially true when it comes to the so-called technical proposals and management proposals that agencies require offerors to submit in response to RFPs.

American legal theory holds that contracts are produced through a process of offer and acceptance that leads to mutual assent, or a meeting of minds. Thus, the first step in negotiating a contract is for one party to submit an offer to another—*offer* in this case meaning a set of promises. However, while FAR Part 15 uses the term *offer*, it more often uses the term *proposal*, and it uses it in ways that can lead to confusion. In some cases, it uses *proposal* as a synonym for *offer*, but in other cases it uses it to denote both the offer and nonpromissory statements of offerors.

What everyone participating in a source selection must understand is that contracts are based on the offers that the government accepts, and that while an offer is a part of every proposal, not every part of a proposal is a part of the offer. Sometimes this is clear from the proposal preparation instructions or from the proposals themselves, but sometimes it is not. Sometimes the parties to the contract understand this, but sometimes they do not.

PROPOSALS AS OFFERS (PROMISES)

The FAR does not define the term *proposal* per se. However, FAR 2.101 defines *offer* as follows:

> "Offer" means a response to a solicitation that, if accepted, would bind the offeror to perform the resultant contract. Responses to invitations for bids (sealed bidding) are offers called "bids or sealed bids;" responses to requests for proposals (negotiation) are offers called "proposals;" responses to requests for quotations (negotiation) are not offers and are called "quotes."

Thus, as defined in FAR 2.101, *proposal* is a synonym for *offer*.

FAR 2.101 seems to define *offer* in the legal sense in which it is defined in § 24 of the *Restatement of the Law, Second, Contracts 2nd, Student Edition* (St. Paul: American Law Institute Publishers, 1981), Pamphlet No. 1, p. 71, which reads as follows:

> An offer is the manifestation of willingness to enter into a bargain, so made as to justify another person in understanding that his assent to that bargain is invited and will conclude it.

In a comment in § 24, the *Restatement* says that when a contract is based upon an exchange of promises, "the offer itself is a promise."

According to the *Restatement,* for an expression to be a promise it must communicate a commitment to do or to refrain from doing something specific. (*Restatement, Second,* Contracts § 2.) Opinions and predictions are not promises. Also, an expression of contingent intention may not be a promise. A court may find that expressions such as "I plan to. . . ," "I intend to. . . ," and "I expect to. . . ," are not expressions of commitment. (*Restatement,* § 2, Comment e.) As John D. Calamari and Joseph M. Perillo point out in *Contracts,* 3rd ed. (St. Paul: West Publishing Co., 1987), § 2-6, p. 35, "Also, in a modern business context, statements of intention to act in a given manner may often be regarded as statements of policy rather than promises." *Offer* is also defined in *Black's Law Dictionary,* 6th ed. (St. Paul: West Publishing Co., 1990), p. 1081, which reads, in part, as follows:

> A proposal to do a thing or pay an amount, usually accompanied by an expected acceptance, counter-offer return promise, or act. A manifestation of willingness to enter into a bargain, so made as to justify another person in understanding that his assent to that bargain is invited and will conclude it. Restatement, Second, Contracts, § 24. A promise; a commitment to do or refrain from doing a specified thing in the future. An act on the part of one person whereby that person gives to another the legal power of creating the obligation called contract. McCarty v. Verson Allsteel Press Co., 44 Ill.Dec. 570, 576, 89 Ill.App.3d 498, 411 N.E.2d 936, 942. The offer creates a power of acceptance permitting the offeree by accepting the offer to transform the offeror's promise into contractual obligation.

Thus, an offer is usually a promise or set of promises, and a contract is formed when the party to whom the offer was made accepts it.

When a government agency issues an RFP, it is requesting offers and information about the firms making the offers. The offers are to be based on the terms in the model contract of the RFP. When offerors fill in the blanks in the model contract, sign the offer form (e.g., Standard Form 33, *Solicitation, Offer, and Award*), and submit it to the agency, they are offering a promise to perform in accordance with the agency's terms at specified prices or estimated costs and fees in exchange for the government's promise to pay the price offered and to do the other things that the contract requires of the government. The government then evaluates the offers, selects one, and makes an award (i.e., accepts the offer), thereby bringing a contract into existence.

PROPOSALS AS MERE INFORMATION

FAR Part 15 uses the term *proposal* in ways that are not entirely consistent with the concept of a proposal as a set of promises. For example, FAR 15.305(a) begins as follows: "Proposal evaluation is an assessment of the proposal and the offeror's ability to perform the prospective contract successfully." Assessment of the offeror's ability to keep its promises ("perform the prospective contract") is not an assessment of the promises themselves. Rather, it is an assessment of facts and assertions about the offeror that have a bearing on the reliability of the offeror's promises.

Thus, as used in FAR Part 15, a proposal includes not only an offeror's promises, but also information about the offeror itself (such as information about its past performance, experience, production capacity, and personnel) and an analysis of the constituent elements of its proposed price or estimated cost. This information tells the agency something about an offeror, but it does not necessarily promise anything. It is an assertion about history or present reality, but it is not a commitment to act or refrain from acting in a specified way. When an agency awards a contract, its source selection decision will reflect some degree of reliance on the validity of this information, but not an *acceptance* of it in the legal sense. It does not become binding on the parties.

TECHNICAL AND MANAGEMENT PROPOSALS

RFPs often instruct offerors to submit *technical proposals* and/or *management proposals*. Such RFP instructions tell the offerors to describe how they will do or manage the work described in the specification or statement of work in the model contract. Such descriptions often must include plans of various kinds, such as quality assurance plans, safety plans, systems engineering plans, configuration management plans, staffing plans, etc., and descriptions of the offeror's proposed organization. Here is an example of such an instruction from a U.S. Navy RFP:

> The Offeror shall provide a plan for the design, development, build, qualification test and incorporation into production of all items as defined in the PIDS [Prime Item Development Specification] and described by First Article Units (FAUs) in the Purchase Description (PD). The plans shall include a description of how each system meets the Open Systems Architecture and PIDS requirements. The proposal shall summarize in one place where there are any problems with PIDS compliance for any of the FAU configurations. The Offeror shall provide adequate justification for not meeting the requirements.
>
> The Offeror shall provide as a part of the Program Management Plan details regarding the evolution of the product(s) and how it plans to provide assurance to the Navy that these changes will continue to function in existing systems. The Offeror shall describe the means whereby it will isolate or insulate the customer from changes that may occur by means of OSA, Application Program Interfaces (APIs) or the use of "middleware."
>
> As a part of this plan the Offeror shall detail how it intends to provide Product Assurance for evolving products from various vendors when there are changes to hardware, firmware, and software. It shall detail how it plans to record those differences and changes made in any of the products, such that if a replacement part is

sent to the fleet which does not match or work properly, it will readily be known what needs to be accomplished to make it function properly.

The Offeror shall detail how it plans to put together a facility to test and evaluate all of the components of hardware, firmware and software that will be delivered and to record differences and fixes that need to be made. It shall specify where that facility will be and what it plans to put into it and how it plans it to evolve and be maintained.

The Offeror shall describe how it plans to achieve maximum commonality. Particular attention should be given to cabinetry, power systems, and functional modules.

The Offeror shall describe how it plans to achieve Technology Insertion. This plan shall include a means for achieving architectural compatibility of the design, and shall describe the processes, including testing, of accomplishing these goals. The Offeror shall also project a schedule of probable need dates for such changes. The methodology for incorporating these additions and/or changes shall be described.

The Offeror shall provide a discussion of what programs it plans to review and continue reviewing in order to be aware of what is going on in the Department of Defense that may have an effect on the Q-70 and the future migration of technology into the Q-70. The Offeror shall at a minimum address the COSIP CRIB, the interface and use of the TAC program, and potential interface with the IT-21 program.

The Offeror shall discuss how it plans to get new items designed, built, tested, and into production. Proposed schedules for circuit cards, functional modules, and assemblies with a list of testing and when that testing will be conducted, shall be provided. This schedule shall include possible conflicts with concurrent developments of other items.

It is important for the parties to reach an express agreement about whether or not the statements in an offeror's technical proposal and management proposal are intended to be promises or merely information that will tell the agency something about the offeror's knowledge of the work and ability to perform. Are they commitments to act or refrain from acting in specified ways, or merely statements of contingent intention or policy? There is no way to answer these questions without seeing the words of the proposals themselves and knowing something about the intentions of the parties. What do the proposals say? Do the parties themselves consider the statements in the proposals to be promises, or merely evidence of knowledge and competence?

The answers to these questions may have a significant bearing on the interpretation of the contract and the resultant responsibilities and rights of the parties. Accordingly, every participant in the source selection process should think about the answers during source selection planning, RFP preparation, proposal preparation, proposal evaluation, and contract negotiation.

COST PROPOSALS

RFPs commonly instruct offerors to submit *cost proposals* that contain information in support of the proposed prices or estimated costs and fees—information such as *cost breakdowns*, or cost or pricing data as defined in FAR 15.401. The following is an example from an Air Force RFP for a combined firm-fixed-price, cost-plus-fixed-fee, cost-plus-award-fee, and time-and-materials contract, quoted in part:

> **6.0 VOLUME III—COST PROPOSAL No Page Limitations.**
>
> Provide the following cost information to support reasonableness and cost realism. (There are specific page

limitations for certain sections of the Cost Proposal Volume. See "section" instructions below).

6.1 Compliance with Instructions: These instructions are to assist you in submitting price information. Compliance with these instructions is mandatory and failure to comply may result in rejection of your proposal.

6.2 Government Furnished Support: If applicable, any government furnished support which you have requested (e.g., GFP, GFE, base support, facilities, test equipment etc.) in addition to that specified in the RFP, shall be listed on a separate schedule by individual item and estimated value.

6.3 Pagination: Every page of the Cost Proposal Volume shall be numbered.

6.4 Volume Organization: The cost/price volume shall be organized as shown below.

SECTION 1— Table of Contents.

SECTION 2— Schedule B.

SECTION 3— Pricing Assumptions.

SECTION 4— Pricing Instructions

SECTION 5— Work Week

SECTION 6— Total Evaluated Price Worksheets

SECTION 7— Forward Pricing Rate Agreements

SECTION 8— Material

SECTION 9— Subcontracts and Inter-Divisional

SECTION 10—Other Direct Costs (ODC) & Travel

SECTION 11—Direct Labor Rates

SECTION 12—Indirect Rates

SECTION 13—Facilities Capital Cost of Money (FCCM)

SECTION 14—Composite Rate Breakout for CPFF/ CPAF rates

SECTION 15—Final Proposal Revision (Note: this section shall only apply if the Contracting Officer requests a Final Proposal Revision.)

This passage was followed by detailed instructions for preparing each of the 15 sections.

An offeror's proposed prices or costs and fees are elements of its offer—that is, part of the promises that will become binding if accepted by the government. However, the information submitted in support of the proposed prices or costs and fee usually is not considered to be part of the offer. Thus, if an offeror proposes a firm-fixed-price of $1,000,000 and breaks this down into components for materials, labor, other direct costs, indirect costs, and profit, the offeror is promising to perform the contract for $1,000,000 but is not promising that actual costs and profit will conform to the cost breakdown in its proposal.

45. What is an *offer*?

FAR 2.101 defines *offer* as follows:

> "Offer" means a response to a solicitation that, if accepted, would bind the offeror to perform the resultant contract. Responses to invitations for bids (sealed bidding) are offers called "bids or sealed bids;" responses to requests for proposals (negotiation) are offers called "proposals;" responses to requests for quotations (negotiation) are not offers and are called "quotes."

This definition is consistent with the common law definition, stated in *Black's Law Dictionary*, 6th ed. (St. Paul: West Publishing Co., 1990), p. 1081, as follows:

> A proposal to do a thing or pay an amount, usually accompanied by an expected acceptance, counter-offer return promise, or act. A manifestation of willingness to enter into a bargain, so made as to justify another person in understanding that his assent to that bargain is invited and will conclude it. Restatement, Second, Contracts, § 24. A promise; a commitment to do or refrain from doing a specified thing in the future. An act on the part of one person whereby that person gives to another the legal power of creating the obligation called contract. McCarty v. Verson Allsteel Press Co., 44 Ill.Dec. 570, 576, 89 Ill.App.3d 498, 411 N.E.2d 936, 942. The offer creates a power of acceptance permitting the offeree by accepting the offer to transform the offeror's promise into contractual obligation.

Thus, an offer submitted in response to a request for proposals is a promise or set of promises that becomes binding upon acceptance. However, proposals include more than just offers; they include information that is not promissory in nature.

46. What are the rules about handling proposals after receipt by the agency?

There are three important rules about how an agency must handle proposals after receipt. First, they must be marked with the date and time of receipt and delivered to the appropriate agency official, usually the contracting officer. Second, the agency must safeguard them from unauthorized disclosure. Third, if any part of a proposal that was submitted electronically or by facsimile is unreadable, the contracting officer must notify the offeror immediately and allow the offeror to resubmit the unreadable portion. These rules appear in FAR 15.207, *Handling of proposals and information*, which reads as follows:

(a) Upon receipt at the location specified in the solicitation, proposals and information received in response to a request for information (RFI) shall be marked with the date and time of receipt and shall be transmitted to the designated officials.

(b) Proposals shall be safeguarded from unauthorized disclosure throughout the source selection process. (See 3.104 regarding the disclosure of source selection information (41 U.S.C. 423)). Information received in response to an RFI shall be safeguarded adequately from unauthorized disclosure.

(c) If any portion of a proposal received by the contracting officer electronically or by facsimile is unreadable, the contracting officer immediately shall notify the offeror and permit the offeror to resubmit the unreadable portion of the proposal. The method and time for resubmission shall be prescribed by the contracting officer after consultation with the offeror, and documented in the file. The resubmission shall be considered as if it were received at the date and time of the original unreadable submission for the purpose of determining timeliness under 15.208(a), provided the offeror complies with the time and format requirements for resubmission prescribed by the contracting officer.

Note that the late proposal rule in FAR 15.208(b) does n apply to the resubmission of unreadable portions of propo als, except with regard to the deadline established by t contracting officer for resubmission.

47. When is a proposal late, and what are the rules about late proposals?

According to FAR 15.208(b)(1), a proposal is *late* when it is received at the government office designated for the receipt of proposals after the "exact" date and time specified in the

RFP. FAR 15.208(b) and (c) prescribe the rules for handling late proposals as follows:

> (b)(1) Any proposal, modification, revision, or withdrawal that is received at the designated Government office after the exact time specified for receipt of proposals is "late" and will not be considered unless it is received before award is made, the contracting officer determines that accepting the late proposal would not unduly delay the acquisition; and—
>
> (i) If it was transmitted through an electronic commerce method authorized by the solicitation, it was received at the initial point of entry to the Government infrastructure not later than 5:00 p.m. one working day prior to the date specified for receipt of proposals; or
>
> (ii) There is acceptable evidence to establish that it was received at the Government installation designated for receipt of proposals and was under the Government's control prior to the time set for receipt of proposals; or
>
> (iii) It was the only proposal received.
>
> (2) However, a late modification of an otherwise successful proposal, that makes its terms more favorable to the Government, will be considered at any time it is received and may be accepted.
>
> (c) Acceptable evidence to establish the time of receipt at the Government installation includes the time/date stamp of that installation on the proposal wrapper, other documentary evidence of receipt maintained by the installation, or oral testimony or statements of Government personnel.
>
> (d) If an emergency or unanticipated event interrupts normal Government processes so that proposals cannot be received at the Government office designated for receipt of proposals by the exact time specified in

> the solicitation, and urgent Government requirements preclude amendment of the solicitation closing date, the time specified for receipt of proposals will be deemed to be extended to the same time of day specified in the solicitation on the first work day on which normal Government processes resume.

The same statements appear in the solicitation provision at FAR 52.215-1, *Instructions to Offerors—Competitive Acquisition,* paragraph (c)(3)(ii).

FAR 15.208(a) states that when an RFP does not specify a time for submission of proposals, the deadline is automatically 4:30 p.m., local time, on the date that the RFP says that proposals are due.

Note that no matter how a proposal is delivered, whether by electronic commerce, U.S. Postal Service, private carrier such as Federal Express or United Parcel Service, or hand-delivered by the offeror itself, it must have been received at the government installation *before* the date and time set for receipt of proposals if it is to be eligible for consideration. In the past, proposals delivered by the U.S. Postal Service Express, registered, or certified mail that were received after the exact date and time for submission of proposals could be considered under some conditions.

Of course, if a proposal is the only one received, these rules do not apply, and the agency may consider it, since doing so would not affect other offerors. Note, too, that FAR 15.208(b)(2) says that an agency will consider a late *modification* to an otherwise successful proposal if it makes the proposal more favorable to the government. This makes sense, since if the offeror has already won the contract, accepting a late modification that makes the proposal better would not be unfair to the other offerors. Apparently, this rule does not apply to proposal *revisions,* as defined in FAR 15.001.

When a proposal is late and is not eligible for consideration in accordance with FAR 15.208(b), FAR 15.208(f) through (h) provide as follows:

> (f) The contracting officer must promptly notify any offeror if its proposal, modification, or revision was received late, and must inform the offeror whether its proposal will be considered, unless contract award is imminent and the notice prescribed in 15.503(b) would suffice.
>
> (g) Late proposals and modifications that are not considered must be held unopened, unless opened for identification, until after award and then retained with other unsuccessful proposals.
>
> (h) If available, the following must be included in the contracting office files for each late proposal, modification, revision, or withdrawal:
>
> (1) The date and hour of receipt.
>
> (2) A statement regarding whether the proposal was considered for award, with supporting rationale.
>
> (3) The envelope, wrapper, or other evidence of date of receipt.

48. What are *proposal modifications* and *proposal revisions*, and what is the significance of the distinction between them?

Proposal modifications and *proposal revisions* are changes that an offeror makes to its proposal. FAR 15.001 defines the terms as follows:

> *Proposal modification* is a change made to a proposal before the solicitation closing date and time, or made in

> response to an amendment, or made to correct a mistake at any time before award.
>
> *Proposal revision* is a change to a proposal made after the solicitation closing date, at the request of or as allowed by a contracting officer, as the result of negotiations.

To change a proposal, an offeror must exchange information with the government. Such exchanges are governed by FAR 15.306, *Exchanges with offerors after receipt of proposals*, and are classified as *clarifications*, *communications*, or *discussions*. Different rules apply to each type of exchange; thus the significance of the distinction between a *proposal modification* and a *proposal revision*.

It is clear that if an agency allows any offeror to *revise* its proposal, such a *proposal revision* would constitute *discussions*, as defined in FAR 15.306(d), and would obligate the agency to establish a competitive range in accordance with FAR 15.306(c), conduct discussions with any other offerors in the competitive range in accordance with FAR 15.306(d), and then allow them to submit final proposal revisions in accordance with FAR 15.307(b). The question raised by these definitions is whether an agency can allow an offeror to *modify* its proposal without conducting discussions with all offerors in the competitive range.

A *proposal modification*, unlike a *proposal revision*, should not trigger the requirement to conduct discussions with all offerors in the competitive range. Based on the plain language of the FAR, agencies may allow an offeror to *modify* its proposal without conducting discussions or allowing any offerors a chance to revise their proposals, because FAR 15.306(d) defines *discussions* as "Negotiations. . . undertaken with the intent of allowing offerors to *revise* their proposals. . ." (italics added), and FAR 15.001 defines *proposal revisions* as changes made "as the result of negotiations." Since the FAR makes a clear distinction between *proposal modifications* and *proposal revisions*, and since it defines discussions as exchanges in which offerors are allowed to *revise* their proposals, it follows that exchanges that allow offerors to *modify* their proposals are not discussions and do not require agencies to establish a competitive range, conduct discussions, or let offerors submit final proposal revisions. GAO, however, appears to use the terms *modification* and *revision* interchangeably.

49. What is a *streamlined solicitation for commercial items*?

A *streamlined solicitation for commercial items* is an announcement in the Governmentwide Point of Entry (see FAR 2.101) that combines a synopsis with either an invitation for bids or a request for proposals. FAR 12.603 prescribes the content and format of streamlined solicitations for commercial items. Such streamlined solicitations eliminate the need to prepare and distribute separate solicitation documents when the government buys commercial items.

50. What are *solicitation provisions* and *contract clauses*?

Solicitation provisions are terms in an RFP that have a bearing on the contract formation process but do not apply during the performance of the resultant contract (see the definition at FAR 2.101). Solicitation provisions establish the groundrules for the source selection process. When an RFP has been prepared in the Uniform Contract Format, solicitation provisions should appear only in RFP Sections K, L, or M.

Most solicitation provisions in an RFP will be standard text (boilerplate) prescribed in FAR Part 52 or in an agency FAR supplement. An example of such a solicitation provision is FAR 52.215-1, *Instructions to Offerors—Competitive*

Acquisition, which agencies must include in Section L of all RFPs. See FAR 15.209(a). But some solicitation provisions, such as proposal preparation instructions, must be specially written for each RFP, although agencies frequently "cut and paste" from one RFP to another.

Contract clauses are terms in an RFP that will appear in the resulting contract and apply during contract performance (see the definition at FAR 2.101). The term *clause* denotes the standard texts chosen from FAR Part 52 and agency FAR supplements and also to clauses specially written for a particular contract. Clauses appear in the *model contract* of the RFP (mainly in Sections E, F, H, and I of the Uniform Contract Format), although—despite the clear instructions in the FAR—agencies have been known to insert clauses in any section of the RFP.

Government contract clauses are often lengthy texts comprising several paragraphs [e.g, FAR 52.227-12, *Patent Rights—Retention by the Contractor (Long Form) (JAN 1997)*], which includes 15 main paragraphs and many subparagraphs. Several FAR clauses incorporate other parts of the FAR into the contract. For example, the clause at FAR 52.216-7, *Allowable Cost and Payment (FEB 1998),* incorporates FAR Subpart 31.2 into the contract; the clause at FAR 52.245-2, *Government Property (Fixed-Price)(DEC 1989),* makes FAR Subpart 45.5 a part of the contract.

Most solicitation provisions and contract clauses are incorporated into the RFP by reference rather than in full text. FAR 52.102, *Incorporating provisions and clauses by reference,* provides as follows:

> (a) Provisions and clauses should be incorporated by reference to the maximum practical extent, rather than being incorporated in full text, even if they—
>
> (1) Are used with one or more alternates or on an optional basis;

(2) Are prescribed on a "substantially as follows" or "substantially the same as" basis, provided they are used verbatim;

(3) Require modification or the insertion by the Government of fill-in material (see 52.104); or

(4) Require completion by the offeror or prospective contractor. This instruction also applies to provisions completed as annual representations and certifications.

(b) Except for provisions and clauses prescribed in 52.107, any provision or clause that can be accessed electronically by the offeror or prospective contractor may be incorporated by reference in solicitations and/or contracts. However, the contracting officer, upon request, shall provide the full text of any provision or clause incorporated by reference.

(c) Agency approved provisions and clauses prescribed in agency acquisition regulations, and provisions and clauses not authorized by Subpart 52.3 to be incorporated by reference, need not be incorporated in full text, provided the contracting officer includes in the solicitation and contract a statement that—

(1) Identifies all provisions and clauses that require completion by the offeror or prospective contractor;

(2) Specifies that the provisions and clauses must be completed by the offeror or prospective contractor and must be submitted with the quotation or offer; and

(3) Identifies to the offeror or prospective contractor at least one electronic address where the full text may be accessed.

(d) An agency may develop a group listing of provisions and clauses that apply to a specific category of contracts. An agency group listing may be incorporated by reference in solicitations and/or contracts in lieu of citing the provisions and clauses individually, provided the group listing is made available electronically to offerors and prospective contractors.

(e) A provision or clause that is not available electronically to offerors and prospective contractors shall be incorporated in solicitations and/or contracts in full text if it is—

(1) A FAR provision or clause that otherwise is not authorized to be incorporated by reference (see Subpart 52.3); or

(2) A provision or clause prescribed for use in an agency acquisition regulation.

(f) Provisions or clauses may not be incorporated by reference by being listed in the—

(1) Provision at 52.252-3, Alterations in Solicitations; or

(2) Clause at 52.252-4, Alterations in Contract.

The complete texts of solicitation provisions and contract clauses are found in FAR Subpart 52.2 and in the corresponding part of agency FAR supplements. A proper reference to a provision or clause includes three elements: (1) the provision or clause number (FAR subsection number); (2) the title; and (3) the date [e.g., 52.203-2, *Certificate of Independent Price Determination (APR 1985)*]. There are three elements to every FAR solicitation provision and contract clause: (1) the prescription; (2) the preface; and (3) the text. The prescription and the preface are not parts of the provision or clause, per se, but they contain important information about it.

The *prescription* is the section of the FAR that prescribes the use of the provision or clause. For example, the use of the clause at FAR 52.243-1, *Changes—Fixed-Price (AUG 1997)*, is prescribed in FAR 43.205(a), as follows:

> (a)(1) The contracting officer shall insert the clause at 52.243-1, Changes—Fixed-Price, in solicitations and contracts when a fixed-price contract for supplies is contemplated.
>
> (2) If the requirement is for services, other than architect-engineer or other professional services, and no supplies are to be furnished, the contracting officer shall use the clause with its Alternate I.
>
> (3) If the requirement is for services (other than architect-engineer services, transportation, or research and development) and supplies are to be furnished, the contracting officer shall use the clause with its Alternate II.
>
> (4) If the requirement is for architect-engineer or other professional services, the contracting officer shall use the clause with its Alternate III.
>
> (5) If the requirement is for transportation services, the contracting officer shall use the clause with its Alternate IV.
>
> (6) If it is desired to include the clause in solicitations and contracts when a research and development contract is contemplated, the contracting officer shall use the clause with its Alternate V.

The number of the provision or clause provides a clue as to which part of the FAR prescribes its use. Every provision and clause number begins with 52.2, and the numbers between 52.2 and the dash identify the part of the FAR that includes its prescription. For example, the use of the provision at FAR 52.215-4, *Type of Business Organization (OCT 1997)*, is prescribed in FAR Part 15. The use of the clause at FAR 52.225-10, *Duty-Free Entry (APR 1984)*, is prescribed in FAR Part 25.

The *preface* is found in FAR Subpart 52.2 immediately before the text of the provision or clause. Most prefaces simply say, "As prescribed in . . . insert the following provision (or clause)." Sometimes, however, the preface will tell the agency to insert a provision or clause "substantially as follows" or "substantially the same as" the FAR text, in which case an agency may make minor modifications to the FAR text. [See the definitions in FAR 52.101(a).] Sometimes a preface will provide more detailed instructions, such as the preface to the clause at FAR 52.216-23, *Execution and Commencement of Work (APR 1984)*, which reads as follows:

> As prescribed in 16.603-4(b)(1), insert the following clause in solicitations and contracts when a letter contract is contemplated, except that it may be omitted from letter contracts awarded on SF [Standard Form] 26.

The text of a solicitation provision or contract clause is what actually appears in the request for proposals or is incorporated by reference in the solicitation and contract. When the FAR or an agency FAR supplement requires the use of a standard solicitation provision or contract clause, an agency may not modify the text unless the regulation says that the provision or clause may be used "substantially as follows" or "substantially the same as," or the agency has obtained approval to deviate from regulation. FAR 52.101 defines those phrases as follows:

> "Substantially as follows" or "substantially the same as," when used in the prescription and preface of a provision or clause, means that authorization is granted to prepare and utilize a variation of that provision or clause to accommodate requirements that are peculiar to an individual acquisition; provided, that the variation includes the salient features of the FAR provision or clause, and is not inconsistent with the intent, principle, and substance of the FAR provision or clause or related coverage of the subject matter.

(See FAR Subpart 1.4 for deviation policies and procedures.) If an agency has modified a provision or clause in accordance with an approved deviation, the agency must insert "(DEVIATION)" after the provision or clause date.

Agencies have to include solicitation provisions from FAR Part 52 in RFPs only when they are applicable, i.e., when prescribed. The contract clauses in FAR Part 52 are classified as: (1) required, (2) required-when-applicable, or (3) optional. The overwhelming majority of clauses are required-when-applicable.

Offerors should read RFPs carefully, check to ensure that they include the applicable provisions and clauses, and inquire about apparent omissions before submitting a proposal. To do this, offerors must determine which provisions and clauses are applicable—a tedious task at best. FAR 52.301 includes a matrix of solicitation provisions and contract clauses that makes it easier to check for missing provisions and clauses. Offerors should keep in mind that the FAR changes frequently, and printed versions of the matrix may not be up to date. An electronic version of the matrix is available at www.managementconcepts.com/publications and at www.acqnet.gov/far.

51. What is a *draft request for proposals*?

A *draft request for proposals* (DRFP) is a preliminary version of an RFP that an agency publishes in order to obtain comments and suggestions from industry before actually soliciting proposals. FAR 15.201(c)(6) mentions DRFPs but does not prescribe formal procedures for preparing or issuing them. However, some agencies have issued extensive rules about them. Consider the following excerpt from the NASA FAR Supplement at 1815.201:

> **Exchanges with industry before receipt of proposals.**
>
> (c)(6)(A) Except for acquisitions described in 1815.300-70(b) contracting officers shall issue draft requests for proposals (DRFPs) for all competitive negotiated acquisitions expected to exceed $10,000,000 (including all

options or later phases of the same project). DRFPs shall invite comments from potential offerors on all aspects of the draft solicitation, including the requirements, schedules, proposal instructions, and evaluation approaches. If the DRFP contains Government-unique standards, potential offerors should be invited to identify voluntary consensus standards that meet the Government's requirements as alternatives to Government-unique standards cited as requirements, in accordance with FAR 11.101 and OMB Circular A-119. Comments should also be requested on any perceived safety, occupational health, security (including information technology security), environmental export control, and/or other programmatic risk issues associated with performance of the work. When considered appropriate, the statement of work or the specifications may be issued in advance of other solicitation sections.

(B) Contracting officers shall plan the acquisition schedule to include adequate time for issuance of the DRFP, potential offeror review and comment, and NASA evaluation and disposition of the comments.

(C) When issuing DRFPs, potential offerors should be advised that the DRFP is not a solicitation and NASA is not requesting proposals.

(D) Whenever feasible, contracting officers should include a summary of the disposition of significant DRFP comments with the final RFP.

(E) If performance-based payments are planned to be used in a competitive negotiated acquisition, the DRFP shall request potential offerors to suggest terms, including performance events or payments criteria. Contracting officers shall use that information to establish a common set of performance-based payments parameters in the formal RFP when practicable.

(F) The procurement officer may waive the requirement for a DRFP upon written determination that the expected

> benefits will not be realized given the nature of the supply or service being acquired. The DRFP shall not be waived because of poor or inadequate planning.

While DRFPs can be useful, some agencies have gone overboard with them. It costs money to prepare DRFPs, as well as to review them and prepare comments to an agency about a DRFP. Issuing DRFPs prematurely (or merely to comply pro forma with an agency policy or out of an excess of enthusiasm for the latest "procurement reform" technique), or issuing multiple drafts, will increase the cost of competition for both government and industry, and the costs may ceed the benefits. Agencies should issue DRFPs selectively, serving the technique mainly for new requirements and ge acquisitions. The draft issued for comment should be se to final, but not so final as to preclude changes based industry comments.

2. What is a *presolicitation conference*?

A *presolicitation conference* is a public meeting conducted an agency before it issues an RFP. The purpose of the meeting is to tell prospective offerors about an upcoming procurement, to describe the terms of the prospective RFP, and, perhaps, to request public comment about a draft RFP. [See FAR 15.201(c)(8).]

53. What is a *synopsis*?

As described in FAR Subpart 5.2, a *synopsis* is a brief description of either a proposed contract action or of a contract award that is published at the website known as the Governmentwide Point of Entry, i.e., http://www.fedbizopps.gov, in order to notify the public. FAR 5.207 explains how to format and transmit synopses. The following is a typical synopsis of a proposed contract action:

PART: U.S. GOVERNMENT PROCUREMENTS

SUBPART: SERVICES

CLASSCOD: H—Quality Control, Testing and Inspection Services

OFFADD: VA N.I.H.C.S, 1700 E 38th St, Marion, IN 46953

SUBJECT: H—TESTING LABORATORY SERVICES

SOL 610-06-00

DUE 022500

POC Marcia Guenin 765-677-3177

DESC: Contractor to provide all labor, materials, equipment, laboratory services, and expert supervision to provide testing laboratory services in accordance with the specifications. Services shall include, but not be limited to inspection, testing, reports and input on materials furnished or work performed, by the construction contractor as they relate to the construction specifications requirements. Materials/work requiring testing include earthwork, landscaping, concrete and masonry. Estimate: Between $25,000 and $100,000. This solicitation is a SMALL BUSINESS SET-ASIDE. SIC 8734, $5.0 million. Approximate issue date: February 7, 2000. Commercial Service

Here is a typical synopsis of an award:

PART: CONTRACT AWARDS

SUBPART: SERVICES

CLASSCOD: K—Modification of Equipment

OFFADD: Director of Strategic Systems Programs, 3801 Nebraska Avenue, Washington, DC 20393-5440

SUBJECT: K—FIRE CONTROL LOGISTICS PROGRAM

POC Linda Haggerty 413 494-6021

CNT N0003098G0051-NJ85

AMT $600000

DTD 123099

TO General Dynamics, 100 Plastics Avenue, Pittsfield, MA 01201

54. When does an agency have to publish a synopsis?

The rules about publishing synopses are in FAR Part 5, *Publicizing Contract Actions*. FAR 5.101(a)(1) requires agencies to publish synopses of proposed contract actions that are expected to exceed $25,000. This requirement is repeated in FAR 5.201. FAR 5.202 establishes 14 exceptions to this requirement.

FAR 5.203(a) says that an agency must publish its synopsis at the Governmentwide Point of Entry 15 days before it issues its RFP, unless the acquisition is for commercial items, in which case the agency can establish a shorter period. When agencies buy commercial items, FAR 12.603 allows them to combine the synopsis and the RFP in a single announcement.

With respect to contract awards, FAR 5.301 requires agencies to publish announcements at the Governmentwide Point of Entry of awards in excess of $25,000 that meet specified criteria.

55. What is the *advisory multistep process*?

The *advisory multistep process* is a procedure for reviewing the qualifications of prospective offerors and advising them about whether or not the government thinks that they have a realistic chance to win a source selection. FAR 15.202 describes the process as follows:

> (a) The agency may publish a presolicitation notice (see 5.204) that provides a general description of the scope or purpose of the acquisition and invites potential offerors to submit information that allows the Government to advise the offerors about their potential to be viable competitors. The presolicitation notice should identify the information that must be submitted and the criteria that will be used in making the initial evaluation. Information sought may be limited to a statement of qualifications and other appropriate information (e.g., proposed technical concept, past performance, and limited pricing information). At a minimum, the notice shall contain sufficient information to permit a potential offeror to make an informed decision about whether to participate in the acquisition. This process should not be used for multi-step acquisitions where it would result in offerors being required to submit identical information in response to the notice and in response to the initial step of the acquisition.
>
> (b) The agency shall evaluate all responses in accordance with the criteria stated in the notice, and shall advise each respondent in writing either that it will be invited to participate in the resultant acquisition or, based on the information submitted, that it is unlikely to be a viable competitor. The agency shall advise respondents considered not to be viable competitors of the general basis for that opinion. The agency shall inform all respondents that, notwithstanding the advice provided by the Government in response to their submissions, they may participate in the resultant acquisition.

FAR 15.202 does not tell agencies how to go about making their advisory assessments; however, it does say that agencies must provide "sufficient information to permit a potential offeror to make an informed decision about whether to participate in the acquisition." So while agencies may use informal assessment processes, they must prepare enough documentation to explain the bases for their assessments.

An agency's opinion is strictly advisory, and a firm may submit a proposal in response to the agency's RFP even if the agency determines that it is not a viable competitor. The agency must evaluate any such proposal on the basis of the evaluation factors described in the RFP. Agencies must evaluate each offeror anew for purposes of the source selection and may not use their previous advisory assessments since offerors may have used those assessments to improve themselves.

It is hard to see the advantages of this procedure from the standpoint of an agency source selection team. While in theory it could reduce the number of proposals received in response to an RFP and thus reduce the team's source selection workload, there is no guarantee that the firms seeking advisory opinions will be serious competitors; they may be conducting market research in anticipation of future acquisitions. There also is no guarantee that serious competitors who receive unfavorable assessments will decide not to compete. The procedural costs associated with developing the advisory assessments may exceed the benefits to a government team that is trying to buy specific products or services.

The advisory procedure has obvious advantages for firms that are willing to accept the government's assessment of their chances of winning or use them to improve themselves. The procedure can save them many thousands of dollars of bid and proposal costs that would otherwise be wasted in the pursuit of contracts that they have little or no chance to win, or it could provide them with inexpensive advice about what they need to do to be more competitive.

56. How should agencies organize and write their proposal preparation instructions?

The proposal preparation instructions in an RFP describe the information that the issuing agency needs from offerors in order to evaluate their proposals against the agency's evaluation factors for award. Thus, every set of proposal preparation instructions ought to be unique to the extent that evaluation factors differ from one procurement to another. However, there are some standard principles about how agencies should instruct offerors about how to organize their proposals.

An RFP should instruct offerors to organize their proposals in three parts: (1) the offer; (2) information about the offeror; and (3) information about prices or costs.

A good set of proposal preparation instructions includes four parts:

- Introduction
- Instructions about preparing and submitting the offer
- Instructions about preparing and submitting information about the offeror
- Instructions about preparing and submitting information about the offeror's prices or costs.

THE INTRODUCTION

The introduction to the proposal preparation instructions should inform offerors about the agency's proposal specifications, such as organization, binding, limitations on the number of pages that the proposal can include, page layout (e.g., margins, line spacing), font style, font size, character spacing, etc. It should state the number of copies to be submitted. The introduction should also include any procedural information that the agency wants to provide to the offerors, such as procedures for submitting questions about the RFP and information about the agency's source selection process.

THE OFFER

The offer is the part of the proposal that will become binding upon acceptance by the agency. It consists of a set of promises. The most fundamental promise the government should want from offerors is the promise to perform in accordance with the terms of the RFP if awarded the contract.

The RFP should instruct offerors to include the following in their offers: (1) a signed offer form (e.g., Standard Form 33, *Solicitation, Offer, and Award*); (2) a schedule of proposed contract line item prices; (3) any information that the agency wants the offeror to insert in blanks in the RFP; (4) proposed small disadvantaged business participation, if applicable; (5) proposed small business subcontracting plan, if applicable; and (6) completed representations, certifications, and other statements of the offerors or respondents.

The RFP should advise offerors that the agency will consider the submission of an offer to be a manifestation of the offeror's assent to the terms of the RFP, except as otherwise indicated by the offeror. It should also state whether or not the government is willing to entertain alternate proposals—i.e., exceptions to the terms of the RFP, offeror-proposed revisions to the specifications or clauses in the RFP, or offeror-proposed specifications or clauses—or whether such exceptions or conditions would make an offer unacceptable.

INFORMATION ABOUT THE OFFEROR

This is information that the agency will use to assess the offerors as firms, but that will not become a part of the contract. The RFP should describe the information that offerors must submit about their qualifications to perform, such as their experience, their past performance (i.e., references), the names and qualifications of their key personnel, and any other information the government wants (e.g., information about the offeror's organization, affiliates, subsidiaries, subcontractors, and performance plans and methods).

INFORMATION ABOUT PRICES OR COSTS

An offeror's proposed prices, hourly labor rates, or estimated costs and fees are part of the offer. But the information described in this third part of the proposal consists of supporting information—*information other than cost or pricing data,* as defined in FAR 15.401. This is information that the agency wants for price or cost analysis purposes, such as cost breakdowns that include descriptions of the types of labor that the offeror plans to employ, estimated labor hours, labor rates, material and equipment costs, indirect cost rates, descriptions of items of other direct cost, and the amount included for profit or fee.

57. How should agencies describe their *evaluation factors for award*?

The FAR does not provide much guidance about how to describe *evaluation factors for award* in an RFP. FAR 15.204-5(c), which applies to RFPs prepared in the Uniform Contract Format, states:

> Section M, Evaluation factors for award. Identify all significant factors and any significant subfactors that will be considered in awarding the contract and their relative importance (see 15.304(d)). The contracting officer shall insert one of the phrases in 15.304(e).

FAR 15.304(d) and (e) state:

> (d) All factors and significant subfactors that will affect contract award and their relative importance shall be stated clearly in the solicitation (10 U.S.C. 2305(a)(2)(A)(i)

> and 41 U.S.C. 253a(b)(1)(A)) (see 15.204-5(c)). The rating method need not be disclosed in the solicitation. The general approach for evaluating past performance information shall be described.
>
> (e) The solicitation shall also state, at a minimum, whether all evaluation factors other than cost or price, when combined, are—
>
> (1) Significantly more important than cost or price;
>
> (2) Approximately equal to cost or price; or
>
> (3) Significantly less important than cost or price (10 U.S.C. 2305(a)(3)(A)(iii) and 41 U.S.C. 253a(c)(1)(C)).

GAO has also provided little in the way of guidance. In *Foundation Health Federal Services, Inc.; Humana Military Healthcare Services, Inc.* (B-278189.3; B-278189.4, February 4, 1998), GAO said:

> Section 2305 of Title 10 of the United States Code requires that solicitations "at a minimum" include "a statement of—(i) all significant factors and significant subfactors which the head of the agency reasonably expects to consider . . . ; [and] (ii) the relative importance assigned to each of those factors and subfactors. . . ." 10 USC sec. 2305(a)(2)(A) (1994). Where an agency fails to advise offerors of the evaluation factors and the relative importance of those factors, there is no assurance that in selecting an offer for award it is obtaining what is most advantageous to the government, all factors considered. Richard S. Cohen, B-256017.4, B-256017.5, June 27, 1994, 94-1 CPD ¶ 382 at 6; see generally Fiber Materials, Inc., 57 Comp. Gen. 527, 530 (1978), 78-1 CPD ¶ 422 at 5.

and:

> Where the solicitation is silent as to the relative importance of the subfactors, as was the case here, Serv-Air, Inc., B-194717, Sept. 4, 1979, 79-2 CPD ¶ 176 at 5, 8, of-

> ferors can assume that the subfactors are approximately equal. Stone & Webster Eng'g Corp., B-255286.2, Apr. 12, 1994, 94-1 CPD ¶ 306 at 5; Informatics, Inc., B-194734, Aug. 22, 1979, 79-2 CPD ¶ 144 at 6.

However, in *Laidlaw Environmental Services (GS), Inc.* (B-271903, August 6, 1996), GAO noted:

> [W]e point out that not every evaluation consideration has to be set forth in an RFP—agencies properly may consider evaluation elements that logically are encompassed by the evaluation factors and subfactors contained in the RFP. See generally Akal Sec., Inc., B-271385.3, July 10, 1996, 96-2 CPD ¶ .

In *J. A. Jones Grupo de Servicios, SA*, B-283234 (October 25, 1999), GAO said:

> While we have held that the RFP must advise offerors of the criteria by which the agency will judge the merit of their proposals, an agency may consider specific, albeit not expressly identified, matters logically encompassed by or related to the stated criteria. Science Management Corp., B-207670, Sept. 23, 1983, 83-2 CPD ¶ 362 at 5.

Evaluation factors are attributes (i.e., features, qualities, or characteristics) of an offeror and of its offer that an agency either wants or wants to avoid. An agency should describe those attributes as clearly as possible so that an offeror can provide them or avoid them, as appropriate. In this light, consider the following proposal preparation instructions from an actual RFP:

> The Offeror shall describe for each element listed below the Offeror's strategic approach to managing NFO, including how the Offeror's strategic approach would be applied to the Pantex Plant; and the Offeror's methodology used in implementing its strategic approach, including how the Offeror's methodology would be applied to the Pantex Plant.

1. Implementing an integrated safety management system (ISMS) that clearly communicates the environment, safety and health roles, responsibilities, and authorities of line managers, and that holds line managers accountable for the performance of work in a manner that ensures protection of workers, the public and the environment.

2. Performing adequate and timely start up and restart of nuclear facilities including operation readiness reviews.

3. Developing and maintaining a technically proficient onsite authorization basis capability to perform comprehensive hazard analysis and change control for non-reactor nuclear facilities and operations.

4. Defining, performing and maintaining authorization basis documentation and analyses for nuclear facilities operations.

5. Reviewing and evaluating current plant activities along with any new information to determine implications on the safety of plant operations.

6. Developing, implementing and maintaining technical safety requirements. This would include development of written procedures for operations, maintenance, testing, and training of associated personnel.

7. Corporate commitment and resources to provide support, assistance and technical expectations in managing NFO.

Now read the description of the evaluation factor that is related to those proposal preparation instructions:

> DOE will evaluate the Offeror's strategic approach to managing ES&H in nuclear facility operations, including how the Offeror's strategic approach would be applied to the Pantex Plant; and the Offeror's methodology used in

> implementing its strategic approach, including how the Offeror's methodology would be applied to the Pantex Plant.

The description of the evaluation factor says that the agency will evaluate each offeror's "strategic approach" and the "methodology" that it will use to implement that approach. Even if we assume that everyone understands what the agency means by strategic approach and methodology, neither the description of the evaluation factor nor the proposal preparation instructions say what features, qualities, or characteristics the agency will look for. For example, the proposal preparation instructions tell the offerors to describe their strategic approach and methodology to implementing an integrated range safety system. The range safety system must possess the attributes of clearly communicating roles and responsibilities and holding line managers accountable; but the description of the evaluation factor does not describe the attributes that the agency would like a strategic approach and a methodology to have, even though those are the things that the agency says it will evaluate. There may be many ways to "approach" implementing a range safety system and many ways to "implement" such approaches, each with different attributes, but unless the agency gives prospective offerors more information, they will have to guess what the agency wants.

A well-written description of evaluation factors for award should describe: (1) *what things* the agency is going to evaluate and (2) *what attributes* the agency would like those things to have. Only then can offerors intelligently develop proposals that provide or avoid those things.

58. What is an *executive summary*, and when should an agency ask for one?

An *executive summary* is a brief document—often between 10 and 25 pages in length—that summarizes the contents of an offeror's proposal. The FAR makes no mention of executive summaries, but some agencies ask for them routinely. Agencies usually request executive summaries for one or more of the following reasons: (1) for the information of senior agency executives who will not be active participants in the evaluation process; (2) for the information of the source selection authority or other senior members of the evaluation team who will not read the detailed proposals; or (3) so that the working members of the evaluation team can obtain an overview of the proposals before beginning their detailed assessment. Agencies usually do not evaluate or score executive summaries.

The following is an instruction for the submission of an executive summary quoted from a Navy RFP:

> Executive Summary. The Executive Summary shall provide the Offeror's overview of how it intends to manage all tasks and integrate them into a comprehensive plan to take over the configuration management of the drawing package, start a JITS Support System for existing and future items, build First Article Units, get them qualified through testing, and begin production of Q-70 systems, as well as take on the overall life cycle support of the program. It should describe how the proposed solution meets the OSA requirement as set forth in the PIDS. In addition it should summarize how it will take on the engineering efforts involved in designing those systems which are new efforts and getting them into production at a firm fixed price. Prices should not be stated except in the price volume. The executive summary will not be included in the page count limit but, shall be no longer than six (6) pages.

Senior agency managers and decision makers who read executive summaries may develop strong first impressions of the offerors as a result, so some offerors devote a lot of effort to designing and writing executive summaries in an effort to make a good first impression. This can make executive summaries very expensive, so agencies should request executive summaries only when absolutely necessary. They should do so only after thinking very clearly about whom the summaries are to be written for, what those readers want to learn from the executive summaries, and how the readers will use that information. During the source selection planning phase, agency planners should try to get some idea from prospective offerors about how much an executive summary would cost to produce, and then try to do some cost/benefit analysis.

59. What is a *proposal compliance matrix*?

A *proposal compliance matrix* is a table in a proposal that cross-references the parts of a proposal with the parts of the RFP. It is designed to help members of the evaluation team find specific information in a large proposal and to show that the proposal is responsive to the instructions in the RFP and is compliant with all requirements.

Table III-2 shows a simple proposal compliance matrix. This matrix cross-references paragraphs in a statement of work to pages in a proposal and provides space for the evaluators to indicate whether the proposal is compliant with the specification or statement of work. There are many possible variations on this format.

TABLE III-2
PROPOSAL COMPLIANCE MATRIX

SOW Paragraph	*Proposal Volume and Page*	*Fully Compliant*	*Partially Compliant*	*Fully Noncompliant*
3.1.1	I-3-4	✔		
3.1.2	I-3-10		✔	
3.2	II-2-1	✔		
3.3.1	II-3-3			✔
3.3.2	II-3-8	✔		

Proposal compliance matrices are very useful devices, as they serve as guides and checklists for both agency evaluation teams and offeror proposal development teams. Their use can reduce the chances that proposals will be incomplete or otherwise deficient. Many companies include compliance matrices in their proposals even when RFPs do not request or require them. They can also be used with oral presentations to relate the presentation slides to the topics specified in the RFP.

60. What are the rules about facsimile submission of proposals?

FAR 2.101 defines *facsimile* as follows:

> "Facsimile" means electronic equipment that communicates and reproduces both printed and handwritten material. If used in conjunction with a reference to a document, e.g., facsimile bid, the term refers to a document (in the example given, a bid) that has been transmitted to and received by the Government via facsimile.

FAR 15.203(d) authorizes agencies to let offerors submit proposals, proposal revisions, and proposal modifications by facsimile, as follows:

> Contracting officers may issue RFPs and/or authorize receipt of proposals, modifications, or revisions by facsimile.
>
> (1) In deciding whether or not to use facsimiles, the contracting officer should consider factors such as—
>
> (i) Anticipated proposal size and volume;
>
> (ii) Urgency of the requirement;
>
> (iii) Availability and suitability of electronic commerce methods; and

(iv) Adequacy of administrative procedures and controls for receiving, identifying, recording, and safeguarding facsimile proposals, and ensuring their timely delivery to the designated proposal delivery location.

(2) If facsimile proposals are authorized, contracting officers may request offeror(s) to provide the complete, original signed proposal at a later date.

FAR 15.209(e) requires that RFPs include the solicitation provision at FAR 52.215-5, *Facsimile Proposals,* when agencies decide to permit facsimile submission. That provision reads as follows:

Facsimile Proposals (Oct 1997)

(a) Definition. Facsimile proposal, as used in this provision, means a proposal, revision or modification of a proposal, or withdrawal of a proposal that is transmitted to and received by the Government via facsimile machine.

(b) Offerors may submit facsimile proposals as responses to this solicitation. Facsimile proposals are subject to the same rules as paper proposals.

(c) The telephone number of receiving facsimile equipment is: [insert telephone number].

(d) If any portion of a facsimile proposal received by the Contracting Officer is unreadable to the degree that conformance to the essential requirements of the solicitation cannot be ascertained from the document—

(1) The Contracting Officer immediately shall notify the offeror and permit the offeror to resubmit the proposal;

(2) The method and time for resubmission shall be prescribed by the Contracting Officer after consultation with the offeror; and

> (3) The resubmission shall be considered as if it were received at the date and time of the original unreadable submission for the purpose of determining timeliness, provided the offeror complies with the time and format requirements for resubmission prescribed by the Contracting Officer.
>
> (e) The Government reserves the right to make award solely on the facsimile proposal. However, if requested to do so by the Contracting Officer, the apparently successful offeror promptly shall submit the complete original signed proposal.

61. What are the rules about submission of proposals via electronic commerce?

FAR 2.101 defines *electronic commerce* as follows:

> *Electronic commerce* means electronic techniques for accomplishing business transactions including electronic mail or messaging, World Wide Web technology, electronic bulletin boards, purchase cards, electronic funds transfer, and electronic data interchange.

The FAR coverage of electronic commerce is not extensive. FAR 4.502 says:

> (a) The Federal Government shall use electronic commerce whenever practicable or cost-effective. The use of terms commonly associated with paper transactions (*e.g.*, "copy," "document," "page," "printed," "sealed envelope," and "stamped") shall not be interpreted to restrict the use of electronic commerce. Contracting officers may supplement electronic transactions by using other media to meet the requirements of any contract action governed by the FAR (*e.g.*, transmit hard copy of drawings).

(b) Agencies may exercise broad discretion in selecting the hardware and software that will be used in conducting electronic commerce. However, as required by Section 30 of the OFPP Act (41 U.S.C. 426), the head of each agency, after consulting with the Administrator of OFPP, shall ensure that systems, technologies, procedures, and processes used by the agency to conduct electronic commerce—

(1) Are implemented uniformly throughout the agency, to the maximum extent practicable;

(2) Are implemented only after considering the full or partial use of existing infrastructures, (*e.g.*, the Federal Acquisition Computer Network (FACNET));

(3) Facilitate access to Government acquisition opportunities by small business concerns, small disadvantaged business concerns, and women-owned small business concerns;

(4) Include a single means of providing widespread public notice of acquisition opportunities through the Governmentwide point of entry and a means of responding to notices or solicitations electronically; and

(5) Comply with nationally and internationally recognized standards that broaden interoperability and ease the electronic interchange of information, such as standards established by the National Institute of Standards and Technology.

(c) Before using electronic commerce, the agency head shall ensure that the agency systems are capable of ensuring authentication and confidentiality commensurate with the risk and magnitude of the harm from loss, misuse, or unauthorized access to or modification of the information.

(d) Agencies may accept electronic signatures and records in connection with Government contracts.

FAR 15.203(c) says:

> Electronic commerce may be used to issue RFPs and to receive proposals, modifications, and revisions. In this case, the RFP shall specify the electronic commerce method(s) that offerors may use (see subpart 4.5).

Some agencies now make their RFPs available on the Internet, either at their own web pages or at centralized websites such as the Electronic Posting System maintained by the U.S. General Services Administration at www.eps.gov/. While there have been some experiments in the electronic submission of proposals, it is still in the planning stage in most agencies.

Nonetheless, it is clear that electronic submission of proposals will be standard practice for some agencies in the not-too-distant future. This should be evident from the number of advertisements for seminars and consultants providing training and advice about how to prepare for paperless contracting with the government.

62. What are the rules about proposal format restrictions?

Agencies restrict proposal formats in various ways. Format restrictions include organizational specifications, limitations on the number of pages, page layout restrictions, font (type) restrictions, etc. The following is a classic example from an RFP, quoted by GAO in *Centech Group, Inc.* (B-278904.4, April 13, 1998):

> All materials submitted shall be in typeface Times New Roman 12 Point, doubled spaced on 8½ inch by 11 inch white paper with one inch margins all around and printed on one side. The Technical and Business Management Proposal shall not contain more than 150 numbered pages inclusive of the table of contents, charts, exhibits, and any other materials the Offeror deems required....

The key question about such restrictions is what an agency should do if an offeror does not comply. The answer is that agencies should not reject proposals merely because of a technical violation of a proposal preparation instruction, but they must take steps to ensure that such a violation does not give an offeror an unfair advantage over offerors that did comply.

ORGANIZATIONAL SPECIFICATIONS

The most common organizational specifications require the packaging of proposal information in separate volumes. RFPs frequently instruct offerors to submit separate *technical, management,* and *cost* volumes. Most commonly, agencies require submission of technical and price information in separate volumes and state that technical volumes must not include any information about price or cost. Failure to comply with these kinds of restrictions may be a nuisance to an agency but probably will not confer much of a competitive advantage on the offending offeror. If failure to comply does confer an unfair advantage, then the restriction must somehow be enforced.

PAGE LIMITATIONS

A proposal page limitation is an instruction in an RFP that limits the number of pages that an offeror may include in its proposal. Agencies set page limits in an effort to curb the tendency of some offerors to throw everything except the kitchen sink into their proposals, hoping to hit as many of the evaluators' hot buttons as possible. The FAR does not mention proposal page limitations, but agencies have set page limits in their RFPs for many years, and these have been the most controversial proposal format restrictions.

GAO has issued a number of decisions that establish rules about page limitations. The most basic rule is that an agency must enforce any limit that it sets. GAO's decision in *Techsys Corporation* (B-278904.3, April 13, 1998) is typical. In that case, an agency had set a limit of 150 pages, as follows:

> The Technical and Business Management Proposal shall not contain more than 150 numbered pages inclusive of the table of contents, charts, exhibits, and any other materials the Offeror deems required for each functional area for which an offer is being made.

Notwithstanding those reasonably clear instructions, the protester submitted a proposal that exceeded the page limit by 28 pages. The agency removed the excess pages before evaluating the proposal, which resulted in a relatively low evaluation score for the protester and award of the contract to a competitor. The protest followed, and GAO denied it, stating:

> Offerors are required to prepare their proposals within the format limitations set out in the solicitation, including the page limits at issue here, and assume the risk that proposal pages beyond the page limits will not be considered because consideration of an offeror's excess proposal pages could give that offeror an unfair competitive advantage. All Star Maintenance, Inc., B-244143, Sept. 26, 1991, 91-2 CPD ¶ 294 at 3-4; Infotec Dev., Inc., B-238980, July 20, 1990, 90-2 CPD ¶ 58 at 4-5.
>
> Here, the RFP clearly provided for a 150-page limit on technical proposals and in response to specific questions concerning the page limit, DOE indicated by amendment that any page that an offeror deemed necessary to include in its proposal would be included in the page count, including the table of contents and tab dividers. Thus, offerors were on notice both of the 150-page limitation and that any and all pages, including unmarked pages, table of contents pages and all narratives would be considered in the page calculation. Techsys's proposal clearly failed to comply with the solicitation format re-

> quirements. Techsys did not protest the page limits of the RFP, but chose to exceed the proposal page limitation set forth in the RFP, thereby assuming the risk that excess pages in its proposal would be rejected for noncompliance with the page limits. Infotec Dev., Inc., supra, at 4.
>
> While Techsys argues that DOE should have been more flexible in the handling of the page limitation, an agency that has set out a clear page limitation in a solicitation is not obligated to sort through hundreds of pages to decide which pages should or should not be counted toward that limitation. HSQ Tech., B-277048, Aug. 21, 1997, 97-2 CPD ¶ 57 at 3 n.1. Further, where, as here, the agency has set specific page limits and indicated that any and all pages submitted would count toward that limit, the agency was not obligated to ask the offeror, after submission of its proposal, to "clarify" its proposal by selecting which pages it wants counted. Infotec Dev., Inc., supra, at 5. Under these circumstances, the agency reasonably computed the 150 pages and properly declined to consider those portions of Techsys's proposal that exceeded the stated limits. All Star Maintenance, Inc., supra, at 3-4.

Clearly, the wisest course of action for any company submitting a proposal in response to an RFP is to comply with the page limitation, if any.

In the Techsys case, the agency did the right thing by counting and removing the pages in excess of the page limit and then evaluating what remained. But may an agency discard the *entire* proposal on the basis of the technicality that the proposal exceeds a page limitation? GAO's decisions indicate that the answer depends on the wording of the RFP. If the RFP says that any proposal which exceeds the limit "shall" be rejected without evaluation, then the answer appears to be yes. But if the RFP states that any proposal that exceeds the limitation "may" or "could" be rejected, then the answer is no.

In *Macfadden & Associates, Inc.* (B-275502; February 27, 1997), the RFP set a limit of 100 pages and said, as quoted by GAO, "[f]ailure of a proposal to comply with these instructions may be grounds for exclusion of the proposal from further consideration." The protester's proposal exceeded the page limit, and the agency rejected the entire proposal without evaluating any part of it. The protester argued that it was at least entitled to have the first 100 pages of its proposal evaluated before rejection. GAO agreed with the protester and sustained the protest, stating:

> The agency and the protester properly acknowledge that a contracting agency may not accept excess proposal pages in contravention of a solicitation page limitation when that action would result in unequal treatment of offerors. However, Macfadden argues that it is entitled to an evaluation of the pages of its proposal that do not exceed the 100-page limit. In this instance, the Customs Service failed to conduct any technical evaluation of the pages of Macfadden's proposal that were within the page limits, based on its belief that a review of the first 97 pages of the proposal would have been "contrary to law." The agency argues that Macfadden ignored the RFP's instructions at its own peril and asserts that Macfadden's proposal is simply not entitled to further consideration because of this violation.
>
> Where an appendix included with a proposal causes the proposal to exceed a page limit established in the RFP, it would be improper for the agency to consider the appendix because to do so would confer upon the offeror furnishing the appendix a competitive advantage over those offerors whose proposals complied with the page limit. <u>ITT Electron Technology Div.</u>, B-242289, Apr. 18, 1991, 91-1 CPD ¶ 383. Accordingly, where solicitations have imposed page and type limits, we have found reasonable the agency's removing pages beyond the solicitation limit and evaluating only those pages within the limit. <u>All Star Maintenance, Inc.</u>, B-244143, Sept. 26, 1991, 91-2 CPD ¶ 294; <u>Infotec Dev., Inc.</u>, B-

> 238980, July 20, 1990, 90-2 CPD ¶ 58. See Management & Indus. Technologies Assocs., B-257656, Oct. 11, 1994, 94-2 CPD ¶ 134; S.T. Research Corp., B-233115, Feb. 15, 1989, 89-1 CPD ¶ 159. Whether the approach taken by the agency here—automatic rejection of an entire proposal exceeding a page limit rather than evaluation of only the proposal pages within the limit—is proper depends, in the first instance, upon the language of the solicitation. If the solicitation provides that a proposal exceeding a specified page limit will be rejected and an offeror, without protesting that provision, chooses to compete in accordance with the RFP's terms but nevertheless submits a proposal that exceeds the limit, rejection of the proposal, at least in general, would seem to be unobjectionable. Where, however, the solicitation states that a proposal exceeding a page limit may be excluded from consideration, we think offerors are reasonably put on notice that rejection for exceeding the page limit will not be automatic but instead will occur only if there is a reasonable basis for such action.

Thus, it appears that GAO would support rejection of the *entire* proposal only if an RFP says that exceeding the page limit "shall" result in the elimination of the entire proposal without evaluation. In *HSQ Technology* (B-277048, August 21, 1997), GAO held that "could be rejected" and "may be rejected" mean the same thing.

What counts as a "page" when an agency sets page limits? The answer depends on what the RFP says. In *Centech Group, Inc.* (B-278904.4; April 13, 1998), the protester complained that the agency improperly included a cover sheet, blank section dividers, and a table of contents in its page count, and that it was unreasonable for the agency to include such pages, which resulted in the elimination of pages containing substantive information. GAO disagreed, saying:

> [T]he RFP clearly provided for a 150-page limit on technical proposals and in response to specific questions concerning the page limit, DOE indicated by amend-

> ment that any page that an offeror deemed necessary to include in its proposal would be included in the page count, including the table of contents and tab dividers. Thus, offerors were on notice both of the 150-page limitation and that any and all pages, including coversheets, dividers, and table of contents pages would be considered in the page calculation.

An agency should set a proposal page limit whenever it decides to ask for essay-type technical or management proposals. This will prevent offerors from overwhelming the agency with reams of material. When setting a page limit, an agency should think hard about what information it wants from offerors, describe that information as clearly and as specifically as possible in its proposal preparation instructions, and then think hard about how much space offerors will need to provide the requested information in adequate detail. The agency should also define what it will count as a "page." The proposal preparation instructions should state whether the count will include covers, inside title pages, tables of contents, section dividers, blank pages, appendices, etc. The instructions should also state that the contracting officer will count the pages in every proposal and remove any pages in excess of the page limit before evaluating the proposal.

Agencies should not set page limits on price or cost proposals when they will require offerors to submit cost or pricing data in accordance with FAR 15.403-4. Such a page limit could be construed as conflicting with the requirement that offerors' submissions of cost or pricing data be complete. (See FAR 15.408, Table 15-2.)

PAGE LAYOUT RESTRICTIONS

The most common page layout restrictions require double-spacing and one-inch margins. If these restrictions are established in conjunction with page limitations, an agency's failure to enforce either of them would allow an offeror that violated one or both of them to put more words in front of the evaluators than offerors that complied. Thus, an agency that imposes such restrictions should enforce them. But how? The answer is that the agency should determine how many more words the offending offeror managed to squeeze in by violating the restrictions and then remove enough pages from the end of its proposal to delete those extra words.

FONT RESTRICTIONS

Some agencies instruct offerors to use a certain size of a certain font—e.g., 12-point Times New Roman. Agencies began to resort to these kinds of restrictions when some offerors responded to page limitations by using small font sizes in order to squeeze more words onto a page. Agencies should enforce font restrictions by determining how many extra words a violation allowed the offending offeror to squeeze onto a page and then deleting enough pages to eliminate any improper advantage.

Agencies should take care to specify font size restrictions properly. They should be careful about how they use terms like *point, pitch,* and *characters per inch* in an instruction. The height of the characters in a font is measured in units called *points,* with one point being equal to 1⁄72 of an inch. Height is measured from the top of the letter ascenders to the bottom of the descenders. When it comes to width, fonts are either proportional or monospaced. Most digital (computer) fonts are proportional. The number of characters per inch in a line of proportional type varies with the letters in the line. Typewriter fonts are monospaced. The number of characters per inch in a line of monospaced type is standard. Times New Roman is a proportional font. Courier is a monospaced font. The terms *pitch* and *characters per inch* (cpi) apply to monospaced fonts. A 10-point monospaced font has a pitch of 12 cpi and is called *pica* type; a 12-point monospaced font has a pitch of 10 cpi and is called *elite* type.

The following instruction from an RFP is an example of an inappropriate font restriction:

> The proposal page shall be printed on both sides (head to head) in *a type size not less than 12 point* with space and a half between lines. The type font shall use *12 characters to an inch* and use *Times New Roman font.* [Italics added.]

The problem with this instruction is that offerors cannot comply with all three restrictions—12 point, 12 characters to an inch, and Times New Roman—at the same time. Times New Roman is a proportional font; some inches of 12 point Times New Roman might contain 12 characters, but some might contain more, and others might contain less, depending on the width of the letters in the particular inch being measured. At best, a proposal could try to comply with the 12 cpi requirement on average. If the specified font had been monospaced, 12 points would be inconsistent with 12 cpi. A more appropriate font restriction in the era of digital type would be 12-point Times New Roman, with *normal character spacing* (instead of *characters per inch*). Agencies should take care when establishing font restrictions.

63. What are *cost or pricing data*?

FAR 2.101 defines *cost or pricing data* as follows:

> *Cost or pricing data* (10 U.S.C. 2306a(h)(1) and 41 U.S.C. 254b) means all facts that, as of the date of price agreement or, if applicable, an earlier date agreed upon between the parties that is as close as practicable to the date of agreement on price, prudent buyers and sellers would reasonably expect to affect price negotiations significantly. Cost or pricing data are data requiring certification in accordance with 15.406-2. Cost or pric-

> ing data are factual, not judgmental; and are verifiable. While they do not indicate the accuracy of the prospective contractor's judgment about estimated future costs or projections, they do include the data forming the basis for that judgment. Cost or pricing data are more than historical accounting data; they are all the facts that can be reasonably expected to contribute to the soundness of estimates of future costs and to the validity of determinations of costs already incurred. They also include such factors as:
>
> *(1)* Vendor quotations;
>
> *(2)* Nonrecurring costs;
>
> *(3)* Information on changes in production methods and in production or purchasing volume;
>
> *(4)* Data supporting projections of business prospects and objectives and related operations costs;
>
> *(5)* Unit-cost trends such as those associated with labor efficiency;
>
> *(6)* Make-or-buy decisions;
>
> *(7)* Estimated resources to attain business goals; and
>
> *(8)* Information on management decisions that could have a significant bearing on costs.

This definition is complex and has been the source of much litigation.

One key to the definition of cost or pricing data is the statement that the data consist of facts, not judgments. As a general rule, cost estimates are not cost or pricing data, because they are not facts, they are judgments. Cost or price breakdowns are also judgments. Another key is the statement that cost or pricing data include "*all* the facts that can be reasonably expected to contribute to the soundness of estimates of future costs and to the validity of determinations of costs already incurred." This statement should lead to the realization that cost or pricing data may be quite voluminous and exceedingly expensive to gather, format, and submit, even for procurements of modest size.

64. What is *information other than cost or pricing data*?

FAR 2.101 defines *information other than cost or pricing data* as follows:

> *Information other than cost or pricing data* means any type of information that is not required to be certified in accordance with 15.406-2 and is necessary to determine price reasonableness or cost realism. For example, such information may include pricing, sales, or cost information, and includes cost or pricing data for which certification is determined inapplicable after submission.

It should be clear from the definition that *information other than cost or pricing data* includes judgments as well as facts. It also includes cost or price breakdowns and information that would be cost or pricing data if it had to be certified. Agencies must specify what information they want when they ask for information other than cost or pricing data.

65. What is the Truth in Negotiations Act, and when do offerors have to submit cost or pricing data with their proposals?

The Truth in Negotiations Act (TINA) is a law enacted in 1962 (Public Law 87-653) that requires contracting officers to obtain *cost or pricing data* from a firm when negotiating a contract for which the price of the estimated cost and fee is expected to exceed a specified dollar value (the "TINA threshold") and when economic forces are not at work that would force the firm to propose a fair and reasonable price. The goal of the law is to ensure that the government has at its disposal the same information about costs that the firm has. The firm must submit the cost or pricing data to the government for its use in performing cost and price analysis, and then, upon reaching agreement with the government on the contract price or estimated cost and fee, it must certify that the data it submitted were accurate, complete, and current as of the time of price agreement. If it later turns out that any of the data were not accurate, complete, or current ("defective pricing"), and if the government agreed to a higher price than it would have if the data had been accurate, complete, and current, then the government will be entitled to a price reduction.

The FAR implements TINA in Subpart 15.4. The requirements for the submission of cost or pricing data are in FAR 15.403-4. The rules about the certification of cost or pricing data are in FAR 15.406-2. The rules about defective pricing are in FAR 15.407-1. Currently, the TINA threshold is $550,000. The value of a contract for the purposes of applying the threshold includes the values of contract options. See FAR 1.108(c).

FAR 15.403-1 prohibits agencies from asking offerors to submit cost or pricing data when any of the following five conditions exists: (1) prices are expected to be based on adequate price competition; (2) prices are expected to be based on prices set by law or regulation; (3) the government is buying a commercial item; (4) a waiver to the requirement for the submission of cost or pricing data has been granted; or (5) the acquisition is for the modification of a contract or subcontract for commercial items. FAR 15.403-1(c) establishes standards for each of these exceptions. FAR 15.403-4 says that agencies must request that offerors submit cost or pricing data when none of these exceptions applies, and offerors must comply to be eligible for award. The nature of the five exceptions is such that agencies should rarely, if ever, request cost or pricing data in a competitive procurement. If an agency does request cost or pricing data, and if an offeror thinks that one of the exceptions applies, FAR 52.215-20 provides that the offeror may submit a written request for the exception. The contracting officer may ask for information to support that request.

FAR 15.403-4 instructs agencies to obtain *information other than cost or pricing data* when the rules do not require the submission and certification of cost or pricing data and when the contracting officer needs the information in order to determine the fairness and reasonableness of proposed prices.

66. Who is entitled to receive a copy of the request for proposals?

For all practical purposes, an agency must give a copy of its RFP to anyone who asks for it unless the information about the procurement is classified for security reasons, in which case it can limit distribution to authorized persons and organizations. FAR 5.102(a) states the rules about the availability of solicitations as follows:

> (a)(1) Except as provided in paragraph (a)(4) of this section, the contracting officer must make available through the GPE solicitations synopsized through the GPE, including specifications and other pertinent information determined necessary by the contracting officer. Transmissions to the GPE must be in accordance with the interface description available via the Internet at http://www.fedbizopps.gov.
>
> (2) The contracting officer is encouraged, when practicable and cost-effective, to make accessible through the GPE additional information related to a solicitation.

(3) The contracting officer must ensure that solicitations transmitted to FACNET are forwarded to the GPE to satisfy the requirements of paragraph (a)(1) of this section.

(4) The contracting officer need not make a solicitation available through the GPE when—

(i) Disclosure would compromise the national security (e.g., would result in disclosure of classified information) or create other security risks. The fact that access to classified matter may be necessary to submit a proposal or perform the contract does not, in itself, justify use of this exception;

(ii) The nature of the file (e.g., size, format) does not make it cost-effective or practicable for contracting officers to provide access through the GPE;

(iii) The agency's senior procurement executive makes a written determination that access through the GPE is not in the Government's interest; or

(iv) The contracting office lacks the capability to access the GPE and the synopsis is issued prior to October 1, 2001.

Refusal of a request for a copy of an RFP will almost certainly provoke a protest or a Freedom of Information Act request, or even a protest to GAO.

67. What is a *preproposal conference*?

A *preproposal conference* is a public meeting conducted by an agency after it has released its RFP in order to give offerors additional information about the government's requirements and answer questions about the contents of the RFP. If the procurement will entail performance at a government facility, a preproposal conference may include a chance to visit the site.

The FAR now mentions preproposal conferences only in passing. See, e.g., FAR 15.201. Before the FAR Part 15 Rewrite, however, it provided detailed guidance, as follows:

> **15.409 Pre-proposal conferences.**
>
> (a) A pre-proposal conference may be held to brief prospective offerors after a solicitation has been issued but before offers are submitted. Generally, the Government uses these conferences in complex negotiated acquisitions to explain or clarify complicated specifications and requirements.
>
> (b) The contracting officer shall decide if a pre-proposal conference is required and make the necessary arrangements, including the following:
>
> (1) If notice was not in the solicitation, give all prospective offerors who received the solicitation adequate notice of the time, place, nature, and scope of the conference.
>
> (2) If time allows, request prospective offerors to submit written questions in advance. Prepared answers can then be delivered during the conference.
>
> (3) Arrange for technical and legal personnel to attend the conference, if appropriate.
>
> (c) The contracting officer or a designated representative shall conduct the pre-proposal conference, furnish all prospective offerors identical information concerning the proposed acquisition, make a complete record of the conference, and promptly furnish a copy of that record to all prospective offerors. Conferees shall be advised that—
>
> (1) Remarks and explanations at the conference shall not qualify the terms of the solicitation; and

(2) Terms of the solicitation and specifications remain unchanged unless the solicitation is amended in writing.

Although this passage no longer appears in the FAR, the guidance is still sound.

68. What is an *RFP amendment,* and what are the rules for amending RFPs?

An *amendment* is a change to an RFP. (Changes to contracts are called *modifications*.) Agencies usually make amendments on Standard Form 30, *Amendment of Solicitation/Modification of Contract,* although use of the form is not mandatory. The rules about amending RFPs are in FAR 15.206, *Amending the solicitation,* which reads as follows:

(a) When, either before or after receipt of proposals, the Government changes its requirements or terms and conditions, the contracting officer shall amend the solicitation.

(b) Amendments issued before the established time and date for receipt of proposals shall be issued to all parties receiving the solicitation.

(c) Amendments issued after the established time and date for receipt of proposals shall be issued to all offerors that have not been eliminated from the competition.

(d) If a proposal of interest to the Government involves a departure from the stated requirements, the contracting officer shall amend the solicitation, provided this can be done without revealing to the other offerors the alternate solution proposed or any other information that is entitled to protection (see 15.207(b) and 15.306(e)).

(e) If, in the judgment of the contracting officer, based on market research or otherwise, an amendment proposed for issuance after offers have been received is so substan-

> tial as to exceed what prospective offerors reasonably could have anticipated, so that additional sources likely would have submitted offers had the substance of the amendment been known to them, the contracting officer shall cancel the original solicitation and issue a new one, regardless of the stage of the acquisition.
>
> (f) Oral notices may be used when time is of the essence. The contracting officer shall document the contract file and formalize the notice with an amendment (see subpart 4.5, Electronic Commerce in Contracting).
>
> (g) At a minimum, the following information should be included in each amendment:
>
> (1) Name and address of issuing activity.
>
> (2) Solicitation number and date.
>
> (3) Amendment number and date.
>
> (4) Number of pages.
>
> (5) Description of the change being made.
>
> (6) Government point of contact and phone number (and electronic or facsimile address, if appropriate).
>
> (7) Revision to solicitation closing date, if applicable.

An agency can amend its RFP at any time before contract award, even after the evaluation of proposals, but it may not do so with the specific objective of changing any particular offeror's standing in the competition. In *SMS Data Products Group, Inc.* (B-280970.4, January 29, 1999), GAO said:

> An agency may amend a solicitation, and request and evaluate further offers where the record shows that the agency made the decision to take this action in good

> faith, without the specific intent of changing a particular offeror's technical ranking or avoiding an award to a particular offeror. See PRC, Inc., B-233561.8, B-233561.9, Sept. 29, 1992, 92-2 CPD ¶ 215 at 3-4; Burns & Roe Servs. Corp., B-248394, Aug. 25, 1992, 92-2 CPD ¶ 124 at 5; Unisys Corp., B-230019.2, July 12, 1988, 88-2 CPD ¶ 35 at 5.

GAO has even allowed agencies to change their evaluation factors after contract award in response to a protest. (See *Roxco, Ltd.*, B-277545, October 27, 1997.)

As indicated in FAR 15.206(b) and (c), an agency must furnish a copy of an RFP amendment to every firm that received a copy of the RFP or to every offeror that is still in the competition, depending on whether the amendment was issued before or after the receipt of proposals. However, GAO has consistently taken the position that offerors bear the risk of not receiving amendments as long as the agency has not acted in bad faith or unreasonably. In its decision in *CardioMetrix* (B-270701, March 13, 1996), GAO stated:

> The protester also complains that it failed to receive a copy of amendment No. 0002 until 3 minutes prior to the revised closing time and thus did not have time to review the contents of the amendment and submit an offer prior to closing. A prospective offeror, however, bears the risk of not receiving a solicitation amendment unless it is shown that the contracting agency made a deliberate effort to exclude the firm from competing, or that the agency failed to furnish the amendment inadvertently after the firm availed itself of every reasonable opportunity to obtain the amendment. Sentinel Security & Patrol Servs., B-261018, Aug. 9, 1995, 95-2 CPD ¶ 67.

Thus, offerors would be wise to contact the agency that issued the RFP periodically to ask whether it has issued any amendments.

69. What can agency personnel talk about before the receipt of proposals?

Exchanges of information between an agency and prospective offerors before the receipt of proposals are governed by the rules in FAR 3.104 and 15.201. Before the receipt of proposals, agency personnel can discuss a procurement as long as they do so in a way that does not give any offeror an unfair informational advantage and as long as they do not disclose any firm's proprietary information or any *source selection information*. (See the definition of the latter term in FAR 2.101.) Exchanges before the receipt of proposals are not *discussions* as defined in FAR 15.306(d).

The rules encourage open exchanges between the government and prospective offerors. Note that FAR 15.201(f) and 15.303(c)(1) state that after the RFP has been released the contracting officer must be the "focal point" for all communications between an agency and prospective offerors.

70. How can prospective offerors get answers to questions about an RFP?

Prospective offerors should submit all questions about an RFP to the contracting officer in writing. The best way to submit questions in writing is via U.S. Postal Service Express Mail or Federal Express. These services deliver quickly and keep records of the date and time of delivery. (Federal Express cannot deliver to post office boxes.) The contracting officer may be willing to receive questions by facsimile, but these can more easily get lost or misdirected. Increasingly, contracting officers are accepting questions by e-mail. Rarely will a contracting officer be willing to accept or respond to any but the simplest administrative questions by telephone.

The best course of action for a prospective offeror is to convene its proposal team to go through the RFP sentence by sentence, page by page, as soon as it is received, noting questions for which answers are needed. This process should be pursued aggressively until the entire RFP has been scoured. Questions should then be submitted to the contracting officer at the earliest possible date. The sooner questions are submitted, the sooner the answers will be obtained. Any delay in submitting questions may result in a costly delay in getting information that is crucial to sound proposal development.

Prospective offerors must be prepared to wait for answers; agencies are usually not staffed to provide immediate answers or are unwilling to do so. In many cases the contracting officer will have to obtain the answers from other offices, and answers may have to be vetted with an agency attorney. Contracting officers usually collect the questions and answer them en masse in an RFP amendment rather than answer each one individually. Agencies generally are not obligated to postpone a proposal due date to respond to questions, and questions submitted at the last minute may not receive an answer in time for proposal submission.

Offerors should submit *all* questions about a competitive procurement to the contracting officer to avoid violations of the Procurement Integrity Act (41 U.S.C. 423; see FAR 3.104). Merely asking for or accepting information from another person, even without offering any gratuity or bribe, violates the Act, which provides for civil and criminal penalties. GAO has allowed agencies to disqualify offerors based on violations of the Procurement Integrity Act. For example, in *Guardian Technologies International* (B-270213; B-270213.2; B-270213.3, February 20, 1996), GAO said:

> When it appears that an offeror may have prepared its proposal with knowledge of source selection information, such an appearance taints the integrity of the procurement process, regardless of whether any source selection information was actually obtained or used, and

the agency may disqualify the offeror from the competition. See Compliance Corp. v. United States, 22 Cl. Ct. 193 (1990), aff'd, 960 F.2d 157 (Fed. Cir. 1992).

71. What information may an agency disclose to the public before it receives proposals?

An agency may disclose any information about an upcoming procurement to the public that it chooses to disclose, except for a firm's proprietary information. For example, an agency may disclose its budget, cost estimate, evaluation plan, and so forth. However, if it chooses to disclose such information, it must do so in ways that do not give any competitor an unfair informational advantage.

FAR 15.201 establishes rules about exchanging information with industry before the receipt of proposals, as follows:

> **Exchanges with industry before receipt of proposals.**
>
> (a) Exchanges of information among all interested parties, from the earliest identification of a requirement through receipt of proposals, are encouraged. Any exchange of information must be consistent with procurement integrity requirements (see 3.104). Interested parties include potential offerors, end users, Government acquisition and supporting personnel, and others involved in the conduct or outcome of the acquisition.
>
> (b) The purpose of exchanging information is to improve the understanding of Government requirements and industry capabilities, thereby allowing potential offerors to judge whether or how they can satisfy the Government's requirements, and enhancing the Government's ability to obtain quality supplies and services, including construction, at reasonable prices, and increase efficiency in

proposal preparation, proposal evaluation, negotiation, and contract award.

(c) Agencies are encouraged to promote early exchanges of information about future acquisitions. An early exchange of information among industry and the program manager, contracting officer, and other participants in the acquisition process can identify and resolve concerns regarding the acquisition strategy, including proposed contract type, terms and conditions, and acquisition planning schedules; the feasibility of the requirement, including performance requirements, statements of work, and data requirements; the suitability of the proposal instructions and evaluation criteria, including the approach for assessing past performance information; the availability of reference documents; and any other industry concerns or questions. Some techniques to promote early exchanges of information are-

(1) Industry or small business conferences;

(2) Public hearings;

(3) Market research, as described in part 10;

(4) One-on-one meetings with potential offerors (any that are substantially involved with potential contract terms and conditions should include the contracting officer; also see paragraph (f) of this section regarding restrictions on disclosure of information);

(5) Presolicitation notices;

(6) Draft RFPs;

(7) RFIs;

(8) Presolicitation or preproposal conferences; and

(9) Site visits.

(d) The special notices of procurement matters at 5.205(c), or electronic notices, may be used to publicize the Government's requirement or solicit information from industry.

(e) RFIs may be used when the Government does not presently intend to award a contract, but wants to obtain price, delivery, other market information, or capabilities for planning purposes. Responses to these notices are not offers and cannot be accepted by the Government to form a binding contract. There is no required format for RFIs.

(f) General information about agency mission needs and future requirements may be disclosed at any time. After release of the solicitation, the contracting officer shall be the focal point of any exchange with potential offerors. When specific information about a proposed acquisition that would be necessary for the preparation of proposals is disclosed to one or more potential offerors, that information shall be made available to the public as soon as practicable, but no later than the next general release of information, in order to avoid creating an unfair competitive advantage. Information provided to a particular offeror in response to that offeror's request shall not be disclosed if doing so would reveal the potential offeror's confidential business strategy, and would be protected under 3.104 or subpart 24.2. When a presolicitation or preproposal conference is conducted, materials distributed at the conference should be made available to all potential offerors, upon request.

One of the objectives of the FAR Part 15 Rewrite was to encourage agencies to share more information with prospective offerors. The Summary of Changes that accompanied the publication of the Rewrite in the *Federal Register* said that one of the goals was to "reengineer" the acquisition process by "supporting more open exchanges of information between the Government and industry, allowing industry to better understand the requirement and the Government to better understand industry proposals." (See 62 Fed. Reg. 51224, September 30, 1997.) Keep in mind, however, that the Procurement Integrity Act, which is implemented in FAR 3.104, prohibits certain persons from disclosing *contractor bid or proposal information* (see the definition in FAR 3.104-1) or *source selection information* (see the definition in FAR 2.101), except as authorized in accordance with agency procedures.

72. When can an agency cancel an RFP?

FAR 15.206(e) says that if an agency decides to amend its RFP after the receipt of proposals in a way that drastically changes the agency's requirements, then it must cancel the RFP and issue a new one. The regulation reads as follows:

> If, in the judgment of the contracting officer, based on market research or otherwise, an amendment proposed for issuance after offers have been received is so substantial as to exceed what prospective offerors reasonably could have anticipated, so that additional sources likely would have submitted offers had the substance of the amendment been known to them, the contracting officer shall cancel the original solicitation and issue a new one, regardless of the stage of the acquisition.

GAO says that an agency can cancel an RFP whenever it has a valid reason to do so. In its decision in *Encore Management, Inc.* (B-278903.2, February 12, 1999), GAO found:

> In a negotiated procurement, such as this, the contracting officer has broad discretion in deciding whether to cancel a solicitation; the contracting officer need only have a reasonable basis to do so, as opposed to the cogent and compelling reason required for the cancellation of a solicitation after sealed bids have been opened. G.K.S. Inc., B-235208, Aug. 9, 1989, 89-2 CPD ¶ 117 at 3. An agency may properly cancel a solicitation no matter

when the information precipitating the cancellation first surfaces or should have been known, even if the solicitation is not canceled until after offers have been submitted and evaluated. Jack Faucett Assocs., supra. Cancellation of a solicitation is proper where award under the solicitation would not serve the government's actual needs. Constructive Solutions, Inc., B-278227, Jan. 9, 1998, 98-1 CPD ¶ 9 at 2; Waste Management Envtl. Servs., Inc., B-252553, July 12, 1993, 93-2 CPD ¶ 14 at 4-5. It is the responsibility of the contracting activity to determine its requirements, and our Office will defer to the activity's judgment in that regard. Peterson-Nunez Joint Venture, B-258788, Feb. 13, 1995, 95-1 CPD ¶ 73 at 4.

WALMART $24.97
Lee.com $32.97
Flanner Jeans (lined)

571-375-7914 BA1
703-481 0912-
Check www.acqnet.gov/far

37/7

~~TAj Mahal~~

~~ORChid~~

Presidents

Washington

Roosevelt

Lincoln

Painters

PIcasso

Michelangelo

DA VINCI

~~Cruise~~

~~Orchid~~

~~Sunset~~

Authors

Hemingway

Shakespeare

Twain / Dickens

Grisham / Seuss

PART IV

Proposal Evaluation

The questions in this part address the process of evaluating proposals, including the processes of evaluation experience, past performance, and cost or price. They address key definitions such as *deficiency* and *weakness,* and *minor informality or irregularity*. They also address techniques such as the evaluation of sample tasks and oral presentations.

73. What is *evaluation*?

Evaluation is the process of determining the relative merits of competing proposals on the basis of criteria (evaluation factors) specified in a request for proposals (RFP). The value in an offeror and its offer comes from the presence of desired attributes and the absence of undesired attributes. Evaluating entails ascertaining the degree to which desired and undesired attributes are present in an offeror and its offer and then comparing each offeror and its offer to the others on that basis in order to rank them from best to worst.

Do not confuse *evaluation* with *scoring*. *Scoring* is the process of using numbers, adjectival expressions (e.g., "very good"), or other symbols to describe the findings of an evaluation. Evaluation must be done before scoring can be done. Evaluation results can be described in prose. Scoring simplifies complex prose descriptions, making it easier for the decision maker to compare the findings about offerors.

The FAR addresses proposal evaluation in section 15.305, *Proposal evaluation*, as follows:

> (a) Proposal evaluation is an assessment of the proposal and the offeror's ability to perform the prospective contract successfully. An agency shall evaluate competitive proposals and then assess their relative qualities solely on the factors and subfactors specified in the solicitation. Evaluations may be conducted using any rating method or combination of methods, including color or adjectival ratings, numerical weights, and ordinal rankings. The relative strengths, deficiencies, significant weaknesses, and risks supporting proposal evaluation shall be documented in the contract file.
>
> (1) Cost or price evaluation. Normally, competition establishes price reasonableness. Therefore, when contracting on a firm-fixed-price or fixed-price with economic price adjustment basis, comparison of the proposed prices will usually satisfy the requirement to perform a price analysis, and a cost analysis need not be performed. In limited situations, a cost analysis (see 15.403-1(c)(1)(i)(B)) may be appropriate to establish reasonableness of the otherwise successful offeror's price. When contracting on a cost-reimbursement basis, evaluations shall include a cost realism analysis to determine what the Government should realistically expect to pay for the proposed effort, the offeror's understanding of the work, and the offeror's ability to perform the contract. Cost realism analyses may also be used on fixed-price incentive contracts or, in exceptional cases, on other competitive fixed-price-type contracts (see 15.404-1(d)(3)). The contracting officer shall document the cost or price evaluation.
>
> (2) Past performance evaluation. (i) Past performance information is one indicator of an offeror's ability to perform the contract successfully. The currency and relevance of the information, source of the information, context of the data, and general trends in contractor's performance shall be considered (41 U.S.C. 401). This

comparative assessment of past performance information is separate from the responsibility determination required under subpart 9.1.

(ii) The solicitation shall describe the approach for evaluating past performance, including evaluating offerors with no relevant performance history, and shall provide offerors an opportunity to identify past or current contracts (including Federal, State, and local government and private) for efforts similar to the Government requirement. The solicitation shall also authorize offerors to provide information on problems encountered on the identified contracts and the offeror corrective actions. The Government shall consider this information, as well as information obtained from any other sources, when evaluating the offeror past performance. The source selection authority shall determine the relevance of similar past performance information.

(iii) The evaluation should take into account past performance information regarding predecessor companies, key personnel who have relevant experience, or subcontractors that will perform major or critical aspects of the requirement when such information is relevant to the instant acquisition.

(iv) In the case of an offeror without a record of relevant past performance or for whom information on past performance is not available, the offeror may not be evaluated favorably or unfavorably on past performance.

(3) Technical evaluation. When tradeoffs are performed (see 15.101-1), the source selection records shall include—

(i) An assessment of each offeror's ability to accomplish the technical requirements; and

(ii) A summary, matrix, or quantitative ranking, along with appropriate supporting narrative, of each technical proposal using the evaluation factors.

> (4) Cost information. Cost information may be provided to members of the technical evaluation team in accordance with agency procedures.
>
> (b) The source selection authority may reject all proposals received in response to a solicitation, if doing so is in the best interest of the Government.
>
> (c) For restrictions on the use of support contractor personnel in proposal evaluation, see 37.203(d).

FAR 15.305 neither prescribes nor prohibits the use of any particular method of evaluation. The greatest single emphasis in FAR 15.305 is on documentation of the evaluation findings.

Proposal evaluation is a two-step process. Step 1 is to determine how much of each evaluation factor is present in an offeror or its offer. Step 2 is to compare each proposal to each of the other proposals on the basis of those determinations in order to rank them in order of merit. This is done by comparing two offerors at a time to determine which of each pair is the better value; this process is called "paired" or "pairwise" comparison. Step 2 may or may not entail making tradeoffs, depending on whether an agency is using the tradeoff process described in FAR 15.101-1 or the lowest price technically acceptable process described in FAR 15.101-2.

74. What are the different approaches to evaluation?

There are two basic approaches to evaluation. The first approach treats the evaluation factors as variables that can take on any value within a range. For example, if the evaluation factor is the weight of a proposed product, such that the lower the weight the better, the value of the item would be a function of its weight—the lower the weight the greater the value. This variable approach is used in the *tradeoff process* method of source selection, which is described in FAR 15.101-1. *Best value* (see FAR 2.101) is determined by comparing the total value of each offeror to the total value of each of the other offerors and ranking them from best to worst.

The second approach to evaluation is to treat the evaluation factors as limits—minimums or maximums—and to evaluate proposals on a pass or fail (acceptable or unacceptable, go/no go) basis. Thus, if the weight of a proposed product is at or below the specified maximum weight, the product passes and is acceptable; otherwise, it fails and is rejected as unacceptable. In this pass or fail approach, evaluators do not compare proposals to each other on the basis of the pass or fail factors. For example, if the evaluation factor is weight and the RFP requires that a proposed product not exceed a maximum weight, a lighter product does not receive a more favorable evaluation and a higher score than a heavier product. They both receive the same score—"pass" or "acceptable." Pass or fail factors do not play any role in the ranking of offerors from best to worst.

This pass or fail approach to evaluation is used to determine technical acceptability in the *lowest price technically acceptable* method of source selection described in FAR 15.101-2. It can also be used in the tradeoff process with respect to *some* nonprice evaluation factors, such as "compliance with requirements." When using the lowest price technically acceptable method of source selection, agencies evaluate *all* nonprice ("technical") factors on a pass or fail basis; cost or price is the only variable factor, and the only basis on which the agency compares the offerors to each other.

An agency should use the pass or fail approach to evaluation if it cares only that the offeror or its offer includes at least a minimum amount of a positive attribute or no more than a maximum amount of a negative attribute, and if it does not care about differences among offerors in the amounts above the minimum or below the maximum. But an agency should use the variable approach if differences in the amount of an attribute matter.

Agencies must always evaluate cost or price on a variable basis and compare the offerors on the basis of their proposed costs or prices to determine which is best. This is essential to meaningful competition. Agencies may not evaluate price or cost on a pass or fail basis. For example, in *Electronic Design, Inc.* (B-279662.2, August 31, 1998), GAO considered a situation where the agency evaluated price by determining whether or not a proposed price was within the agency's budget for the procurement. The agency did not compare the offerors to each other on the basis of price. GAO ruled that such a pass or fail approach to price evaluation does not satisfy the requirements of the Competition in Contracting Act of 1984. Specifically, GAO said:

> As a general rule, the Competition in Contracting Act of 1984 (CICA) requires contracting agencies to include cost or price as a significant evaluation factor that must be considered in the evaluation of proposals. 10 U.S.C. §§ 2305(a)(2)(A), 2305(a)(3)(A)(ii); Boeing Sikorsky Aircraft Support, B-277263.2, B-277263.3, Sept. 29, 1997, 97-2 CPD ¶ 91 at 9-10; see FAR § 15.605(b)(1)(i) (June 1997). An evaluation and source selection which fails to give significant consideration to cost or price is inconsistent with CICA and cannot serve as a reasonable basis for award. Boeing Sikorsky Aircraft Support, supra. Cost or price has not been accorded significant consideration if the agency's evaluation and source selection decision so minimizes the potential impact of cost or price as to make it a nominal evaluation factor. Coastal Science and Eng'g, Inc., B-236041, Nov. 7, 1989, 89-2 CPD ¶ 436 at 3.
>
> Here, the agency states that price was considered only to determine whether a proposal was eligible for award. Proposals with prices greater than the budget were not

> eligible for, nor considered for award. Once three of the proposals were determined eligible for award based on price, the Navy states that it did not consider the relative differences in price among the proposals, and did not perform a price/technical tradeoff; rather, technical merit was the sole consideration in the selection decision. Thus, to the extent the agency did consider price in this procurement, it was solely to determine basic eligibility for award. Such a consideration of price is nominal; indeed, anything less would be to ignore price completely. [Footnote omitted.]
>
> We conclude that the Navy's evaluation and source selection decision did not give significant consideration to price, and therefore was inconsistent with CICA and cannot form the basis for an award.

Agencies must develop factor measurement scales in order to make a rational evaluation. A factor measurement scale enables evaluators to consistently distinguish among different factor levels. The concept of a scale includes notions of unit of measure and range; however, factor measurement scales do not have to be quantitative or numerical. Factor measurement scales should not be confused with scoring scales, such as "excellent, very good, good, marginal, and poor," or 0 to 100 points. Scoring converts diverse factor measurements or descriptions to a common scale. Figure IV-1 illustrates the difference between factor measurement scales and scoring scales.

There are widely accepted scales (sometimes called *natural* scales) for some factors, such as price, weight, volume, speed, acceleration, loudness, electrical output, reliability in mean hours between failure, etc. However, the use of factors such as "soundness of approach" and "environmental impact" will require the development of what are called "constructed scales" for "soundness" and "impact." This is essential to rational evaluation. [For more detailed discussions about scales, including guidance in the development

FIGURE IV-1
COMPARISON OF FACTOR MEASUREMENT SCALES AND SCORING SCALES

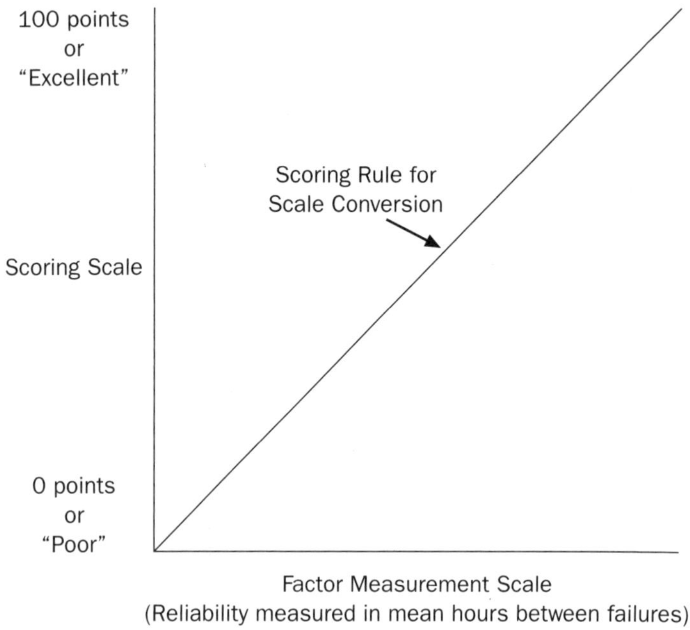

of constructed scales, see Ralph L. Keeney, *Value-Focused Thinking: A Path to Creative Decisionmaking* (Cambridge, MA: Harvard University Press, 1992), pp. 101–112; and Detlof von Winterfeldt and Ward Edwards, *Decision Analysis and Behavioral Research* (Cambridge, UK: Cambridge University Press, 1986), pp. 221–223.]

75. What is *scoring*?

The FAR does not use the terms *score* and *scoring*. Scoring is the process of using symbols to represent and simplify complex evaluation findings. Scoring converts evaluation measurements and findings that are expressed in a variety of forms—such as quantities and verbal descriptions—to a common scale, such as 0 to 100 points or *excellent, very good, satisfactory, marginal,* and *poor*. This conversion simplifies more complex information, making it easier to comprehend and to use to compare the competing proposals. Thus, scoring is helpful, but not essential, to source selection.

A good scoring system includes: (1) a scale—numbers such as 0 to 100 points, or adjectives such as *exceptional, good, marginal,* and *poor*; and (2) a rule for converting evaluation measurements to a point on the scoring scale. A scoring rule should take the logical form: If the factor measurement is *x*, then the score is *y*. Such scoring rules ensure consistency among evaluators when assigning scores.

GAO has consistently held that scores are not binding on decision makers. For example, in *Veda Incorporated* (B-278516.2, March 19, 1998), GAO stated:

> Where, as here, a negotiated procurement provides for award after cost/technical tradeoff, point scores and adjectival ratings are guides to assist contracting agencies in evaluating proposals; they do not mandate automatic selection of a particular proposal. Grey Advertising, Inc., 55 Comp. Gen. 1111, 1118-1121 (1976), 76-1 CPD ¶ 325 at 9-12. In deciding between competing proposals, cost/technical tradeoffs may be made, the propriety of which turns not on the difference in technical scores or ratings per se, but on whether the source selection official's judgment concerning the significance of the difference was reasonable and adequately justified in light of the RFP evaluation scheme. Southwestern Marine, Inc.; American Sys. Eng'g Corp., supra, at 17; DynCorp, B-245289.3, July 30, 1992, 93-1 CPD ¶ 69 at 8.

All scoring, no matter what symbols are used—numbers, adjectives, color codes, stars, etc.—entails the suppression of detailed evaluation information; that is how it simplifies, and that is why agency decision makers must not base their source selection tradeoff decisions on simple score/price comparisons. Agencies may use scores to make preliminary analyses but should refer to detailed evaluation information when making tradeoffs. They should never justify tradeoff decisions merely by reference to scores.

GAO does not like what it calls "mechanical" use of scores, and decision justifications based on differences in scores are red flags in the event of a protest. For example, in *Opti-Lite Optical* (B-281693; March 22, 1999), GAO sustained a protest when an agency failed to document any basis for its source selection decision other than differences among scores:

> [I]t is clear from the record that the source selection decision was based on a purely mechanical application of the numerical scores for the technical factors and price....
>
> The contracting officer's original and revised award memorandum and his statement submitted in response to this protest provide only the total technical and price scores for the proposals evaluated and in each instance state that the total score for technical and price would determine the final ranking of vendors and award. The contracting officer's award memorandum contains no hint as to the basis for the scoring of the proposals and provides no assessment of the strengths and weaknesses in the various proposals. While, in response to the protest, the contracting officer makes references to certain identified deficiencies in the protester's proposal, the contracting officer does not provide any explanation of how, based on these deficiencies in the protester's low priced proposal, or based on strengths in Classic's proposal, Classic's proposal was determined to be the more advantageous; rather he maintains his position that the total point scores per se justified the award to Classic.
>
> Where a price/technical tradeoff is made, the source selection decision must be documented, and the documentation must include the rationale for any tradeoffs made, including the benefits associated with additional costs. Federal Acquisition Regulation § 15.308 (FAC 97-

> 02). It is improper to rely, as the agency did here, on a purely mathematical price/technical tradeoff methodology. See Teltara, Inc., B-280922, Dec. 4, 1998, 98-2 CPD ¶ at 4; General Offshore Corp.-Riedel Co., a Joint Venture, B-271144.2, B-271144.3, July 2, 1996, 96-2 CPD ¶ 42 at 8. In this case the tradeoff is inadequate because, beyond the mechanical comparison of the total point scores, the contracting officer made no qualitative assessment of the technical differences between the offers from Classic and Opti-Lite to determine whether Classic's technical superiority justified the cost premium involved. [Footnote omitted.]

Most agencies use either numerical or adjectival scoring. A scale of 0 to 100 points or 0 to 10 points is quite common, but other schemes are also used. For example, the Environmental Protection Agency's (EPA) FAR Supplement 1515.305-70 describes the following scheme (Table IV-1):

TABLE IV-1
ENVIRONMENTAL PROTECTION AGENCY SCORING SCALE

Value	*Descriptive Statement*
0	The factor is not addressed, or is totally deficient and without merit.
1	The factor is addressed, but contains deficiencies and/or weaknesses that can be corrected only by major or significant changes to relevant portions of the proposal, or the factor is addressed so minimally or vaguely that there are widespread information gaps. In addition, because of the deficiencies, weaknesses, and/or information gaps, serious concerns exist on the part of the technical evaluation team about the offeror's ability to perform the required work.
2	Information related to the factor is incomplete, unclear, or indicates an inadequate approach to, or understanding of the factor. The technical evaluation team believes there is question as to whether the offeror would be able to perform satisfactorily.

continues

TABLE IV-1 continued

3	The response to the factor is adequate. Overall, it meets the specifications and requirements, such that the technical evaluation team believes that the offeror could perform to meet the Government's minimum requirements.
4	The response to the factor is good with some superior features. Information provided is generally clear, and the demonstrated ability to accomplish the technical requirements is acceptable with the possibility of more than adequate performance.
5	The response to the factor is superior in most features.

Note that in this scheme the "descriptive statement" is a scoring rule—e.g.: If the offeror's response to the factor is superior in most features, then the score is 5. The problem with the scoring rules in EPA's descriptive statements is that they are generic. They do not relate to measurements associated with any particular factor. Thus, they beg the question of what makes a proposal "totally deficient," "inadequate," "adequate," "good," or "superior."

Adjectival schemes that use scales such as *exceptional, acceptable, marginal,* and *unacceptable,* or *excellent, very good, good, satisfactory, marginal,* and *poor,* are also common. The Air Force uses an adjectival "performance confidence" scale to score past performance; Air Force Mandatory Procedure MP5315.3, dated 17 May 2005, describes that scale as shown in Table IV-2).

TABLE IV-2
AIR FORCE PERFORMANCE CONFIDENCE ASSESSMENT RATINGS

Rating	*Description*
High Confidence	Based on the offeror's performance record, the government has high confidence the offeror will successfully perform the required effort.
Significant Confidence	Based on the offeror's performance record, the-government has significant confidence the offeror will successfully perform the required effort.
Satisfactory Confidence	Based on the offeror's performance record, the government has confidence the offeror will successfully perform the required effort. Normal contractor emphasis should preclude any problems.
Unknown Confidence	No performance record is identifiable.
Little Confidence	Based on the offeror's performance record, substantial doubt exists that the offeror will successfully perform the required effort.
No Confidence	Based on the offeror's performance record, extreme doubt exists that the offeror will successfully perform the required effort.

One or two agencies—mainly the Air Force—use a color rating scheme in association with adjectival ratings to score proposals. The colors are used on briefing charts to describe evaluation findings to the source selection authority. Air Force Mandatory Procedure MP5315.3, dated 17 May 2005, describes one such scheme for rating technical proposals as shown in Table IV-3.

TABLE IV-3
AIR FORCE COLOR RATING SCALE

Color	*Rating*	*Definition*
Blue	Exceptional	Exceeds specified minimum performance or capability requirements in a way beneficial to the Air Force.
Green	Acceptable	Meets specified minimum performance or capability requirements necessary for acceptable contract performance.
Yellow	Marginal	Does not clearly meet some specified minimum performance or capability requirements necessary for acceptable contract performance, but any proposal inadequacies are correctable.
Red	Unacceptable	Fails to meet specified minimum performance or capability requirements. Proposals with unacceptable rating are not awardable.

If the purpose of scoring is to simplify complex information, then numerical scoring systems are best because they offer the most simplification; the scores for each of the various evaluation factors can be added together into a single, overall score. However, some agencies prohibit or discourage the use of numerical scoring on the grounds that source selection decision making entails subjectivity, and numerical scoring falsely suggests that evaluation findings are precise and objective. Detlof von Winterfeldt and Ward Edwards dealt with this issue in their book, *Decision Analysis and Behavioral Research,* referenced above, on page 20:

> Almost all numbers that describe the physical world, as well as those that describe judgments, are imprecise to some degree. . . .*The advantage of numerical subjectivity is simply that expressing judgments in numerical form makes it easy to use arithmetical tools to aggregate them.* The aggregation of various kinds of judgments is the essential step in every meaningful decision. [Italics added.]

Despite the evident advantages of numerical scoring systems, some individuals are so prejudiced against them that it is probably fruitless to argue this point.

76. What is the difference between *evaluating* and *scoring*?

Agencies must *evaluate* proposals, but they do not have to *score* proposals. Evaluating is a two-step process. In step 1, the evaluators examine each proposal to determine how good it is with respect to each evaluation factor. This step may be called the measuring step. Thus, if the evaluation factor is "soundness of approach," step 1 is to determine how sound each proposal is. This step does not entail comparing each proposal to the others.

In step 2, the evaluators or source selection authority compare each proposal to each of the others to determine its rank and to identify the differences among the proposals. This is the tradeoff analysis, in which the agency decides whether the nonprice differences between any two proposals is worth any difference between them in price.

Scoring merely converts the findings of step 1 to symbols in order to make step 2 easier. Scoring is useful, but not essential to source selection.

77. What is the difference between *rating* and *scoring*?

FAR Part 15 does not use the terms *score* and *scoring*, but it does use the terms *rated* and *rating* in several places, including 15.101-1(a), 15.304(d), 15.305(a), 15.306(b)(2), 15.306(c)(1) and (2), and 15.306(d)(4). It seems clear from these usages that *rating* is just another name for *scoring*.

78. Can agencies score cost or price?

Yes. There is no rule in the FAR that prohibits the assignment of scores to cost or price. However, some agencies prohibit or discourage the practice.

GAO does not object to the assignment of scores to costs or prices, and has even permitted agencies to use totally numerical scoring systems in which the request for proposals states that the agency will award the contract to the offeror who receives the highest total score. However, GAO has called such scoring systems "unwise." (See *Harrison Systems, Ltd.*, B-212675, May 24, 1984.)

Despite the fact that neither the FAR nor GAO prohibits the assignment of scores to cost or price, it is probably not a good idea to do so. First, converting a cost or price to a score may obscure significant dollar differences between proposals if not done properly. Second, source selection tradeoffs ultimately must be based on the determination of whether nonprice differences between competing offerors are worth any difference in the offerors' proposed costs or prices. Converting the offerors' costs or prices to scores and adding those scores to others does not assist in that determination and may actually impede effective tradeoff analysis.

One scheme that has been used in the past is the dollar-per-point assessment. Proposals are given a numerical score to reflect how well they perform on the nonprice evaluation factors, then the proposed price in each proposal is divided by the number of points given to the proposal to develop a dollar-per-point ratio. As explained in one agency's handout:

> **Scoring Cost Data/Projected Cost to Government.** Although translating cost data into a scorable numerical representation may be difficult, and is not recommended, any rational and logical method may be acceptable.

Some suggested methods are the intermediate step of assigning a rating adjective, and the "point score per dollar ratio." Using the second method, ratings for all technical and management factors/sub-factors are developed for each offeror's proposal. The evaluation panel applies the predetermined weights to each offeror's ratings, extends and totals each to obtain an overall score for the technical proposal. The overall projected cost to the Government for each proposal is also reported to the evaluation panel. The evaluation panel then divides the overall score for each technical proposal by the overall projected cost to determine the "point score per dollar ratio."

To illustrate, assume three proposals are technically acceptable.

OFFEROR	SCORE	PROJECTED COST	RATIO SCORE
A	925	$350M	264
B	870	$310M	281
C	830	$300M	277

Offeror A has a technical proposal that has been evaluated as superior to either B or C (925 points). However, the projected cost from Offer A is higher. (Consistent with the language in the RFP, which stated that the cost factor was to be considered of equal importance with the technical factor, the question to be decided is whether Offeror A's proposal is worth the extra cost.) The illustration clearly shows that Offeror B's proposal produces more points per dollar (Ratio: 281) than either A or C. Based on the sketchy information provided in the illustration, the additional 55-point score differential between Offeror A and B at a probable additional cost of $40 million may not be a worthwhile gain.

The analytical usefulness of such schemes has been questioned.

79. What do *acceptable* and *unacceptable* mean?

The FAR does not define *acceptable* and *unacceptable,* and the terms are used in two ways. First, they are used to describe the legal status of an offer. In this legal sense, an offer is *acceptable* when it manifests the offeror's assent to all requirements in the request for proposals. An agency may not accept an offer that does not assent to all the material terms of an RFP. Such *materially nonconforming* offers are *unacceptable.*

GAO has sustained many protests because agencies have accepted proposals that deviated from the terms of the RFP. In the matter of *Beckman Coulter* (B-281030, December 21, 1998), for example, an offeror included terms in its best and final offer that were inconsistent with terms in the government's RFP, including a deviation from the specified pricing scheme and a clause that would have allowed either party to terminate the contract with 30 days' notice. The government accepted the offer anyway, and a competitor protested. GAO sustained the protest, saying:

> In negotiated procurements, any proposal that fails to conform to material terms and conditions of the solicitation should be considered unacceptable and may not form the basis for an award. Barents Group, L.L.C., B-276082, B-276082.2, May 9, 1997, 97-1 CPD ¶ 164 at 10; Martin Marietta Corp., B-233742.4, Jan. 31, 1990, 90-1 CPD ¶ 132 at 7....

Second, agencies use the terms *acceptable* and *unacceptable* as scores to signify the value or merit of a proposal, without regard to its legal status, as in the following scheme: *exceptional, acceptable, marginal,* and *unacceptable.* When used in this way, they indicate a degree of value. This seems to be the most common usage of the terms *acceptable* and *unacceptable.* GAO provided an example of this usage in its decision in the matter of *Laidlaw Environmental Services (GS), Inc.* (B-

271903, August 6, 1996). In that case, the protester objected to the evaluation of its proposal as merely "acceptable":

> Specifically, Laidlaw complains that its proposal was rated acceptable under the experience and past performance evaluation subfactor, while Philip's proposal was rated highly acceptable....
>
> The TEB concluded that Laidlaw's proposal demonstrated an extensive range of prior experience, including the current contract; a similar contract for the Public Works Center, San Francisco; and numerous other contracts with the Defense Marketing and Reutilization Service. The TEB noted, however, that Laidlaw had experienced performance problems in its current contract, particularly with respect to returning manifests within the times required by the contract; modifying manifests after shipment; and receiving wastes without signing the required manifest. The TEB not only concluded that these were weaknesses in Laidlaw's past performance, but that these practices violated applicable regulations controlling waste disposal.

The issue in this case was the quality of the protester's past performance, not whether or not the protester had assented to the requirements in the RFP. GAO found the agency's evaluation to be reasonable and denied the protest.

In another case, *Dimensions International/QSOFT, Inc.* (B-270966, May 28, 1996), the evaluation team rated a proposal "unacceptable":

> Dimensions's unacceptable proposal received marginal ratings for four of the sample tasks and unacceptable ratings for the other four sample tasks. The Navy found that Dimensions's proposal did not demonstrate an understanding of the sample tasks or provide evidence that it could provide a reasonable logical approach to satisfying the government's requirements; that the responses to the tasks, even those rated marginal, were not written

> in a clear or complete manner and failed in many parts to specifically address the required elements beyond a cursory level; that overall the sample tasks failed to meet the minimum requirements and had many gross omissions; and that the proposal would have to be completely rewritten in order to be made acceptable. The Navy further concluded that, given Dimensions's apparent lack of understanding of the sample tasks, it was not reasonable to assume that its proposed price represented an accurate forecast of the work to be performed under the contract.

This, too, was a matter of merit, rather than assent to terms in the RFP.

The differing usages of the terms *acceptable* and *unacceptable* are potentially confusing. A proposal could be rated unacceptable based on merit but be acceptable in the strictly legal sense. It would be best if agencies used these terms exclusively to denote the legal status of proposals.

80. What is a *deficiency*?

FAR 15.001 defines *deficiency* as follows:

> Deficiency is a material failure of a proposal to meet a Government requirement or a combination of significant weaknesses in a proposal that increases the risk of unsuccessful contract performance to an unacceptable level.

A deficiency is either the absence of something that is necessary to satisfy a requirement, or the presence of something that is inconsistent with the requirement or that will make it more difficult to satisfy the requirement. It appears that a deficiency makes a proposal unacceptable, since it signifies an actual or potential failure to satisfy a requirement.

81. What is a *weakness*?

FAR 15.001 defines *weakness* as follows:

> Weakness means a flaw in the proposal that increases the risk of unsuccessful contract performance. A "significant weakness" in the proposal is a flaw that appreciably increases the risk of unsuccessful contract performance.

Most dictionaries say that a flaw is an imperfection. Unlike a deficiency, which signifies failure to satisfy a requirement of the RFP, a weakness does not necessarily make a proposal unacceptable.

82. What is a *strength*?

The FAR neither uses nor defines the term *strength*. However, the term is commonly used to denote a favorable attribute of an offeror or of its offer. For example, GAO's protest decision in *Laidlaw Environmental Services (GS), Inc.* (B-271903, August 6, 1996) stated:

> The Laidlaw proposal, ranked first technically, received an exceptional rating under all technical evaluation factors. The evaluators determined that Laidlaw had notable strengths in that its past and current contract work on government contracts as a prime contractor was very similar to the work required by the solicitation. Agency Report, Tab 7, at 6. Laidlaw's references stated that Laidlaw's timeliness, quality control, cooperation and customer satisfaction were above average and it received exceptional ratings for all factors. Id. The evaluators especially noted Laidlaw's above average performance and outstanding customer service in identifying and fixing major compliance problems at Public Works Center San Francisco.

Air Force Mandatory Procedure MP5315.3, dated 17 May 2005, defines *strength* as follows:

> "Strength" is a significant, outstanding or exceptional aspect of an offeror's proposal that has merit and exceeds specified performance or capability requirements in a way that is advantageous to the government, and either will be included in the contract or is inherent in the fferor's process.

What is a *discriminator*?

e FAR neither uses nor defines the term *discriminator*. rtheless, the term is often used to refer to an evaluation r that helps an agency identify meaningful differences ng competing offerors in terms of their prospects for ying the agency's requirements. An evaluation factor t a discriminator if the competing offerors are not significantly different in that regard. Another use of the term is to refer to some feature in a proposal that distinguishes an offeror from its competitors.

84. What is a *minor informality or irregularity* in a proposal?

FAR Part 15 neither defines nor uses the term *minor informality or irregularity*. Before the FAR Part 15 Rewrite, FAR 15.607(a) did use the term, referring to the definition in FAR 14.405; however, the provisions of FAR 15.607(a) were deleted by the Rewrite. Some individuals continue to use the term to describe something that a contracting officer can talk to an offeror about without conducting *discussions*, as defined in FAR 15.306(d), or something that the contracting officer can talk about during *clarification*, as defined in FAR 15.306(a), and still make an award without discussions.

The definition of *minor informality or irregularity* that appears in FAR 14.405 reads as follows:

A minor informality or irregularity is one that is merely a matter of form and not of substance. It also pertains to some immaterial defect in a bid or variation of a bid from the exact requirements of the invitation that can be corrected or waived without being prejudicial to other bidders. The defect or variation is immaterial when the effect on price, quantity, quality, or delivery is negligible when contrasted with the total cost or scope of the supplies or services being acquired. . . .Examples of minor informalities or irregularities include failure of a bidder to—

(a) Return the number of copies of signed bids required by the invitation;

(b) Furnish required information concerning the number of its employees;

(c) Sign its bid, but only if—

(1) The unsigned bid is accompanied by other material indicating the bidder's intention to be bound by the unsigned bid (such as the submission of a bid guarantee or a letter signed by the bidder, with the bid, referring to and clearly identifying the bid itself); or

(2) The firm submitting a bid has formally adopted or authorized, before the date set for opening of bids, the execution of documents by typewritten, printed, or stamped signature and submits evidence of such authorization and the bid carries such a signature;

(d) Acknowledge receipt of an amendment to an invitation for bids, but only if—

(1) The bid received clearly indicates that the bidder received the amendment, such as where the amendment added another item to the invitation and the bidder submitted a bid on the item; or

(2) The amendment involves only a matter of form or has either no effect or merely a negligible effect on price, quantity, quality, or delivery of the item bid upon and

(e) Execute the representations with respect to Equal Opportunity and Affirmative Action Programs, as set forth in the clauses at 52.222-22, Previous Contracts and Compliance Reports, and 52.222-25, Affirmative Action Compliance.

85. What are the rules about correcting mistakes in proposals before contract award?

An agency must notify an offeror before accepting its offer if it knows or suspects that the offer contains a mistake. Failure to do so could enable the contractor to avoid the contract. [See *Restatement of the Law, Second, Contracts 2d,* § 153, especially Comment e; and John Cibinic, Jr., and Ralph C. Nash, Jr., *Administration of Government Contracts,* 3rd ed. (Washington, D.C: The George Washington University, 1995), pp. 334–340.] This requirement raises the question of whether allowing an offeror to correct a mistake in its offer constitutes *discussions* as defined in FAR 15.306(d). If so, letting the offeror correct the mistake would preclude an award without discussions and would make it necessary to conduct discussions with all offerors in the competitive range.

FAR Part 15 states no clear rule about correcting mistakes in proposals. This is not a problem if an agency is planning to conduct discussions before making an award, because an offeror can correct mistakes in its proposal during the discussions. But the lack of a clear rule is a matter of concern if the agency would like to make an award without discussions.

Before the FAR Part 15 Rewrite, the rules for correcting mistakes before an award without discussions were clear and simple: An offeror who claimed to have made a mistake could withdraw its offer or ask to correct it. The agency could allow the offeror to correct the mistake and then make an award without discussions if the offeror could prove: (1) that it had made a mistake; and (2) what it had intended to propose, based on the text of the RFP and its offer, without reference to work papers. But if the offeror had to refer to documents other than the RFP and the offer to prove either that it had made a mistake or what it had intended to propose, then the agency had to conduct discussions to let the offeror correct the mistake.

Those pre-FAR Part 15 Rewrite rules had appeared in FAR 15.607, *Disclosure of mistakes before award,* which read as follows:

> (a) Contracting officers shall examine all proposals for minor informalities or irregularities and apparent clerical mistakes (see 14.405 and 14.407). Communication with offerors to resolve these matters is clarification, not discussion within the meaning of 15.610. However, if the resulting communication prejudices the interest of other offerors, the contracting officer shall not make award without discussions with all offerors within the competitive range.
>
> (b) Except as indicated in paragraph (c) of this section, mistakes not covered in paragraph (a) above are usually resolved during discussion (see 15.610).
>
> (c) When award without discussion is contemplated, the contracting officer shall comply with the following procedure:
>
> (1) If a mistake in a proposal is suspected, the contracting officer shall advise the offeror (pointing out the suspected mistake or otherwise identifying the area of the proposal where the suspected mistake is) and request verification. If the offeror verifies its proposal, award may be made.

(2) If an offeror alleges a mistake in its proposal, the contracting officer shall advise the offeror that it may withdraw the proposal or seek correction in accordance with subparagraph (c)(3) of this section.

(3) If an offeror requests permission to correct a mistake in its proposal, the agency head (or a designee not below the level of chief of the contracting office) may make a written determination permitting the correction; *provided*, that—

(i) Both the existence of the mistake and the proposal actually intended are established by clear and convincing evidence from the solicitation and the proposal; and

(ii) Legal review is obtained before making the determination.

(4) If the determination under subparagraph (c)(3) of this section cannot be made, and the contracting officer still contemplates award without discussion, the offeror shall be given a final opportunity to withdraw or to verify its proposal.

(5) Verification, withdrawal, or correction under subparagraphs (c)(1) through (4) of this section is not considered discussion within the meaning of 15.610. If, however, correction of a mistake requires reference to documents, worksheets, or other data outside the solicitation and proposal in order to establish the existence of the mistake, the proposal intended, or both, the mistake may be corrected only through discussions under 15.610.

(d) If a proposal received at the Government facility in electronic format is unreadable to the degree that conformance to the essential requirements of the solicitation cannot be ascertained from the document, the contracting officer immediately shall notify the offeror and provide the opportunity for the offeror to submit clear and convincing evidence—

> (1) Of the content of the proposal as originally submitted; and
>
> (2) That the unreadable condition of the proposal was caused by Government software or hardware error, malfunction, or other Government mishandling.

The FAR Part 15 Rewrite eliminated the rules that had been in FAR 15.607. The Rewrite established different rules for correcting mistakes: (1) before award without discussions; (2) before establishing the competitive range; and (3) during discussions.

CORRECTION OF MISTAKES BEFORE AWARD WITHOUT DISCUSSIONS

FAR 15.306(a)(2) says:

> If award will be made without conducting discussions, offerors may be given the opportunity to clarify certain aspects of proposals (e.g., the relevance of an offeror's past performance information and adverse past performance information to which the offeror has not previously had an opportunity to respond) or to resolve minor or clerical errors.

FAR Part 15 does not define the terms *minor* or *clerical* errors. Note the disjunctive "or" in the phrase "minor *or* clerical." Does this rule really make a distinction between *minor* errors and *clerical* errors, or is that just a careless turn of phrase? Are *minor errors* the same as *minor informalities or irregularities,* as defined in FAR 14.405? Are clerical errors the same as *apparent clerical mistakes,* as defined in FAR 14.407-2?

It seems likely that GAO would let an agency clear up minor informalities or irregularities and apparent clerical mistakes and still make an award without discussions. However, since the effective date of the Rewrite, GAO has not said whether it thinks that the term *minor error* encompasses more than minor irregularities, informalities, and apparent clerical mistakes. Thus, if an agency were to let an offeror change its offer to correct anything more serious than a minor informality or irregularity or an apparent clerical mistake, and then award the contract to that offeror without discussions, it would be taking a chance that GAO would consider the correction to have been discussions and thus sustain a protest against the award. It is not known whether or not GAO would let an agency proceed in accordance with the rules that appeared in the pre-Rewrite FAR 15.607.

On the other hand, FAR 15.306(d) defines discussions as negotiations conducted "with the intent of allowing the offeror to *revise* its proposal." [Italics added.] FAR 15.001 makes a distinction between *proposal modifications* and *proposal revisions*, as follows:

> *Proposal modification* is a change made to a proposal before the solicitation closing date and time, or made in response to an amendment, or *made to correct a mistake in a proposal at any time before award.* [Italics added to last phrase.]
>
> *Proposal revision* is a change made after the solicitation closing date, at the request of or as allowed by a contracting officer, *as the result of negotiations.* [Italics added to last phrase.]

These definitions could be interpreted to mean that a contracting officer could allow an offeror to modify its proposal to correct a mistake and still award without discussions, since the correction would be a proposal modification and not a proposal revision.

CORRECTION OF MISTAKES BEFORE ESTABLISHING THE COMPETITIVE RANGE

FAR 15.306(b) states the rules for correcting mistakes during communications before establishing the competitive range. It reads, in part, as follows:

> Communications are exchanges, between the Government and offerors, after receipt of proposals, leading to establishment of the competitive range. If a competitive range is to be established, these communications....
>
> (2) May be conducted to enhance Government understanding of proposals; allow reasonable interpretation of the proposal; or facilitate the Government's evaluation process. *Such communications shall not be used to cure proposal deficiencies or material omissions, materially alter the technical or cost elements of the proposal, and/or otherwise revise the proposal.* Such communications may be considered in rating proposals for the purpose of establishing the competitive range;
>
> (3) Are for the purpose of addressing issues that must be explored to determine whether a proposal should be placed in the competitive range. *Such communications shall not provide an opportunity for the offeror to revise its proposal,* but may address—
>
> (i) Ambiguities in the proposal or other concerns (e.g., perceived deficiencies, weaknesses, errors, omissions, or mistakes (see 14.407)).... [Italics added.]

Thus, an agency may "address" errors or mistakes, but may it allow an offeror to *correct* them? The answer may depend on whether the correction is considered a proposal revision or a proposal modification, as discussed above. It may be that an agency cannot let an offeror *revise* its offer in order to get into the competitive range, but it can let an offeror *modify* its offer in order to do so.

FAR 15.306(b)(3)(i) refers the reader to FAR 14.407, *Mistakes in bids,* which addresses mistakes found during the sealed bidding process.

FAR 14.407-2 says that agencies may correct apparent clerical mistakes before award; however, the rules about other mistakes are not so simple. FAR 14.407-3, which states the rules for correcting other mistakes, says that the authority to correct mistakes "may not be used to permit correction of [offers] to make them responsive." It is not clear what this means in the context of negotiated procurements, since GAO has long held that the concept of responsiveness generally does not apply to negotiated procurements. (See *Pacificon Prods., Inc.*, B-196371, 80-2 CPD ¶ 58.)

FAR 14.407-3(a) says that an agency may let an offeror correct a mistake if it can produce "clear and convincing evidence" of both the existence of a mistake and of the offer actually intended. However, if correction would result in "displacing" one or more lower proposals, then the agency may allow correction only if both the existence of the mistake and the offer actually intended are ascertainable from the invitation for bids and the bid itself. This sounds like the rule in FAR 15.607 before the FAR Part 15 Rewrite, although it is not clear what "displacing" means in the context of a negotiated procurement, since an agency can include as many proposals in the competitive range as it likes.

FAR 14.407-3(b) and (c) prescribe procedures for letting a bidder withdraw a bid when it claims to have made a mistake. FAR 14.407-3(d) says that an agency head may refuse to allow an offeror to withdraw its bid. These paragraphs do not apply to negotiated procurements, since FAR 15.208(e) says that an offeror may withdraw its proposal at any time before contract award.

CORRECTION OF MISTAKES DURING DISCUSSIONS

The rule about correcting mistakes during discussions is simple. FAR 15.306(d)(3) says that agencies must bring a suspected mistake to the attention of an offeror in the competitive range. FAR 15.307(b) says that agencies must allow offerors in the competitive range to submit final proposal revisions; they can correct any mistakes in their offer at that time, in which case they need not present any evidence of a mistake or of the intended offer.

86. What happens when an offeror does not follow the proposal preparation instructions?

The FAR does not prescribe a course of action in the event that an offeror does not follow the proposal preparation instructions in an RFP, but GAO has established two rules about how an agency should respond. If an offeror fails to follow an RFP instruction, the agency's response must ensure that the failure does not reward the offeror with a competitive advantage. However, the agency should be reasonable and not reject an entire proposal merely because the offeror failed to follow an instruction; the agency's response must reflect the effect that the failure to follow instructions has had on the *content* of the proposal.

An offeror must not be permitted to gain a competitive advantage through its failure to follow an instruction. For example, an offeror must not be allowed to provide an agency with extra information that it could not have provided if it had complied with a page limitation or a type size limitation. In *All Star Maintenance, Inc.* (B-244143, September 26, 1991), for example, the RFP had included page and type size limitations and required that proposals be double spaced; the protester had violated all three restrictions. The agency calculated that the offeror was able to include 59 extra pages worth of information in its proposal as a result and removed the excess pages before evaluating the proposal. This resulted in its rejection of the proposal as "grossly deficient." The offeror protested, and GAO denied the protest, saying:

> All Star argues that its failure to adhere to the proposal preparation instructions should be waived or clarified as a minor informality, irregularity, or apparent clerical mistake. Contrary to All Star's position here, its significant deviation from the proposal preparation instructions was not subject to waiver because the consideration of its proposal in the format submitted would have given All Star a competitive advantage. See ITT Electron Technology Div., B-242289, Apr. 18, 1991, 91-1 CPD ¶ 383.

The second rule is that an agency's response to a failure to comply with proposal preparation instructions must be reasonable. An agency would be unwise to reject a proposal automatically without evaluation merely because the offeror has failed to follow instructions. In *Macfadden & Associates, Inc.* (B-275502, February 27, 1997), GAO reported that an RFP had included a page limitation of 100 pages and required a type size of not less than 12 points. The protester submitted a 97-page technical volume and 94 pages worth of appendices. Furthermore, the first 13 pages of the technical volume were in a type size smaller than the 12-point limit. The agency rejected the entire proposal as "technically unacceptable" without making a detailed evaluation of the technical volume. GAO sustained the protest, saying:

> Where an appendix included with a proposal causes the proposal to exceed a page limit established in the RFP, it would be improper for the agency to consider the appendix because to do so would confer upon the offeror furnishing the appendix a competitive advantage over those offerors whose proposals complied with the page limit. ITT Electron Technology Div., B-242289, Apr. 18, 1991, 91-1 CPD ¶ 383. Accordingly, where solicitations have imposed page and type limits, we have found reasonable the agency's removing pages beyond the solicitation

limit and evaluating only those pages within the limit. All Star Maintenance, Inc., B-244143, Sept. 26, 1991, 91-2 CPD ¶ 294; Infotec Dev., Inc., B-238980, July 20, 1990, 90-2 CPD ¶ 58. See Management & Indus. Technologies Assocs., B-257656, Oct. 11, 1994, 94-2 CPD ¶ 134; S.T. Research Corp., B-233115, Feb. 15, 1989, 89-1 CPD ¶ 159. Whether the approach taken by the agency here—automatic rejection of an entire proposal exceeding a page limit rather than evaluation of only the proposal pages within the limit—is proper depends, in the first instance, upon the language of the solicitation. If the solicitation provides that a proposal exceeding a specified page limit will be rejected and an offeror, without protesting that provision, chooses to compete in accordance with the RFP's terms but nevertheless submits a proposal that exceeds the limit, rejection of the proposal, at least in general, would seem to be unobjectionable.

Where, however, the solicitation states that a proposal exceeding a page limit may be excluded from consideration, we think offerors are reasonably put on notice that rejection for exceeding the page limit will not be automatic but instead will occur only if there is a reasonable basis for such action.

One such reasonable basis, suggested by the cases cited above, is that the proposal, when evaluated after removal of the pages exceeding the limit, is unacceptable or, in cases where a competitive range is established, is otherwise inappropriate for inclusion in the competitive range. Here, although a significant portion of Macfadden's proposal—97 pages—are within the page limit, the agency did not evaluate that portion of the proposal and thus did not determine whether the proposal was actually technically unacceptable or otherwise should be excluded from the competitive range either because the proposal would not have a reasonable chance for award or because its inclusion would be unfair to other offerors.

Our review of the 97-page proposal shows that it includes sections covering the five main areas listed in the RFP: past performance; technical approach; understand-

> ing the requirements; overall operational approach; and personnel resources and staffing and transition plan. The appendices, on the other hand, include documents such as examples of forms that Macfadden has developed to use as worksheets. In this regard, it is commonly understood that an appendix is supplementary material to what is normally a complete text. The 97 pages thus are easily severable from the appendices and cover all of the areas required by the RFP. Thus, there is nothing on the face of the proposal to indicate that the proposal could not be acceptable.

The lesson of this decision is that an agency's response to an offeror's failure to comply with proposal preparation instructions must be appropriate to the offense, designed to eliminate competitive advantage, and not unreasonable.

87. Do the same evaluators have to read all the proposals?

The FAR is silent on this issue, but GAO does not require that the same persons evaluate all proposals. In *Quality Elevator Company, Inc.* (B-276750, July 23, 1997), in a footnote, GAO said:

> Quality [the protester] also complains that the oral presentations of the two offerors were not evaluated by the same three evaluators, allowing for "inconsistency." The agency explains that the change in evaluators was due to scheduling conflicts that arose after the date for Quality's oral presentation—originally scheduled for the same date as Maryland's—was extended at Quality's request. In the absence of any substantive argument to show that the evaluators' conclusions were unreasonable or inconsistent with the solicitation, we have no basis to object to the agency's use of different evaluators under these circumstances. See Innovative Logistics Techniques, Inc., B-275786.2, Apr. 2, 1997, 97-1 CPD ¶ 144 at 9.

Thus, one group of persons might evaluate one proposal while another evaluates a different proposal. Also, one group of persons might evaluate the initial proposals while another group evaluates the revised proposals after discussions.

88. Are the government's technical evaluators permitted to see the price or cost proposals?

Yes. FAR 15.305(a)(4) says, "Cost information may be provided to members of the technical evaluation team in accordance with agency procedures."

89. What do *phased evaluation* and *downselect* mean?

Downselect (sometimes hyphenated as "down-select") is a term used to describe a process of phased evaluation that progressively reduces the number of firms that are competing for a contract or program. In general, a person using the term *downselect* may be using it in one of two ways, which can be distinguished as *source selection downselect* and *programmatic downselect.* FAR Part 15 does not use or define *downselect.*

SOURCE SELECTION DOWNSELECT

Source selection downselect refers to the phased evaluation of competitive proposals. The objective is to streamline the source selection process by reducing the amount of information that an evaluation team must process. In this type of downselect, an agency issues an RFP, receives proposals, evaluates them based on one or more evaluation factors, and eliminates some from further consideration. This concludes the first phase. In the next phase, the agency evaluates the remaining proposals based on other evaluation factors in order to reduce the size of the offeror pool further or to make a source selection decision. This phased evaluation process eliminates the need to evaluate a complete proposal from every offeror. Unlike the advisory multistep process described in FAR 15.202, this elimination terminates an offeror's right to be considered for award.

For example, an agency might: (1) evaluate the proposals based on price; (2) eliminate some offerors whose prices are obviously too high; (3) evaluate the remaining offerors based on price, experience, and past performance, and eliminate some more; and then (4) evaluate the remaining offerors based on price and oral presentations before making a final nonprice/price tradeoff analysis in order to pick the winner.

[Note: In this example, the decision to eliminate an offeror at the end of a phase is not a competitive range determination, and the rules in FAR 15.306(c) for establishing a competitive range do not apply. The purpose of establishing a competitive range is to decide which offerors to invite to discussions. Offerors eliminated as described above should be considered to have been "otherwise eliminated from the competition," as provided in FAR 15.503(a)(1). See: Department of Commerce—Request for Modification of Recommendation (B-283137.7, February 14, 2000), Footnote 1.]

Notwithstanding the obvious advantages of such a downselect procedure, the decision to use it may be controversial. The first drafts of the FAR Part 15 Rewrite expressly provided for the use of such a procedure. [See: 61 Fed. Reg. 48380, 48383 (September 12, 1996) and 62 Fed. Reg. 26640, 26644 (May 14, 1997).] However, no such procedure was included in the final rule. Moreover, the summary of changes that accompanied the final rule emphasized that "no offeror, otherwise eligible to submit a proposal in response to a Government solicitation, will be excluded from the competitive range without its proposal being initially reviewed and evaluated solely against *all* the evaluation factors and significant subfactors in the solicitation." [Italics added.] FAR 15.306(c)(1) says:

> Agencies shall evaluate all proposals in accordance with 15.305(a), and, if discussions are to be conducted, establish the competitive range. Based on the ratings of each proposal against *all* evaluation criteria, the contracting officer shall establish a competitive range comprised of all of the most highly rated proposals, unless the range is further reduced for purposes of efficiency pursuant to paragraph (c)(2) of this section. [Italics added.]

It appears that some agency officials interpret the word "all" in FAR 15.306(c)(1) to mean that an agency may not apply the evaluation factors in phases in order to progressively reduce the size of the offeror pool. There seems to be no basis for this thinking, since the second (May 14, 1997) draft of the FAR Part 15 Rewrite also used the phrase "each proposal against all evaluation criteria," but expressly provided for phased evaluation. In any event, the FAR does not expressly prohibit phased evaluations, so the use of the technique is consistent with the guiding principles in FAR 1.102(d) and 1.102-4(e).

Agencies that are planning to evaluate proposals in phases should describe their process in the RFP and state which evaluation factors they will apply in each phase of the evaluation. When evaluating proposals in phases, agencies must ensure that price or cost to the government is an evaluation factor in each phase. In *Kathpal Technologies, Inc.; Computer & Hi-Tech Management, Inc.* (B-283137.3, December 30, 1999), GAO ruled that an agency cannot eliminate a technically acceptable proposal from consideration without evaluating price or cost, saying:

> We disagree with the agency that it could ignore price in its initial screening evaluation. Cost or price to the government must be included in every RFP as an evaluation factor, and agencies must consider cost or price to the government in evaluating competitive proposals. 41 U.S.C. § 253a(c)(1)(B) (1994); FAR § 15.304(c)(1); S.J. Thomas Co., Inc., B-283192, Oct. 20, 1999, 99-2 CPD

¶ __ at 3. This requirement means that an agency cannot eliminate a technically acceptable proposal from consideration for award without taking into account the relative cost of that proposal to the government. SCIENTECH, Inc., B-277805.2, Jan. 20, 1998, 98-1 CPD ¶ 33 at 7.

PROGRAMMATIC DOWNSELECT

The second usage of the term *downselect* refers to a procedure sometimes used in large system development programs. The primary users of this type of procedure have been the military services and the National Aeronautics and Space Administration (NASA).

A programmatic downselect might proceed as follows: In the first phase, the agency issues an RFP for system concept studies and notifies prospective offerors that in order to participate in subsequent phases, a firm must be selected to participate in the first phase. The agency then awards small contracts (e.g., firm-fixed-price level-of-effort research and development contracts) to three or four firms. The contracts require each offeror to deliver a proposal for the next phase. Upon completion of these initial contracts, the agency evaluates the quality of the contractors' work and their proposals for the next phase and downselects to two or three firms, awarding them contracts for preliminary designs and for proposals for full-scale development without soliciting proposals from other firms. Upon completion of the preliminary design work, the agency evaluates the contractors' performance in the second phase and their proposals for full-scale development, including production of one or more prototypes. It then downselects to one or two contractors. The agency might proceed to the final phase (production) by testing the prototypes and evaluating the contractors' production proposals, and then selecting the contractor that represents the best value. This is only one way to do it; several variations on this approach are possible.

NASA has issued the most detailed rules about programmatic downselects. [See the NASA FAR Supplement (NFS) at 1817.73, *Phased Acquisition*.] NASA distinguishes between what it calls *phased acquisitions*, in which a solicitation is issued at the start of each phase (as described above), and *progressive acquisitions*, in which a solicitation is issued for the first phase, but less formal procedures (e.g., a letter) are used to solicit proposals for the subsequent phases.

NFS 1817.7301-4(a)(7) and 1817.7301-5(b) state that NASA contracting officers soliciting proposals for later phases of the acquisition must accept and evaluate proposals received from all offerors, including those that did not participate in the preceding phase. It should be clear to all but blue-sky optimists that offerors that did not participate in the earlier phases will have little chance of receiving an award for a later phase.

90. What is *experience*?

The FAR uses the term *experience* but does not define it. Some agencies use *experience* interchangeably with *past performance*. Others distinguish between experience and past performance, defining *experience* as the kind and amount of work an offeror has done, and *past performance* as an assessment of how well the offeror did its work in the past.

Since we value experience because of what it teaches us, it could be defined as "the opportunity to learn by doing." Learn what? Experience teaches us what can go wrong with a plan and what kinds of preventive and corrective actions are likely to be effective. Thus, each instance in which a firm has had an opportunity to learn what can go wrong during the performance of certain kinds of work is an instance of relevant experience with that work—an opportunity to learn what can go wrong and what to do to prevent it or fix it.

Experience is relevant when it confronted a firm with the same kinds of challenges the firm is likely to encounter while performing the work contemplated by the new procurement. As a general rule, agencies should not measure experience in years, but in numbers of instances of performance—that is, numbers of opportunities to learn.

91. What is *past performance,* and how should agencies evaluate it?

The FAR does not define the term *past performance,* but FAR 15.304(c)(3) requires agencies to evaluate it during source selection. Past performance should be considered a measure of how well an offeror performed on similar work in the past, as assessed on the basis of its customers' expressions of satisfaction (or the lack thereof) and other information. Work in the past is "similar" or "relevant" when it involved the same kinds of challenges and difficulties that will confront the contractor on the prospective contract.

Although the FAR does not define *past performance* per se, FAR 42.1501 describes *past performance information* as follows:

> [R]elevant information, for future source selection purposes, regarding a contractor's actions under previously awarded contracts. It includes, for example, the contractor's record of conforming to standards of good workmanship; the contractor's record of forecasting and controlling costs; the contractor's adherence to contract schedules, including the administrative aspects of performance; the contractor's history of reasonable and cooperative behavior and commitment to customer satisfaction; and generally, the contractor's business-like concern for the interest of the customer.

Agencies should evaluate past performance by collecting information from an offeror's customers about how they think the offeror performed in the past. They should also collect information from other sources, such as government law enforcement agencies, better business bureaus and consumer protection organizations, credit organizations, and business press reports.

The most important customer information is the agency's own experience with an offeror, which should be obtained from past performance files and interviews with agency technical and contracting personnel. Agency evaluators should collect information from an offeror's other customers by telephone, asking if they would be willing to share their opinions, and then sending them a brief (no more than 15 questions) questionnaire. The evaluators should not ask the customers to complete and mail the questionnaires, but should go through the questionnaire with the customer on the telephone. This approach minimizes the demands on the customers, and thus increases the likelihood of getting a response.

Agencies should not mail out lengthy questionnaires asking for factual details. Most customers will not have specific facts at their fingertips and may not be willing to dig them out of old files. Agencies should not rely too heavily on reports of one or two instances of good or bad past performance, but should look for indications of performance trends.

SUBCONTRACTORS, MANAGERS, AND KEY PERSONNEL

An issue that comes up repeatedly is whether or not to credit an offeror with the past performance of its individual managers, key personnel, and subcontractors. FAR 15.305(a)(2)(iii) says:

> The evaluation should take into account past performance information regarding predecessor companies,

> key personnel who have relevant experience, or subcontractors that will perform major or critical aspects of the requirement when such information is relevant to the instant acquisition.

There are two ways to comply with the regulation in this regard. One way is to credit the offeror with the past performance of its managers, key personnel, and subcontractors; the other way is to evaluate the offeror strictly on the basis of its own record and evaluate the past performance of its managers, key personnel, and subcontractors separately. The first method may obscure the fact that the offeror, as a firm, has no record or has done poorly in the past, thus making the offeror seem a better choice than it actually is. This is a matter of special concern when the offeror's managers or key personnel are new to the company, hired in order to make the offeror more palatable to the government. It is also of concern when a subcontractor has not worked with the offeror in the past.

GAO will allow an agency to evaluate an offeror's past performance on the basis of the record of the offeror's managers, key personnel, or subcontractors as it sees fit, as long as the evaluation is reasonable and consistent with the terms of the request for proposals. In *The Paintworks, Inc.* (B-292982, December 23, 2003), GAO said:

> Paintworks argues that MMF has no experience installing paint booths, and thus does not warrant a past/present performance rating of very good. In this regard, the protester acknowledges that MMF's subcontractor, Spray Systems, may have substantial experience manufacturing and installing paint booths. Paintworks argues, however, that the agency unreasonably credited MMF with the experience of its subcontractor, since the solicitation did not expressly provide for consideration of subcontractor experience and, in any event, while Spray Systems is manufacturing the paint booth, MMF plans to install it.... The record here shows that in evaluating MMF's

> past/present performance, the agency gave MMF credit for Spray Systems' substantial experience in manufacturing and providing paint booths, for which Spray Systems received ratings of very good and exceptional from each of its references. The experience of a proposed subcontractor properly may be considered in determining whether an offeror meets experience or past performance requirements where the solicitation does not expressly prohibit its consideration.

Footnote omitted. See, too, *Northrop Grumman Technical Services, Inc.; Raytheon Technical Services Company* (B-291506, January 14, 2003), for a similar ruling about joint ventures.

On the other hand, GAO does not require an agency to credit an offeror with the experience of a subcontractor if the agency thinks it would not be reasonable to do so. See *Joint Management & Technology Services* (B-294229, September 22, 2004).

92. How should agencies evaluate the past performance of new companies or companies that have never done similar work?

Agencies should evaluate the past performance of new companies or companies that have never done similar work as "no record" or "none." FAR 15.305(a)(iv) says:

> In the case of an offeror without a record of relevant past performance or for whom information on past performance is not available, the offeror may not be evaluated favorably or unfavorably on past performance.

This has been called *the neutral rule*, because an earlier version of the FAR required agencies to give such offerors "a neutral evaluation." The FAR Part 15 Rewrite dropped that phrase, adopting instead the language quoted above, which is similar to the language in the governing statute, 41 U.S.C. 405(j)(2). The commonsense meaning of this rule is that you cannot evaluate something that does not exist. Thus, if an offeror has not done *relevant* work in the past, then you cannot say anything about its past performance, good or bad; so the appropriate thing to do is to write down "no record," "not applicable," or "none."

This does not mean that, when comparing offerors to each other, agencies have to consider "none" to be as good as "good." GAO has ruled on several occasions that an agency may consider an offeror with a record of good past performance and a higher price to be a better value than an offeror with no record and a lower price. For example, in *Phillips Industries, Inc.* (B-280645, September 17, 1998), GAO said:

> As we stated in Excalibur, supra, at 3, [Excalibur Systems, Inc., B-272017, July 12, 1996] the use of a neutral rating approach, to avoid penalizing a vendor without prior experience and thereby enhance competition, does not preclude, in a best value procurement, a determination to award to a higher-priced offeror with a good past performance record over a lower-cost vendor with a neutral past performance rating. Indeed, such a determination is inherent in the concept of best value.

The GAO decisions notwithstanding, some individuals think that it is wrong to choose a higher priced experienced offeror over a lower priced inexperienced offeror, because they say it "penalizes" the lower priced offeror merely because it lacks a record of past performance. There is no legal basis for this position.

If an agency defines *relevant* broadly enough, relevant work can include virtually any type of work done in the past, and the agency can thus avoid having to make a finding of "no record." Furthermore, even though an offeror, as a firm, has not done relevant work in the past, FAR 15.305(a)(2)(iii) encourages (but does not require) agencies to credit the offeror with work done by predecessor companies, key personnel, and even subcontractors.

The *neutral rule* has caused much confusion. The quality of a firm's past work is a risk indicator, and common sense suggests that it is bad business to do business with a firm that has a reputation for doing poor work. But when a firm has no record of relevant past performance, what bothers people is that the firm lacks *experience*, which is different from having a reputation for doing poor work. The *neutral rule* is not so much a *past performance* issue as an *experience* issue, yet the law applies the *neutral rule* to the evaluation of past performance, not to the evaluation of experience.

To understand the true meaning of the *neutral rule*, read Office of Federal Procurement Policy Letter No. 92-5, *Past Performance Information*, dated December 30, 1992. Paragraph 6.d of that letter says, "Allow newly established firms to compete for contracts even though they lack a history of past performance." That's it: The lack of experience is not to be a bar to competing for government contracts. Somehow, this clear statement of policy became the obscure statement that "the offeror may not be evaluated favorably or unfavorably on past performance."

The way to eliminate the confusion would be to rewrite the rule, saying that agency decision makers must not reject a firm's offer merely because the firm does not have experience, but must thoughtfully assess the government's risk/cost tradeoffs before deciding to pay a higher price rather than rely on an inexperienced firm.

Some individuals think that agencies ought to credit offerors with the past performance of managers, key personnel, subcontractors, or joint-venture partners in order to provide an offeror with a record of past performance and thus avoid application of the neutral rule. While they may do so, GAO does not require them to do so. See *Joint Management & Tech-*

nology Services (B-294229, September 22, 2004), in which GAO said:

> JMTS argues that the agency improperly assigned it a rating of 5 under the past performance criterion. According to the protester, this was improper because three of the four JMTS team members (D.N. American, EG&G and SAIC) received high ratings on their past performance surveys (in the exceptional or outstanding rating categories), and JMTS did not have any significant experience and therefore should have received a neutral rating. JMTS concludes that an averaging of three high ratings with one neutral rating should have resulted in a score higher than merely satisfactory, and that the agency, by assigning only a satisfactory rating, essentially penalized the firm for JMTS's lack of past performance, and improperly ignored the past performance ratings of the other entities comprising the JMTS team.
>
> The evaluation in this area was reasonable. The record shows that the agency assigned the satisfactory rating due to concerns that JMTS, the managing concern for performance of the contract, did not have any meaningful past performance, AR, exh. E-2, at 44, and that JMTS itself did not have any past performance, having been created solely for purposes of submitting a proposal for this requirement. Id. The agency's assigning of a rating of 5 effectively the midpoint on the evaluation scoring scale, which did not include a neutral category amounted to a neutral (i.e., a neither favorable nor unfavorable) evaluation of the firm's past performance, consistent with regulations applicable where an offeror has no past performance.... We find nothing improper in the agency's focusing, in particular, on the joint venture's lack of past performance, even though the JMTS team includes D.N. American, a mentor firm with a record of past performance, as well as the two subcontractors, also with records of past performance. In this regard, agencies are permitted, but not required, to consider the individual experience and past performance of other entities such as individual members of a mentor-protege joint venture

> or other subcontractors comprising a team being offered to perform a requirement.... Thus, there was nothing unreasonable in the agency's not according some greater weight to the positive past performance surveys of those team members having past performance.

93. What is a *sample task*?

A *sample task* is a proposal evaluation technique that is used in source selections for task order contracts. Task order contracts are indefinite-delivery/indefinite-quantity (ID/IQ) contracts for services. See FAR 16.501-1 and 16.504. They allow agencies to defer specification and ordering of services until after contract award. The statements of work in such contracts usually describe the contract work in broad terms; when the agency wants the contractor to do some work, it issues a task order (see the definition in FAR 2.101) that contains a detailed statement of work. The parties to such contracts negotiate descriptions of labor categories and associated labor rates. When the buyer wants to issue a task order, the parties negotiate an agreement on the kinds and quantities of labor that will be needed and then apply the appropriate labor rates to determine the price of the order.

It is difficult to evaluate proposed prices for ID/IQ contracts, because the buyer has no idea how efficient each offeror will be during performance and how many hours each will spend to perform a given task. One offeror may propose higher labor rates than another, but that offeror may be more efficient; despite the higher labor rates, it may need fewer hours and be able to do the work for a lower total price. One way to test this is to give each of the offerors a sample task that is representative of the kinds of tasks that the buyer intends to order under the contract, and instruct the offerors to estimate the labor categories and hours they would need to do the work. The estimates can then be used to evaluate the prospective labor efficiency of each of the offerors.

Another use of sample tasks is to test offerors' understanding of the work by asking them to describe how they would plan, organize, staff, direct, and control the performance of the task. The government can evaluate the offerors' understanding of the work based on the quality of their responses to the sample task. This can be done either by furnishing the sample task with the RFP and instructing the offerors to include a written response as part of their proposals, or by asking the offerors to respond orally in a presentation to the government's source selection team.

Two criticisms are often made of the sample task technique. The first criticism is that sample task pricing is not binding, so competition may encourage the offerors to understate the number of hours that they will really need to do the work in order to obtain the best possible price evaluation. The second criticism is that one or two sample tasks may not be sufficiently representative of all the types of work that the offeror will have to do under the contract and thus will not be adequate tests of the offeror's understanding. Both criticisms have merit; nevertheless, the sample task is a popular evaluation technique.

GAO has ruled that when sample tasks are used to test offerors' understanding of the work, the government is not obligated to disclose deficiencies in their responses during discussions or allow them to correct the deficiencies by revising their responses, since this would defeat the purpose of the test. In *Syscon Services, Inc.* (B-235647, September 21, 1989), GAO found:

> We have consistently stated that in order for discussions on a negotiated procurement to be meaningful, contracting agencies must furnish information to all offerors in the competitive range as to the areas in their proposals which are believed to be deficient so that offerors may have an opportunity to revise their proposals to fully satisfy the government's requirements. Pan Am World

Servs., Inc., et al., B-231840, Nov. 7, 1988, 88-2 CPD ¶ 466. However, the content and extent of discussions is a matter of the contracting officer's judgment based on the particular facts of the procurement. Huff & Huff Serv. Corp., B-235419, July 17, 1989, 89-2 CPD ¶ 55. . . .

Here, the sole purpose of evaluating offerors' responses to the sample tasks was not to assess the sufficiency of the offerors' technical approach *per se*, but, as expressly stated in the RFP and repeatedly emphasized during discussions, to evaluate the offerors' understanding. If the Navy had simply spoon fed Syscon each of the noted deficiencies for every sample task, it may have led Syscon to simply repeat back the Navy's concerns pont by point, which would defeat the primary purpose of the sample task scenario—to test the offerors' demonstrated understanding of the technical requirements of the contemplated contract. Eagan, McAllister Assocs., Inc., B-231983, supra. That is, if such extensive discussions were conducted, the agency would be provided with no assurance that the offeror independently appreciated the problems identified by the agency. Fairchild-Weston Sys., Inc., B-229568.2, Apr. 22, 1988, 88-1 CPD ¶ 394. Consequently, we find that where an offeror's understanding is being tested, as opposed to evaluating the adequacy of its technical approach to the contract work, the agency need not specify during discussions all identified deficiencies. Eagan, McAllister Assocs., Inc., B-231983, supra; see also Hills's Capitol Sec., Inc., B-233411, Mar. 15, 1989, 89-1 CPD ¶ 274 at 6; Fairchild-Weston Sys., Inc., B-229568.2, supra.

94. What is the *contingency procedure for proposal evaluation*?

The *contingency procedure for proposal evaluation* allows an agency to resort to a phased evaluation if it receives an unexpectedly large number of proposals. In this way, it can eliminate some of the offerors without first having to evaluate them on the basis of all the evaluation factors that are described in the RFP. To use the contingency procedure, an agency must notify prospective offerors in advance by describing the procedure in its RFP.

Suppose that an agency issues an RFP that states that it will evaluate proposals on the basis of the following factors: (1) offer acceptability; (2) understanding of the work (based on an oral presentation); (3) experience; (4) past performance; and (5) price. Suppose then that the agency had anticipated receiving about 10 proposals, but that it actually receives 36 proposals, an unexpectedly large number, and its evaluators now face the unwelcome prospect of having to sit through and evaluate 36 oral presentations. The contingency procedure allows the agency to eliminate some of the proposals before scheduling oral presentations by the remainder.

First, the agency evaluates the technical acceptability of the offers on a pass or fail basis and eliminates any that are unacceptable. An offer is technically unacceptable when: (1) it does not manifest the offeror's unconditional assent to the terms of the RFP; (2) the offeror tries to impose additional terms; (3) the offeror proposes an inadequate amount of small business participation when FAR Subpart 19.12 applies to the procurement; or (4) the offeror's representations, certifications, or other statements indicate that the offeror is not eligible for contract award.

If, after the elimination of offerors whose offers are technically unacceptable, a large number of offerors still remains, the next step is to perform a price analysis, comparing the prices of the remaining offerors to each other and to the government estimate, and eliminating any offeror whose prices are too high. A price is too high when the agency's source selection authority decides that it is significantly higher than the prices of most of the other offerors and that he or she would not select an offeror at that price no matter how good its experience and past performance.

If a large number of offerors still remains, the next step is to evaluate each offeror's experience and past performance and then compare the offerors on the basis of those factors and price, eliminating more of them because they are not sufficiently competitive. The agency can then hear oral presentations from the remaining offerors and make a source selection decision by comparing the remaining offerors on the basis of all the evaluation factors.

The contingency procedure is a type of phased evaluation. For the procedure to be acceptable to GAO, agencies must describe the procedure in their RFPs and consider price before eliminating an offeror in any step of the process after determining the technical acceptability of the offers. (See *Kathpal Technologies, Inc.; Computer & Hi-Tech Management, Inc.*, B-283137.3, December 30, 1999.) An offeror that is eliminated in one of the preliminary steps should be considered *otherwise eliminated from the competition*, as provided in FAR 15.503(a)(1), rather than *excluded from the competitive range*. [See: *Department of Commerce—Request for Modification of Recommendation* (B-283137.7, February 14, 2000), Footnote 1.]

The following is an example of the kind of language that agencies should include in an RFP to notify offerors that they might use the contingency procedure:

> **Contingency Procedure.** If we receive what we consider to be a large number of proposals, then we will evaluate the proposals in phases in order to progressively reduce the number being considered for contract award. The purpose of this contingency procedure is to reduce the time and cost of source selection, both for ourselves and for the competing offerors. We will execute the procedure as follows:
>
> 1. First, we will determine the technical acceptability of each offer in accordance with the acceptability criteria in this RFP. We will eliminate from further consideration

any offerors who submitted technically unacceptable offers.

2. If a large number of offerors still remain in contention after the elimination of offerors whose offers were technically unacceptable, we will then perform a price analysis and eliminate offerors whose prices we consider to be too high to be competitive in light of the prices offered by other offerors.

3. If a large number of offerors still remain after the elimination of offerors based on technical acceptability and price, we will then evaluate the experience, past performance, and prices of the remaining offerors and eliminate any that are not sufficiently competitive to be selected for contract award.

4. Once we have reduced the number of offerors to a manageable number by completing Step 1, and, if necessary, Steps 2 and 3, above, we will schedule oral presentations by the remaining offerors and select the contractor by comparing those offerors on the basis of experience, past performance, understanding of the work, and price, and make an award without discussions.

The decision to eliminate any offeror through this contingency procedure will not constitute the establishment of a competitive range, as described in FAR 15.306(c), and it will not obligate us to conduct discussions or to solicit or entertain proposal revisions. However, we reserve the right to establish a competitive range and conduct discussions if we decide that it is in the best interests of the Government to do so.

In accordance with GAO's protest rules, any prospective offeror who objects to this procedure must file a protest before the closing date and time of the RFP. [See 4 C.F.R. § 21.2(a)(1).]

The contingency procedure has at least two potential pitfalls that agencies should avoid. The first pitfall is establishing a specific number for what constitutes "a large number" or "a manageable number" of proposals. One or more prospective offerors may try to get an agency to commit to a specific number in advance, but an agency would be unwise to make such a commitment. The second pitfall is establishing in advance a formula for determining how high a price has to be to be "too high," another matter about which prospective offerors may try to get a firm commitment from an agency. Such formulae might include a percentage above the average price of all offerors or a percentage above the amount of the government estimate. Both of these advance commitments run the risk of being considered arbitrary and would limit an agency's discretion for no good reason.

95. What is an *oral presentation*?

An *oral presentation* is an oral submission of proposal information. Traditionally, offerors have submitted their entire proposals in writing. But FAR 15.102 now authorizes agencies to require offerors to submit parts of their proposals orally. When an agency requires offerors to make oral presentations, it is using a two-step proposal submission process: In step 1, offerors submit specified written information by a specified deadline; in step 2, they submit additional information orally at a date, time, and place specified by the agency.

Agencies have required offerors to make oral presentations to their evaluation boards for many years, but before 1995 agencies generally did not consider such presentations to be part of an offeror's proposal. Oral presentations were used to familiarize evaluators with the main points of a proposal before they began their evaluation. The evaluators did not evaluate the information provided in the oral presentations, just the information in the written proposal documents.

In 1995, agencies began to experiment by asking offerors to present a part of their proposal information to the evaluation board in an oral presentation, which was to be evaluated immediately. These experiments sought to streamline and expedite the source selection process, and they met with considerable success. In March 1996, the Office of Federal Procurement Policy and the Department of Energy published *Guidelines for the Use of Oral Presentations*, which explains how to use the new approach. Although it is now outdated, it is still available on the Internet at www.pr.doe.gov/oral6.html. Coverage in the FAR did not come until September 1997, as part of the FAR Part 15 Rewrite. The fact that practice has preceded regulation has led to much confusion, in particular with regard to whether oral presentations are *discussions*.

When used properly, oral presentations are neither proposal revisions nor proposal modifications (see FAR 15.001), nor are they clarifications, communications, or discussions about proposals (see FAR 15.306). Rather, they are part of the initial submissions of proposal information. FAR 15.102 addresses the topic of oral presentations at length:

> (a) Oral presentations by offerors as requested by the Government may substitute for, or augment, written information. Use of oral presentations as a substitute for portions of a proposal can be effective in streamlining the source selection process. Oral presentations may occur at any time in the acquisition process, and are subject to the same restrictions as written information, regarding timing (see 15.208) and content (see 15.306). Oral presentations provide an opportunity for dialogue among the parties. Pre-recorded videotaped presentations that lack real-time interactive dialogue are not considered oral presentations for the purposes of this section, although they may be included in offeror submissions, when appropriate.
>
> (b) The solicitation may require each offeror to submit part of its proposal through oral presentations. However, certifications, representations, and a signed offer sheet

(including any exceptions to the Government's terms and conditions) shall be submitted in writing.

(c) Information pertaining to areas such as an offeror's capability, past performance, work plans or approaches, staffing resources, transition plans, or sample tasks (or other types of tests) may be suitable for oral presentations. In deciding what information to obtain through an oral presentation, consider the following:

(1) The Government's ability to adequately evaluate the information;

(2) The need to incorporate any information into the resultant contract;

(3) The impact on the efficiency of the acquisition; and

(4) The impact (including cost) on small businesses. In considering the costs of oral presentations, contracting officers should also consider alternatives to on-site oral presentations (e.g., teleconferencing, video teleconferencing).

(d) When oral presentations are required, the solicitation shall provide offerors with sufficient information to prepare them. Accordingly, the solicitation may describe—

(1) The types of information to be presented orally and the associated evaluation factors that will be used;

(2) The qualifications for personnel that will be required to provide the oral presentation(s);

(3) The requirements for, and any limitations and/or prohibitions on, the use of written material or other media to supplement the oral presentations;

(4) The location, date, and time for the oral presentations;

> (5) The restrictions governing the time permitted for each oral presentation; and
>
> (6) The scope and content of exchanges that may occur between the Government's participants and the offeror's representatives as part of the oral presentations, including whether or not discussions (see 15.306(d)) will be permitted during oral presentations.
>
> (e) The contracting officer shall maintain a record of oral presentations to document what the Government relied upon in making the source selection decision. The method and level of detail of the record (e.g., videotaping, audio tape recording, written record, Government notes, copies of offeror briefing slides or presentation notes) shall be at the discretion of the source selection authority. A copy of the record placed in the file may be provided to the offeror.
>
> (f) When an oral presentation includes information that the parties intend to include in the contract as material terms or conditions, the information shall be put in writing. Incorporation by reference of oral statements is not permitted.
>
> (g) If, during an oral presentation, the Government conducts discussions (see 15.306(d)), the Government must comply with 15.306 and 15.307.

Oral presentations are simply a means of communicating information and do not presuppose any particular content. It should be clear from FAR 15.102(b) and (f) that agencies must not use oral presentations to obtain any part of an offer—i.e., promises that would be binding upon acceptance. Offers should be obtained in writing. Instead, agencies should use oral presentations to obtain proposal information about an offeror's capability, such as information bearing on an offeror's understanding of the work.

Thus, *oral presentation* should not be identified in an RFP as an evaluation factor, but instead as the way offerors must submit information that pertains to an evaluation factor like "understanding of the work."

When agencies first began to use oral presentations to solicit information that would be evaluated, some expressed fears that the procedure would instigate numerous protests and that GAO would consider oral presentations to be improper discussions, thereby blocking an award without discussions. Experience has shown that those fears were unjustified. GAO will not consider an oral presentation to have been discussions as long as the offeror was not given a chance to change its proposal. For example, in *BE, Inc.; PAI Corporation* (B-277978; B-277978.2; December 16, 1997), GAO said:

> The acid test of whether discussions have been held is whether it can be said that an offeror was provided the opportunity to revise or modify its proposal.

Also see *Development Alternatives, Inc.* (B-279920, August 6, 1998).

Oral presentations should be conducted simply and expeditiously. Some agencies have turned oral presentations into major "dog and pony shows," with each offeror presenting hundreds of PowerPoint® slides and with lengthy question-and-answer sessions, conducted in an auditorium filled with nearly 100 government attendees. This is both unnecessary and inappropriate, even for a large procurement. In most cases an oral presentation should be conducted at a conference table, with the government personnel asking a set of prescribed questions, following up as appropriate based on the offeror's answers. Two hours for both the presentation and the question-and-answer session should be sufficient in most cases to judge how well an offeror's key personnel understand the government's requirements. Attendance should be limited to members of the government's evaluation team; "observers" should be excluded. Presentations should be recorded on audio or audio-visual media.

96. What is the difference between an *oral presentation* and an *oral proposal*?

The FAR does not use the term *oral proposal*. When agencies began to use oral presentations to obtain information that they would evaluate, some of them, like the Air Force, began to use the two terms to distinguish between information that would tell evaluators about the contents of written proposals, but that would not be evaluated, and information that would be considered a part of the proposal and would be evaluated as such. For example, the 1996 edition of the Air Force FAR Supplement, in Appendix AA, *Formal Source Selection for Major Acquisitions*, paragraph AA-103, *Definitions*, defined the two terms as follows:

> "Oral Presentation" means essentially one-way communication from the offerors to the Air Force, with written proposals still required.
>
> "Oral Proposal" means allowing two-way communication between the Government and the offeror. This may constitute discussions and take the place of a written proposal.

Since the publication of the FAR Part 15 Rewrite, agencies no longer officially distinguish between oral presentations and oral proposals. Some now use the terms interchangeably.

97. Should the government videotape oral presentations?

The FAR does not require that agencies videotape oral presentations. Some persons have advocated the videotaping of oral presentations so that there would be a record of what was said in the event of a protest, and in at least one case an agency used a videotape to prove to GAO that oral presentations did not constitute discussions (see *SEAIR Transport Services, Inc.*; B-274436; December 12, 1996).

Another argument for videotaping oral presentations is that the evaluators can use the tape to resolve disagreements among themselves about what an offeror said during a presentation. Videotaping need not be expensive or intrusive, and so there is little reason to object to it. When agencies first began to use oral presentations to obtain information for evaluation, videotaping was routine as agencies sought to protect themselves in the event of protests. However, protests about oral presentations have been rare, and it appears that several agencies have decided that videotaping serves little purpose and have stopped doing it.

98. When should agencies use oral presentations?

Agencies should use oral presentations instead of written technical or management proposals whenever they would use the information in such proposals solely to evaluate offerors' capability to perform—that is, their understanding of the work. Oral presentations are an effective way to obtain the kind of information that is included in essay-type technical and management proposals. Agencies should not use oral presentations to obtain promises that are to become binding upon acceptance.

99. What are the different formats for oral presentations?

Three main formats are used for oral presentations: (1) the briefing; (2) the sample task; and (3) the interview. In a briefing, the offeror's representatives make a formal presentation, usually with overhead slides. A briefing is followed by a question-and-answer session. In a sample task, the offeror's representatives are given a written description of a problem that is typical of the type of problem that the offeror will be called upon to solve during contract performance. They are given time—an hour or so—to decide how they would handle the matter, and then they make a presentation of their solution, which is followed by questions and answers. In an interview, the offeror's attendees are asked questions about how they would handle various aspects of performance.

The formal briefing is the most costly and time-consuming of the three formats. Offerors tend to spend large sums of money preparing impressive overhead slides, and then they spend more money rehearsing their presentation. The presentations are not especially revealing when they have been thoroughly rehearsed, and some agencies have reported that the most revealing and informative part of the process is the question-and-answer session.

The sample task procedure is costly when an agency gives the written problem to the offerors in advance, because the offerors will spend a lot of money preparing and rehearsing their presentations. If the agency waits until the day of the presentation to give the written problem to the offerors, it must ensure that the nature of the problem and the kind of answer expected are clear, and they must provide a reasonable amount of time for problem analysis and development of a response.

Of the three formats, the interview is the least costly and the most expedient, since the offerors do not have a chance to spend a lot of money preparing and rehearsing a formal presentation, and they do not have to be given time to read and analyze a written problem and prepare responses on the day of the presentation. Another advantage of the interview is that it can be conducted like an ordinary business meeting between a firm and a prospective client in which the client asks questions about the firm's business policies and practices. But the interview requires skilled questioners, perceptive listeners, and careful note-takers, since the questions and answers will be the only source of information for evaluation.

100. What should agencies ask offerors to talk about during oral presentations?

The most effective topic for oral presentations is the offerors' assessment of the challenges and risks associated with performance of the prospective contract, and how they would manage them. Agencies should ask offerors to identify what kinds of things can go wrong during performance and the preventive and corrective actions that they would take. The depth and thoughtfulness of the responses should reveal a great deal about how much each of the offerors knows about the work. The agency's evaluators should use the offerors' responses as the basis for evaluating their understanding of the agency's requirements.

101. What are the rules about question-and-answer sessions during oral presentations?

FAR 15.102(a) says, in part, "Oral presentations provide an opportunity for dialogue among the parties." Question-and-answer sessions allow the agency evaluators to probe an offeror's understanding by going beyond the practiced part of its presentation and confronting it with "what-if" scenarios: "What would you do if X happened?" "What would you do if that did not work?" "How would you try to prevent X from happening?" By asking such questions, the evaluators can assess the depth of the offeror's understanding of the work and its ability to develop sensible solutions to potential problems. Many agency personnel who have participated in oral presentations have said that the question-and-answer sessions are the most revealing part of the exercise.

Unless the oral presentations are being conducted concurrently with discussions [see FAR 15.306(d)], agency evaluators must not engage in bargaining behavior while conducting question-and-answer sessions. They must neither ask nor allow an offeror to revise the promises that it made in its offer or cure material omissions in the written part of its proposal. If an offeror tries to change its promises or cure material omissions, the evaluators must advise the offeror that they are not engaging in discussions and will not entertain such revisions. FAR 15.102(g) says, "If, during an oral presentation, the Government conducts discussions (see 15.306(d)), then the Government must comply with 15.306 and 15.307."

102. What is *price analysis*?

FAR 15.404-1(b)(1) defines *price analysis* as follows:

> Price analysis is the process of examining and evaluating a proposed price without evaluating its separate cost elements and proposed profit.

Price analysis is the preferred method of evaluating prices proposed for fixed price contracts. FAR 15.305(a)(1) provides as follows:

> Cost or Price Evaluation. Normally, competition establishes price reasonableness. Therefore, when contracting on a firm-fixed-price or fixed-price with economic price adjustment basis, comparison of the proposed prices will usually satisfy the requirement to perform a price analysis, and a cost analysis need not be performed.

[See, also, FAR 15.404-1(a)(2).] For a detailed discussion of price analysis techniques, see: the Federal Acquisition Institute's *Contract Pricing Reference Guides*, Volume I, Price Analysis, which is available on the Internet at www.gsa.gov/fai/; *Pricing and Cost Accounting: A Handbook for Government Contractors, 2nd edition*, by Darrell J. Oyer (Management Concepts, Inc.: Vienna, VA, 2005); and *Guide to Contract*

Pricing, 4th edition., by John Edward Murphy (Management Concepts, Inc.: Vienna, VA, 2005).

103. What is *cost analysis*?

FAR 15.404-1(c)(1) defines *cost analysis* as follows:

> Cost analysis is the review and evaluation of the separate cost elements and profit in an offeror's or contractor's proposal (including cost or pricing data or information other than cost or pricing data), and the application of judgment to determine how well the proposed costs represent what the cost of the contract should be, assuming reasonable economy and efficiency.

FAR 15.404-1(a)(3) requires contracting officers to perform a cost analysis when cost or pricing data are required. Since cost or pricing data are rarely required when the government solicits competitive proposals, agencies should rarely have to perform a cost analysis when conducting a source selection. FAR 15.305(a)(1) says:

> In limited situations, a cost analysis (see 15.403-1(c)(1)(i)(B)) may be appropriate to establish reasonableness *of the otherwise successful offeror's price*. [Italics added.]

This sentence seems to suggest that cost analysis should be limited to the prospective awardee's proposal, and only when the contracting officer believes that the prospective awardee has proposed an unreasonable price. For a detailed discussion of cost analysis techniques, see: Volume III, Cost Analysis, of the Federal Acquisition Institute's *Contract Pricing Reference Guides*, available on the Internet at www.gsa.gov/fai/; *Pricing and Cost Accounting: A Handbook for Government Contractors*, by Darrell J. Oyer (Management Concepts, Inc.: Vienna, VA, 2000); and *Guide to Contract Pricing,*

2nd ed., by Edward Murphy (Management Concepts, Inc.: Vienna, VA, 1997).

104. What is *cost realism analysis*?

FAR 15.404-1(d)(1) defines *cost realism analysis* as follows:

> Cost realism analysis is the process of independently reviewing and evaluating specific elements of each offeror's proposed cost estimate to determine whether the estimated proposed cost elements are realistic for the work to be performed; reflect a clear understanding of the requirements; and are consistent with the unique methods of performance and materials described in the offeror's technical proposal.

FAR 15.305(a)(1) says:

> When contracting on a cost reimbursement basis, evaluations shall include a cost realism analysis to determine what the Government should realistically expect to pay for the proposed effort, the offeror's understanding of the work, and the offeror's ability to perform the contract. Cost realism analyses may also be used on fixed-price incentive contracts or, in exceptional cases, on other competitive fixed-price type contracts (see FAR 15.404-1(d)(3)).

(This question and answer apply to cost-reimbursement contracts. See the next question, *What is price realism analysis?* for a discussion of analysis of the realism of proposals for fixed-price contracts.)

When an offeror submits a proposal for a cost-reimbursement contract, it does not promise to complete the work within the estimated cost. Rather, it promises "to use its best efforts to perform the work specified in the Schedule and all obligations under this contract within the estimated cost. . . ." (See FAR 52.232-20, *Limitation of Cost*, and 52.232-22, *Limitation of Funds*.) If a contractor cannot complete the work within the estimated cost, the government must either allow the contract to end unsuccessfully, or give the contractor more money to keep working. Inability to complete the work within the estimated cost is not grounds, per se, for termination for default. Thus, an offeror that is competing for a cost-reimbursement contract might be inclined to propose an unrealistically low estimated cost because it thinks that the government evaluates low costs favorably and because it knows that if it cannot finish the job for the estimated cost, it will not be stuck for the cost of completion.

In its decision in *DATEX, Inc.* (B-270268.2, April 15, 1996), GAO found:

> When an agency evaluates a proposal for the award of a cost reimbursement contract, an offeror's proposed estimated costs are not dispositive because, regardless of the costs proposed, the government is bound to pay the contractor its actual and allowable costs. Federal Acquisition Regulation § 15.605(c). Consequently, a cost realism analysis must be performed by the agency to determine the extent to which an offeror's proposed costs represents what the contract should cost, assuming reasonable economy and efficiency. McDonnell Douglas Corp., B-259694.2; B-259694.3, June 16, 1995, 95-2 CPD ¶ 51. That is, the purpose of a cost realism analysis is to determine what, in the government's view, it would realistically cost the offeror to perform given the offeror's technical approach. Hager Sharp, Inc., B-258812, Feb. 17, 1995, 95-1 CPD ¶ 93.

The objective of cost realism analysis is to determine whether or not an offeror's cost estimate is too low. To do this, an agency's cost realism evaluators must determine *the most probable cost* (sometimes called *most likely cost* or *evaluated cost*) associated with each offeror's proposed performance. Once the agency has determined each of the offerors' most probable costs, it uses those amounts to compare each offeror to the others to evaluate cost reasonableness (see Table IV-4).

TABLE IV-4

COST REALISM ANALYSIS AND COMPARISON

Offeror	*Proposed Estimated Cost*	*Agency Net Cost Realism Adjustments*	*Most Probable Cost*	*Proposed Fixed Fee*	*Total Most Probable Cost and Fixed Fee*
A	$1,297,000	+$300,000	$1,597,000	$77,820 (6%)	$1,674,820
B	$1,531,400	+$50,000	$1,581,400	$91,884 (6%)	$1,673,284

The table shows that the agency has determined that the most probable cost of contracting with Offeror A would be higher than that offeror's proposed estimated cost by a net amount (increases plus decreases) of $300,000. Offeror B's proposed estimated cost is unrealistic to a lesser degree. Note that the determination of most probable cost does not include any increase in the offeror's proposed fixed fee, since that amount would not change in the event of a cost overrun. In the final analysis, Offeror B represents a lower overall cost to the government than Offeror A, despite the fact that Offeror A proposed a lower estimated cost and fee.

The FAR does not prescribe detailed procedures for cost realism analysis. FAR 15.404-1(d)(2) merely states:

> Cost realism analyses shall be performed on cost-reimbursement contracts to determine the probable cost of performance for each offeror.
>
> (i) The probable cost may differ from the proposed cost and should reflect the Government's best estimate of the cost of any contract that is most likely to result from the offeror's proposal. The probable cost shall be used for purposes of evaluation to determine the best value.

> (ii) The probable cost is determined by adjusting each offeror's proposed cost, and fee when appropriate, to reflect any additions or reductions in cost elements to realistic levels based on the results of the cost realism analysis.

In numerous protest decisions, such as *Systems Integration & Research, Inc.; Presearch Inc.* (B-279759.2; B-279759.3; February 16, 1999), GAO has said, "An agency is not required to perform an in-depth cost analysis to verify each and every item in conducting a cost realism analysis," and "Because the contracting agency is in the best position to make this cost realism determination, our review is limited to determining whether the agency's cost realism analysis is reasonably based and not arbitrary." Nevertheless, GAO has sustained quite a few protests because cost realism analyses have been inadequate or done improperly, and any contracting officer whose duties include performing cost realism analyses in source selections would be wise to study GAO's cost-realism decisions in depth.

GAO has held that the determination of most probable cost must reflect each offeror's particular approach to contract performance. An agency cannot determine most probable cost by assuming a standard approach by all offerors or by applying standard factors to all proposals unless there would be no meaningful differences in the ways that the offerors would perform. For example, an agency cannot determine cost realism by comparing the offerors' proposed estimated costs to a government estimate when each offeror would approach the work differently. GAO sustained a protest against a Navy source selection for this very reason, in *Tidewater Construction Corporation* (B-278360, January 20, 1998):

> The Navy's comparison of the various work item costs in the government estimate to the offerors' target costs for the same line items cannot suffice as a sufficient analysis of cost realism where the agency has not considered the

> offerors' individual technical approaches or determined whether the offerors' proposals are consistent with the technical and cost parameters that were reflected in the government estimate. See ManTech Envtl. Tech., Inc., B-271002 et al., June 3, 1996, 96-1 CPD ¶ 272 at 4-5, 8-12; The Jonathan Corp., Metro Mach. Corp., supra, at 11-13. As indicated above, the agency made no attempt to determine the offerors' technical approaches. Tr. 36-39.

In performing a cost realism analysis, an agency cannot simply rely on inputs from audit organizations, like the Defense Contract Audit Agency (DCAA). In *ManTech Environmental Technology, Inc.* (B-271002; B-271002.2; B-271002.3, June 3, 1996), the Environmental Protection Agency, evaluating proposals for a cost-plus-award-fee, level-of-effort services contract, did little more than rely on a DCAA analysis of a limited number of an offeror's proposed labor rates. GAO sustained a protest against this approach. The decision is worth quoting at length, as follows:

> In support of the reasonableness of its cost realism analysis, the EPA relies upon its cost advisory report, DCAA audit results, pre/post negotiation memorandum, and source selection decision. The three EPA generated documents all rely on the written and oral results of the DCAA audit which purportedly found Dynamac's direct labor rates to be realistic. However, the audit and cost advisory report were qualified, and information on which they were based was incorrect.
>
> Where, as here, the agency sets the level of effort and identifies the specific categories of personnel necessary to perform, the primary inquiry in a cost realism analysis should be the realism of direct labor rates. Sociometrics, Inc., supra. Determining that the rates are realistic depends upon a finding that personnel, at the proposed rates, meet the requirements of the RFP, i.e., that qualified personnel can be employed and retained at those rates. Here, the cost evaluators stated that their review was based on "adequate cost and pricing data"

consisting of a verbal audit report from DCAA, contractor information, and other information contained in agency files. With regard to direct rates, the report states that the "proposed labor rates are actual 1995 rates for a specific individual in each category." Based upon conversations with the cognizant DCAA office, the cost evaluators concluded that the labor rates were acceptable for government pricing purposes. The pre/post negotiation memorandum and source selection decision include determinations of cost realism based upon the DCAA audit and its verification of direct rates.

However, EPA's cost evaluators qualified their recommendations by stating that they did not assess whether the personnel, at the rates proposed, met the RFP requirements. The report also was prepared without the benefit of the cost evaluators being apprised that the TEP had concerns about the low Dynamac rates. In this regard, the TEP had noted that the rate proposed for a P-3 (second highest) level ecologist "seems very low" and that all the new hires were listed at low rates suggestive of entry level positions. The TEP was concerned that "quality people cannot be hired at these rates" and observed that only a few existing employees worked at the rates suggested for new hires.

Further, notwithstanding the agency's reliance on DCAA, there is no evidence that the cost evaluators considered DCAA's qualification of its general recommendation that the proposal was acceptable as a basis for negotiation of a fair and reasonable price. These qualifications included DCAA's need for technical assistance in mapping the proposed labor rates to the RFP and evaluating Dynamac's weighted labor rates. DCAA had requested assistance from the agency in determining whether the personnel, at the rates proposed, were appropriate for the positions identified in the RFP. While the agency did not provide any assistance, Dynamac advised DCAA that its proposal manager had reviewed the RFP and had selected qualified individuals to propose. DCAA verified that the labor rates for named individuals represented actual Dynamac 1995 labor rates.

While this DCAA assessment provides a reasonable basis for accepting labor rates for named individuals, EPA accepted DCAA's limited statement as verification of all direct rates. Since Dynamac had provided verifiable personnel rates for less than half of the 54 labor categories listed in its cost proposal, it was unreasonable for the agency to rely on this aspect of the audit to support a finding of cost realism for all direct rates. Further, there is no indication that the agency attempted to assess the realism of the new hire rates. The EPA explains that it had received oral information from DCAA indicating that DCAA had verified the new hire rates as well. However, during the protest, the agency learned that the DCAA auditor had confused this audit with another Dynamac audit she was conducting at about the same time. She did not verify the new hire rates proposed for the EPA contract, believing that it was unnecessary because the other audit had verified the proposed rates. There is nothing in the record to indicate whether the rates or any other aspects of the verified audit were in any way similar to this contract audit. Thus, there is no way to gauge the reasonableness of the auditor's conclusion in this regard.

While agencies may ordinarily rely on the advice of DCAA when performing a cost realism analysis, see NKF Eng'g, Inc.; Stanley Assocs., B-232143; B-232143.2, Nov. 21, 1988, 88-2 CPD ¶ 497, this does not mean that contracting officials are thereby insulated from responsibility for error. See PAI, Inc., 67 Comp. Gen. 516 (1988), 88-2 CPD ¶ 36. A contracting officer's determination based on incorrect information is not rendered reasonable because the incorrect information was supplied by another organization such as the DCAA. American Management Sys., Inc.; Dep't of the Army—Recon., supra.

Apart from relying on the DCAA audit information, written and oral, EPA apparently conducted no other cost realism analysis of Dynamac's direct labor rates. For example, the agency did not conduct any independent review of the reasonableness of the proposed rates, question any of the rates in discussions, or seek substantiation of the rates through market surveys or historical cost data from similar contracts. See Sociometrics, Inc., supra; The Warner/Osborn/G&T Joint Venture, B-256641.2, Aug. 23, 1994, 94-2 CPD ¶ 76. Further, the record does not include any of the "other" information on which the evaluators said they relied and, at the time of the agency's cost review, Dynamac had not submitted any information, such as labor market surveys, to support its proposed new hire rates.[10] Contrary to what the evaluators accepted from DCAA, not all of the proposed labor rates represented 1995 Dynamac rates and most of the new hire rates were lower than those proposed for comparable personnel currently employed by Dynamac. In this regard, more than half of the 30 new hires proposed were at the P-3 level—requiring 6-12 years of experience, with a masters degree or equivalent—at a labor rate of less than [deleted] per hour. While the agency maintains that the fringe benefits proposed by Dynamac are competitive, there is no evidence that any meaningful tradeoff analysis was made to determine whether the benefits package offset the low new hire rates. Under these circumstances, placing complete reliance on the DCAA's report was unfounded and unreasonable and does not constitute a meaningful cost realism analysis.

[Footnotes omitted.]

As can be seen from the *Tidewater* and *ManTech* decisions, cost realism analysis can be a daunting task. Although agencies do not have to perform comprehensive analyses of all estimated costs, they must perform sufficient analysis to reasonably determine the most probable costs of performance associated with each of the competing offerors. Defective cost realism analysis is one of the most frequently protested issues—and one of the most frequently sustained protests. Agencies must thoughtfully plan and execute this task in order to pass muster before GAO. Specifically, they must: (1) select appropriate cost elements for analysis; (2) obtain appropriate data from the offerors upon which to base their analyses; and (3) use sound analytical techniques.

Finally, cost realism analysis raises one further question. Look again at Table IV-4. Suppose that the agency decides to select Offeror B for award. That offeror proposed an estimated cost of $1,531,400; the agency determined its most probable cost to be $1,581,400. Should the agency: (1) award the contract at the proposed estimated cost of $1,531,400 and set aside a cash reserve in case the overrun actually occurs, or (2) conduct discussions and ask Offeror B to change its estimated cost to $1,581,400? The FAR is silent on this point; thus, it would seem that either answer is acceptable under the regulations.

105. What is *price realism analysis*?

Agencies ordinarily do not evaluate the realism of proposed fixed prices. However, agencies may fear that an unrealistically low price reflects a lack of understanding of their requirements and could lead to poor performance. Thus, FAR 15.305(a)(1) says, "Cost realism analysis may also be used on fixed-price incentive contracts or, in exceptional cases, on other competitive fixed-price type contracts." FAR 15.404-1(d)(3) says:

> Cost realism analyses may also be used on competitive fixed-price incentive contracts or, in exceptional cases, on other competitive fixed-price-type contracts when new requirements may not be fully understood by competing offerors, there are quality concerns, or past experience indicates that contractors proposed costs have resulted in quality or service shortfalls. Results of the analysis may be used in performance risk assessments and responsibility determinations. However, proposals shall be evaluated using the criteria in the solicitation, and *the offered prices shall not be adjusted as a result of the analysis*. [Italics added.]

While FAR uses the term *cost realism* when talking about this type of evaluation of fixed prices, GAO uses the term *price realism.* GAO summed up its position on price realism in the matter of *RMS Information Systems, Inc.* (B-280521.3, October 21, 1998):

> Generally, cost realism (a measurement of the likely cost of performance in a cost reimbursement contract) is not a factor in the evaluation of proposals when a fixed-price contract is to be awarded, since the government's liability is fixed, and the risk of cost escalation is borne by the contractor. PHP Healthcare Corp.; Sisters of Charity of the Incarnate Word, B-251799 et al., May 4, 1993, 93-1 CPD ¶ 366 at 5. However, since the risk of poor performance when a contractor is forced to provide services at little or no profit is a legitimate concern in evaluating proposals, an agency in its discretion may, as it did here, provide for a price realism analysis in the solicitation of fixed-price proposals. Id. The depth of an agency's price realism analysis is a matter within the sound exercise of the agency's discretion. Family Realty, B-247772, July 6, 1992, 92-2 CPD ¶ 6 at 4.

Price realism is really a nonprice (i.e., technical) evaluation factor; it is not a cost or price evaluation factor in the strict sense. GAO says that price analysis must be used to determine how well an offeror understands the work. When used in that way, it is an assessment of the risk of poor performance. Otherwise, an unrealistically low price must be considered a matter of the offeror's responsibility in accordance with FAR Subpart 9.1. In its decision in *HSG-Holzmann Technischer Services GmbH; HSG-GeBe* (B-274992.2; B-274993.2, February 26, 1997), GAO said:

> [A]n agency may, as here, provide for the use of a price realism analysis in a solicitation for the award of a fixed-price contract *for the limited purpose* of measuring an offeror's understanding of the solicitation's requirements, or to assess the risk inherent in an offeror's approach. PHP Healthcare Corp., B-251933, May 13, 1993, 93-1 CPD ¶ 381. [Footnotes omitted.][Italics added.]

Failure to recognize that price realism is really a nonprice factor has led to a number of sustained protests. See, for example, *Possehn Consulting* (B-278579, January 9, 1998).

It is important to note that FAR 15.404-1(d)(3) says, "[T]he offered prices shall not be adjusted as a result of the analysis." This marks a key difference between the evaluation of proposed estimated costs and the evaluation of proposed fixed prices. When analyzing the reasonableness of proposed estimated costs for cost-reimbursement contracts, an agency must compare the offerors to each other on the basis of the agency's determinations of their most probable costs, not their proposed estimated costs. But agencies may not do this when evaluating the reasonableness of proposed fixed prices; they must determine price reasonableness on the basis of the offerors' proposed prices.

106. What evaluation documentation does the government have to prepare?

FAR 15.305(a) says, in part: "The relative strengths, deficiencies, significant weaknesses, and risks supporting proposal evaluation shall be documented in the contract file." FAR 15.305(a)(3) says:

> Technical evaluation. When tradeoffs are performed (see 15.101-1), the source selection records shall include—
>
> (i) An assessment of each offeror's ability to accomplish the technical requirements; and
>
> (ii) A summary, matrix, or quantitative ranking, along with appropriate supporting narrative, of each technical proposal using the evaluation factors.

FAR 15.308 says:

> The source selection authority's (SSA) decision shall be based on a comparative assessment of proposals against

Safeguarding Info
3,104, 15,207, & 15,306(e)

4,703

FAR 4,801(b) says, p261

p 264 - Destruction of documents
could create an impression
of impropriety & or cast doubt
on the professionalism of
the agency's acquisition personnel

FAR 4.803 (a) (13) requires that Source selection documentation be retained in contract file. Being that FAR 4.805 specifies a retention period of 6yrs & 3mths for contract files, it follows that documentation that went into the source selection decision also be retained with files for that long. The 6yr/3mth period in FAR 4.805 also is relevant to Contract Disputes Act so it's logical that an audit trail should be retained for anything to do with the Source Selection.

52.215-2 4.805-Chart

Typically records are retained for the life of the contract plus 3yrs after date of final payment

> all source selection criteria in the solicitation. While the SSA may use reports and analyses prepared by others, the source selection decision shall represent the SSA's independent judgment. The source selection decision shall be documented, and the documentation shall include the rationale for any business judgments and tradeoffs made or relied on by the SSA, including benefits associated with additional costs. Although the rationale for the selection decision must be documented, that documentation need not quantify the tradeoffs that led to the decision.

Additionally, FAR 4.801(b) says:

> The documentation in the files (see 4.803) shall be sufficient to constitute a complete history of the transaction for the purpose of—
>
> (1) Providing a complete background as a basis for informed decisions at each step in the acquisition process;
>
> (2) Supporting actions taken;
>
> (3) Providing information for reviews and investigations; and
>
> (4) Furnishing essential facts in the event of litigation or congressional inquiries.

Agencies must document each step in the evaluation process: (1) the assessments of individual offerors and their offers against the evaluation factors, (2) the comparison and ranking of offerors and their offers, and (3) the determination of which offeror and its offer represent the best value to the government. The documentation should take the form of memoranda, which may be supplemented with evaluator worksheets and notes.

The documentation of Step 1 should demonstrate how well each offeror and its offer performed on each of the relevant evaluation factors. This documentation should consist of statements of verifiable fact and of reasonable opinion, as appropriate.

The documentation of Step 2 should reveal how each offeror and its offer compared to each of the other offerors and their offers in terms of its performance on each of the relevant evaluation factors. It should describe the difference between the offeror and its offer and each of the other offerors and their offers on each of the factors, and state whether the offeror and its offer were considered better than, equal to, or worse than each of the others. If the reason for any conclusion of relative merit is not obvious, the documentation should explain the basis for the conclusion. It should show how the offerors were ranked, from best to worst. Tables should be used to make such comparisons and conclusions as clear as possible.

The documentation of step 3 should explain why the offeror selected for award is considered a better value than any of the other offerors. This should be explained in terms of the pros and cons described in the documentation of steps 1 and 2 and in terms of assessments of net overall value, but need not be explained in monetary terms. (See FAR 15.308.) It is important that this documentation display conscious and reasonable consideration of the differences among the offerors and their offers.

Air Force Mandatory Procedure MP5315.3, dated 17 May 2005, specifies the documentation of the selection decision as follows:

> The Source Selection Decision Document is required and is the single document that provides insight into the Source Selection Authority's integrated assessment and resultant decision. It is important that this document be written clearly and in a manner that allows it to stand on its own without need of referencing other documents. Paragraphs should be written in a concise manner and should flow logically. Ensure that the source selection decision is consistent with the evaluation factors and that each conclusion or decision in the Source Selection

> Decision Document is directly linked to those evaluation factors. In addition, the Source Selection Decision Document must compare aspects of the most competitive offers against each other; e.g., "I have decided Contractor A's approach to factor XX was better than [Contractor B's][all other offerors'] because Contractor A proposed, discussed, resolved, identified, possesses, or whatever." All pertinent information including necessary proprietary information must be included in the Source Selection Decision Document. The Source Selection Decision Document must be fully traceable to the evaluation criteria (Section M or equivalent provision of the solicitation), the evaluation briefing charts, and the PAR [Proposal Analysis Report].

Clearly, the greater the number of evaluation factors used by an agency and the greater the number of offerors included in the comparisons, the more complex and voluminous the evaluation documentation will have to be.

The FAR does not require that individual evaluators document their personal findings and opinions. While FAR 4.801(b) could be interpreted as requiring the preparation and retention of such documentation, GAO has not found the lack of such documentation or the destruction of such documentation to be, in and of itself, grounds for sustaining a protest. Thus, a single memorandum would be sufficient to document a source selection decision as long as it contained all the information required by the FAR. For example, in GAO's protest decision in the matter of *Southwest Marine, Inc.; American Systems Engineering Corporation* (B-265865.3; B-265865.4; January 23, 1996), the Navy destroyed the documentation prepared by individual evaluators. GAO called the Navy's action "improper," but denied the protest on the ground that the Navy's remaining documentation was adequate to support its decision. The protest decision was based on the requirements in FAR 15.608 before the FAR Part 15 Rewrite in 1997. Those requirements were substantially the same as the requirements after the Rewrite.

Although the Navy's destruction of the evaluators' documentation in *Southwest Marine* did not result in a sustained protest, it was extremely unwise. Not only can such conduct create an impression of impropriety, but it can increase the cost of defending a protest if it means that the agency's contracting officer and lawyers have to reconstruct the evaluation. It can certainly cast doubt on the professionalism of the agency's acquisition personnel.

PART V
Competitive Negotiations

The questions in this part address the rules about *exchanges* of information between the government and offerors after the receipt of proposals—*clarifications, communications,* and *discussions*—including both required and prohibited practices. They also address the process of establishing a competitive range and the process of soliciting final proposal revisions.

107. What can an agency talk to offerors about after it receives the proposals?

An agency can talk to offerors about almost anything, even after it receives the proposals, but such talks (including written exchanges) may have procedural consequences. The rules governing exchanges of information between an agency and offerors after the receipt of proposals are in FAR 15.306(a), (b), (d), and (e). These rules establish three categories of exchanges of information: *clarifications, communications,* and *discussions*. These categories are distinguished by their timing and content. The relevant FAR passages read as follows:

> **15.306 Exchanges with offerors after receipt of proposals.**
>
> (a) Clarifications and award without discussions. (1) Clarifications are limited exchanges, between the Government and offerors, that may occur when award without discussions is contemplated.

(2) If award will be made without conducting discussions, offerors may be given the opportunity to clarify certain aspects of proposals (e.g., the relevance of an offeror's past performance information and adverse past performance information to which the offeror has not previously had an opportunity to respond) or to resolve minor or clerical errors.

(3) Award may be made without discussions if the solicitation states that the Government intends to evaluate proposals and make award without discussions. If the solicitation contains such a notice and the Government determines it is necessary to conduct discussions, the rationale for doing so shall be documented in the contract file (see the provision at 52.215-1) (10 U.S.C. 2305(b)(4)(A)(ii) and 41 U.S.C. 253b(d)(1)(B)).

(b) Communications with offerors before establishment of the competitive range. Communications are exchanges, between the Government and offerors, after receipt of proposals, leading to establishment of the competitive range. If a competitive range is to be established, these communications—

(1) Shall be limited to the offerors described in paragraphs (b)(1)(i) and (b)(1)(ii) of this section and—

(i) Shall be held with offerors whose past performance information is the determining factor preventing them from being placed within the competitive range. Such communications shall address adverse past performance information to which an offeror has not had a prior opportunity to respond; and

(ii) May only be held with those offerors (other than offerors under paragraph (b)(1)(i) of this section) whose exclusion from, or inclusion in, the competitive range is uncertain;

(2) May be conducted to enhance Government understanding of proposals; allow reasonable interpretation of

the proposal; or facilitate the Government's evaluation process. Such communications shall not be used to cure proposal deficiencies or material omissions, materially alter the technical or cost elements of the proposal, and/or otherwise revise the proposal. Such communications may be considered in rating proposals for the purpose of establishing the competitive range;

(3) Are for the purpose of addressing issues that must be explored to determine whether a proposal should be placed in the competitive range. Such communications shall not provide an opportunity for the offeror to revise its proposal, but may address—

(i) Ambiguities in the proposal or other concerns (e.g., perceived deficiencies, weaknesses, errors, omissions, or mistakes (see 14.407)); and

(ii) Information relating to relevant past performance; and

(4) Shall address adverse past performance information to which the offeror has not previously had an opportunity to comment.

* * *

(d) Exchanges with offerors after establishment of the competitive range. Negotiations are exchanges, in either a competitive or sole source environment, between the Government and offerors, that are undertaken with the intent of allowing the offeror to revise its proposal. These negotiations may include bargaining. Bargaining includes persuasion, alteration of assumptions and positions, give-and-take, and may apply to price, schedule, technical requirements, type of contract, or other terms of a proposed contract. When negotiations are conducted in a competitive acquisition, they take place after establishment of the competitive range and are called discussions.

(1) Discussions are tailored to each offeror's proposal, and shall be conducted by the contracting officer with each offeror within the competitive range.

(2) The primary objective of discussions is to maximize the Government's ability to obtain best value, based on the requirement and the evaluation factors set forth in the solicitation.

(3) At a minimum, the contracting officer shall, subject to paragraphs (d)(5) and (e) of this section and 15.307(a), indicate to, or discuss with, each offeror still being considered for award, deficiencies, significant weaknesses, and adverse past performance information to which the offeror has not yet had an opportunity to respond. The contracting officer is also encouraged to discuss other aspects of its proposal (such as cost, price, technical approach, past performance, and terms and conditions) that could, in the opinion of the contracting officer, be altered or explained to enhance materially the proposal's potential for award. However, the contracting officer is not required to discuss every area where the proposal could be improved. The scope and extent of discussions are a matter of contracting officer judgment.

(4) In discussing other aspects of the proposal, the Government may, in situations where the solicitation stated that evaluation credit would be given for technical solutions exceeding any mandatory minimums, negotiate with offerors for increased performance beyond any mandatory minimums, and the Government may suggest to offerors that have exceeded any mandatory minimums (in ways that are not integral to the design), that their proposals would be more competitive if the excesses were removed and the offered price decreased.

(5) If, after discussions have begun, an offeror originally in the competitive range is no longer considered to be among the most highly rated offerors being considered for award, that offeror may be eliminated from the competitive range whether or not all material aspects of the

proposal have been discussed, or whether or not the offeror has been afforded an opportunity to submit a proposal revision (see 15.307(a) and 15.503(a)(1)).

(e) Limits on exchanges. Government personnel involved in the acquisition shall not engage in conduct that—

(1) Favors one offeror over another;

(2) Reveals an offeror's technical solution, including unique technology, innovative and unique uses of commercial items, or any information that would compromise an offeror's intellectual property to another offeror;

(3) Reveals an offeror's price without that offeror's permission. However, the contracting officer may inform an offeror that its price is considered by the Government to be too high, or too low, and reveal the results of the analysis supporting that conclusion. It is also permissible, at the Government's discretion, to indicate to all offerors the cost or price that the Government's price analysis, market research, and other reviews have identified as reasonable (41 U.S.C. 423(h)(1)(2));

(4) Reveals the names of individuals providing reference information about an offeror's past performance; or

(5) Knowingly furnishes source selection information in violation of 3.104 and 41 U.S.C. 423(h)(1)(2).

The key to understanding these rules is to know that if, in exchanging information with an offeror after the receipt of proposals, an agency goes beyond *clarification* [see FAR 15.306(a)] and engages in *discussions* [see FAR 15.306(d)], it cannot then make an award without discussions. Instead, it must: (1) establish a competitive range; (2) conduct discussions with all offerors in the competitive range; (3) give each offeror in the competitive range a chance to revise its proposal; and (4) evaluate the revised proposals. Clearly, agencies that would like to award a contract without conducting discussions must take care not to cross the line between *clarifications* and *discussions*.

CLARIFICATIONS DISTINGUISHED FROM *COMMUNICATIONS*

The FAR does not clearly distinguish between *clarifications* and *communications*. It may be that the persons who wrote the regulation had some distinction in mind, but what that might have been is hard to determine based on the language of the regulation itself. What is the difference between giving an offeror "the opportunity to clarify certain aspects of proposals. . .or to resolve minor or clerical errors" [FAR 15.306(a)(2)], and communicating to "enhance Government understanding of proposals; allow reasonable interpretation of the proposal; or facilitate the Government's evaluation process" [FAR 15.306(b)(2)]? In neither case is the offeror to be allowed to revise its proposal, since that may be done only during *discussions*. [See FAR 15.306(a)(3) and 15.306(b)(2) and (3).]

CLARIFICATIONS AND *COMMUNICATIONS* DISTINGUISHED FROM DISCUSSIONS

The distinction between *clarifications* and *communications*, on the one hand, and *discussions* on the other, is that during discussions the government asks or allows the offerors to revise their proposals. Since discussions are also called negotiations, and since FAR 15.306(d) says that negotiations are bargaining sessions, it appears that discussions are exchanges in which the government asks or allows the offerors to change their *offers*—i.e., the promises they have made that would be binding after contract award. After all, why would the government "bargain" about something that would be of no legal consequence during contract performance?

Thus, it seems that as long as the contracting officer does not allow an offeror to change its *offer*—that is, its promises—then he or she has not engaged in discussions and need not allow offerors to submit final proposal revisions. As a general rule, statements pertaining to an offeror's capability to perform, such as experience and past performance, are not promises and are not a part of the offer. However, it is by no means clear that this interpretation of FAR 15.306 is correct.

LIMITS ON THE CONTENT OF EXCHANGES

Breaking the rules in FAR 15.306(e) about limits on exchanges could have serious consequences. For example, unfair treatment of any offeror could result in a sustained protest; disclosing an offeror's "technical solution" might violate the Procurement Integrity Act or the Trade Secrets Act, making the violator vulnerable to criminal prosecution.

108. What are *exchanges*?

The term *exchanges* refers to exchanges of information between the government and an offeror, either orally or in writing. The term came into use with the FAR Part 15 Rewrite. There are two broad categories of exchanges: (1) exchanges with industry before receipt of proposals; and (2) exchanges with offerors after receipt of proposals. The rules about exchanges before receipt of proposals are in FAR 15.201. The rules about exchanges after receipt of proposals are in FAR 15.306.

Exchanges before the receipt of proposals include market research, presolicitation notices (e.g., sources-sought synopses), presolicitation and preproposal conferences, requests for information, draft RFPs, site visits, and one-on-one meetings. These are conducted to notify industry about an upcoming procurement, obtain information from industry about products or services, or obtain industry comments before the completion of a specification or statement of work.

Exchanges after the receipt of proposals are divided into three categories, depending on their timing and content: *clarifications, communications,* and *discussions. Clarifications* are exchanges during the evaluation of initial proposals or proposal revisions that are conducted to "clarify certain aspects of a proposal. . .or to resolve minor or clerical errors." *Communications* are exchanges during the evaluation of initial proposals that are conducted to "enhance Government understanding of proposals; allow reasonable interpretation of a proposal; or facilitate the Government's evaluation of proposals" to determine which offerors are in the competitive range. *Discussions* are exchanges in which the government negotiates, i.e., bargains for better terms or permits an offeror to revise its proposal.

109. What are *clarifications,* and what rules apply to them?

FAR 15.306(a) defines the term *clarifications* and prescribes rules for their conduct as follows:

> Clarifications and award without discussions. (1) Clarifications are limited exchanges, between the Government and offerors, that may occur when award without discussions is contemplated.
>
> (2) If award will be made without conducting discussions, offerors may be given the opportunity to clarify certain aspects of proposals (e.g., the relevance of an offeror's past performance information and adverse past performance information to which the offeror has not previously had an opportunity to respond) or to resolve minor or clerical errors.

> (3) Award may be made without discussions if the solicitation states that the Government intends to evaluate proposals and make award without discussions. If the solicitation contains such a notice and the Government determines it is necessary to conduct discussions, the rationale for doing so shall be documented in the contract file (see the provision at 52.215-1) (10 U.S.C. 2305(b)(4)(A)(ii) and 41 U.S.C. 253b(d)(1)(B)).

The key to understanding this rule is to understand the difference between *clarifications* and *discussions*, since if an agency goes too far when conducting clarifications and crosses the line into discussions, then it may no longer make an award without discussions; it must then determine a competitive range, conduct discussions, and permit proposal revisions.

FAR 15.306(d) defines *discussions* as follows:

> *Exchanges with offerors after establishment of the competitive range.* Negotiations are exchanges, in either a competitive or sole source environment, between the Government and offerors, that are undertaken with the intent of allowing the offeror to revise its proposal. These negotiations may include bargaining. Bargaining includes persuasion, alteration of assumptions and positions, give-and-take, and may apply to price, schedule, technical requirements, type of contract, or other terms of a proposed contract. When negotiations are conducted in a competitive acquisition, they take place after establishment of the competitive range and are called discussions.

Discussions are bargaining sessions in which offerors are allowed or encouraged to revise their proposals in order to improve the bargain that they are offering the government. Clarifications, on the other hand, make an existing proposal clearer but do not change its terms, except to eliminate minor or clerical errors. Thus, if in seeking clarification, an agency gives an offeror a chance to change the terms of its proposal, then it will have crossed the line between clarifications and discussions.

GAO's protest decision in *Development Alternatives, Inc.* (B-279920, August 6, 1998) illustrates the distinction between clarification and discussion. In that case, which is based on the language of the FAR before the FAR Part 15 Rewrite took effect, the Agency for International Development conducted discussions and asked the offerors in the competitive range to submit written revised proposals, to be followed by oral presentations. The protester complained that during one offeror's oral presentation the agency actually conducted a second round of discussions; the protester demanded the chance to submit another revised proposal. GAO denied the protest, saying:

> DAI also alleges that, notwithstanding the agency's intent to the contrary, the questions asked during the oral interview constituted discussions. As a result, DAI argues, the agency was required to request second BAFOs [best and final offers] from the offerors on the competitive range. FAR § 15.611(a) (June 1997).
>
> As set forth in FAR § 15.601 (June 1997), discussions "means any oral or written communication between the Government and an offeror, (other than communications conducted for the purpose of minor clarification) whether or not initiated by the Government, that (a) [i]nvolves information essential for determining the acceptability of a proposal; or (b) [p]rovides the offeror an opportunity to revise or modify its proposal." The acid test of whether discussions have been held is whether it can be said that an offeror was provided the opportunity to revise or modify its proposal. BE, Inc.; PAI Corp., B-277978, B-277978.2, Dec. 16, 1997, 98-1 CPD ¶ 80 at 5.
>
> Whether or not the oral presentation constituted part of the BAFO such that a second round of BAFOs was not required, see Labat-Anderson Inc., B-246071.4, Oct. 9,

> 1992, 92-2 CPD ¶ 244 at 11 n.4, the record shows that the questions asked are in the nature of clarifications—they merely request additional detail concerning information already presented in DAI's proposal as revised by its written BAFO. BE, Inc.; PAI Corp., supra, at 5-6. For example, in its BAFO, DAI reduced by ten the number of Bosnian lending professionals that it would use under the contract. During the oral interview the firm was asked to describe any changes that this reduction would require in the way the lending staff was deployed and organized. Other questions included requests for elaboration on the reasons for selecting particular personnel and on arguments made and positions taken in the BAFO to support a particular approach. Contrary to DAI's position, the fact that some of its scores changed as a result of the oral interview does not show that it was allowed to revise its proposal, but that its explanations of what was already proposed became more clear, at times to the firm's detriment and at times to its benefit.

Thus, despite the fact that the offeror had provided the government with more information, the exchange did not constitute discussions. This decision illustrates the importance of the distinction between the *offer* and the *other information* in a proposal.

110. What are *communications*, and what rules apply to them?

FAR 15.306(b) defines the term *communications* and prescribes rules for their conduct as follows:

> Communications with offerors before establishment of the competitive range. Communications are exchanges, between the Government and offerors, after receipt of proposals, leading to establishment of the competitive range. If a competitive range is to be established, these communications—

(1) Shall be limited to the offerors described in paragraphs (b)(1)(i) and (b)(1)(ii) of this section and—

(i) Shall be held with offerors whose past performance information is the determining factor preventing them from being placed within the competitive range. Such communications shall address adverse past performance information to which an offeror has not had a prior opportunity to respond; and

(ii) May only be held with those offerors (other than offerors under paragraph (b)(1)(i) of this section) whose exclusion from, or inclusion in, the competitive range is uncertain;

(2) May be conducted to enhance Government understanding of proposals; allow reasonable interpretation of the proposal; or facilitate the Government's evaluation process. Such communications shall not be used to cure proposal deficiencies or material omissions, materially alter the technical or cost elements of the proposal, and/ or otherwise revise the proposal. Such communications may be considered in rating proposals for the purpose of establishing the competitive range;

(3) Are for the purpose of addressing issues that must be explored to determine whether a proposal should be placed in the competitive range. Such communications shall not provide an opportunity for the offeror to revise its proposal, but may address—

(i) Ambiguities in the proposal or other concerns (e.g., perceived deficiencies, weaknesses, errors, omissions, or mistakes (see 14.407)); and

(ii) Information relating to relevant past performance; and

(4) Shall address adverse past performance information to which the offeror has not previously had an opportunity to comment.

Unlike discussions, communications do not give an offeror a chance to revise its proposal; thus, communications are like clarifications in that they let an offeror provide more information about information that has already been submitted. Indeed, despite the FAR's lengthier coverage of communications, it is difficult to see any significant difference between communications and clarifications. The main differences appear to be that if the government is going to award the contract without discussions, then such exchanges of information are called *clarifications*, but if the government is going to conduct discussions, then such exchanges are called *communications*; also, clarifications before award without discussions are optional, but communications before the establishment of the competitive range are mandatory when an offeror's inclusion is in doubt because of "adverse" past performance information.

If the government would like to make an award without discussions, then crossing the line between clarifications and discussions when talking to an offeror is a mistake, because it precludes award without discussions. However, crossing the line between communications and discussions would appear to be inconsequential, since the agency is conducting communications because it has already decided to conduct discussions. Thus, no harm, no foul.

What is interesting—and strange—about the clarification and communication rules is that if an agency is going to award without discussions, then it *may* give an offeror a chance to address adverse past performance information, but it does not have to do so [see FAR 15.306(a)(2)]. GAO confirmed this interpretation of the FAR in its decision in *Rohmann Services, Inc.* (B-280154.2, November 16, 1998), in which it held:

> Rohmann [the protester] also argues that the Air Force should have communicated with the firm concerning its performance, even without conducting discussions. Sup-

> plemental Comments at ¶¶ 25-27. In this regard, Rohmann refers to FAR § 15.306(a), which was amended by the Federal Acquisition Circular No. 97-02, which includes the Part 15 rewrite. FAR § 15.306(a)(2) which concerns "Clarifications and award without discussions," states:
>
> > If award will be made without conducting discussions, offerors may be given the opportunity to clarify certain aspects of proposals (e.g., the relevance of an offeror's past performance information and adverse past performance information to which the offeror has not previously had an opportunity to respond) or to resolve minor or clerical errors.
>
> Apparently, it is Rohmann's position that this provision requires a contracting officer to conduct "clarifications" with any offeror where the agency intends to rely on adverse past performance information on which the offeror has not previously had an opportunity to respond. Supplemental Comments at ¶ 27.
>
> We read no such "requirement" into FAR § 15.306(a)(2), which states that "offerors may be given the opportunity to clarify certain aspects of proposals" including past performance information (emphasis added). Similar to the decision whether or not to hold discussions, under the above-quoted language, we think a contracting officer has broad discretion to decide whether to communicate with a firm concerning its performance history. We will review the exercise of such discretion to ensure that it was reasonably based on the particular circumstances of the procurement.

However, the FAR says that if an agency is going to conduct communications, then it *must* disclose adverse past performance information to an offeror and let the offeror tell its side of the story if the adverse past performance would keep the offeror out of the competitive range [see FAR 15.306(b)(1)(i)]. It is unclear why the FAR Council decided that an exchange about adverse past performance information should be optional before award without discussions, but mandatory before the establishment of the competitive range.

111. What is the *competitive range,* and how is it established?

The *competitive range* is the set of "the most highly rated offerors" among the offerors that submitted proposals in response to the RFP. The rules for establishing the competitive range are in FAR 15.306(c), which reads as follows:

> Competitive range. (1) Agencies shall evaluate all proposals in accordance with 15.305(a), and, if discussions are to be conducted, establish the competitive range. Based on the ratings of each proposal against all evaluation criteria, the contracting officer shall establish a competitive range comprised of all of the most highly rated proposals, unless the range is further reduced for purposes of efficiency pursuant to paragraph (c)(2) of this section.
>
> (2) After evaluating all proposals in accordance with 15.305(a) and paragraph (c)(1) of this section, the contracting officer may determine that the number of most highly rated proposals that might otherwise be included in the competitive range exceeds the number at which an efficient competition can be conducted. Provided the solicitation notifies offerors that the competitive range can be limited for purposes of efficiency (see 52.215-1(f)(4)), the contracting officer may limit the number of proposals in the competitive range to the greatest number that will permit an efficient competition among the most highly rated proposals (10 U.S.C. 2305(b)(4) and 41 U.S.C. 253b(d)).
>
> (3) If the contracting officer, after complying with paragraph (d)(3) of this section, decides that an offeror's proposal should no longer be included in the competitive range, the proposal shall be eliminated from consid-

> eration for award. Written notice of this decision shall be provided to unsuccessful offerors in accordance with 15.503.
>
> (4) Offerors excluded or otherwise eliminated from the competitive range may request a debriefing (see 15.505 and 15.506).

After an agency evaluates the proposals in accordance with the terms of the RFP and FAR 15.305, the agency must compare them and rank them from best to worst. The contracting officer then must select "the most highly rated"; these are in the competitive range, and the others are notified that their proposals will receive no further consideration. The contracting officer then invites the offerors in the competitive range to discussions. If the contracting officer thinks that the competitive range contains too many firms, FAR 15.306(c)(2) allows him or her to eliminate some of the most highly rated firms "for purposes of efficiency."

The FAR provides no criterion for inclusion in the competitive range other than the phrase "most highly rated," and the question is how many offerors to include. But in the background material that accompanied the publication of the FAR Part 15 Rewrite in the *Federal Register* on September 30, 1977 (62 Fed. Reg. 51224), the FAR Council hinted that three was the right number. At one point in its regulatory flexibility analysis, commenting on public responses to the competitive range provisions in early drafts of the FAR Part 15 Rewrite, the FAR Council said:

> We also note that comments received from Government agencies indicate that award is nearly always made to one of the three most highly rated offerors in the competitive range. Therefore, including an offeror that is not most highly rated in the competitive range would not likely impact the final award decision. This final rule ensures that offerors are advised early on that their competitive

> position does not merit additional expense in a largely futile attempt to secure the contract.

62 Fed. Reg. 51224, 51226.

At another point, the FAR Council said:

> [A]s noted above, public comments from agencies indicate that awards are nearly always made to one of the three most highly rated proposals going into the competitive range. This is true even when small businesses win full and open competitions. The incidence of award to an offeror other than one of the three such proposals is so small that it does not support keeping any business, particularly a small business with limited bid and proposal resources, in a competition that the business has virtually no chance of winning.

62 Fed. Reg. 51224, 51228.

Hint, hint. The FAR Council probably did not say "the *three* most highly rated proposals" in FAR 15.306(c)(1) because they were under political pressure from the small business lobby during the preparation of the FAR Part 15 Rewrite. That lobby was afraid that contracting officers would use the competitive range process to eliminate small businesses from further competition. In any event, "three" sounds like a sensible number, although contracting officers should not be arbitrary: If other offerors are in close contention with the third, the contracting officer should include them in the competitive range as well.

The emphasis in FAR 15.306(c) is on exclusion, rather than inclusion. The pre-Rewrite version of the competitive range rule, which had appeared in FAR 15.609(a), emphasized the need to keep firms in the competition and said that when there was doubt about a firm's chances of winning the contract, the firm should be included. That was often referred to as the "when in doubt, keep them in" rule. The new rule could be described as "when in doubt, throw them out!"

GAO has confirmed that it is permissible to include only one firm in the competitive range. For example, in *SDS Petroleum Products, Inc.* (B-280430, September 1, 1998), the contracting officer eliminated all but one proposal from the competitive range. SDS had the second-highest score, and it argued that under the "most highly rated proposals" rule, it should have been included in the competitive range, even though its score was significantly lower than the firm that had been included (note that "proposals" is plural). GAO denied the protest, saying:

> SDS seems to argue that, no matter how low its proposal's evaluation rating relative to Tiger's, the agency was required to retain its proposal in the competitive range since it was the second-highest rated. We find no merit in this argument, which is apparently based on the recent rewrite of Part 15 of the Federal Acquisition Regulation (FAR) that changed the language governing competitive range determinations. The earlier language, FAR § 15.609(a) (June 1997), stated that the competitive range "shall include all proposals that have a reasonable chance of being selected for award" and that "[w]hen there is doubt as to whether a proposal is in the competitive range, the proposal should be included." The current language, which governs this procurement, states, "Based on the ratings of each proposal against all evaluation criteria, the contracting officer shall establish a competitive range comprised of all of the most highly rated proposals, unless the range is further reduced for purposes of efficiency pursuant to paragraph (c)(2) of this section." FAR § 15.306(c)(1) (FAC 97-02). We do not read the revised language to require agencies to retain in the competitive range a proposal that the agency reasonably concludes has no realistic prospect of award, even if that proposal is, as here, the second-highest rated proposal.

> The explanatory preamble published at the time the final version of the FAR Part 15 rewrite was issued makes clear that the intent of the revised language was to permit a competitive range more limited than under the prior "reasonable chance of being selected for award" standard. That preamble states that the drafters had elected to require contracting officers to retain in the competitive range "only" the most highly rated offers rather than include in that range the potentially broader range of proposals that could be viewed as having a reasonable chance of award. 62 Fed. Reg. 51,224, 51,226 (1997). Specifically, the preamble stated that the new language would "ensure that offerors with little probability of success . . . are advised early on that their competitive position does not merit additional expense in a largely futile attempt to secure the contract." Id.
>
> Accordingly, we conclude that the Part 15 rewrite does not require that agencies retain in the competitive range a proposal that is determined to have no reasonable prospect of award simply to avoid a competitive range of one. We have long held that there is nothing inherently improper in a competitive range of one, Cobra Techs., Inc., supra, at 3, and we do not view the Part 15 rewrite as effecting a change in that regard; conducting discussions and requesting BAFOs from an offeror with no reasonable chance of award would benefit neither the offeror nor the government. See 62 Fed. Reg. 51,226 (retaining marginal offers in competitive range imposes additional and largely futile effort and cost on government and industry).

112. What does an agency have to talk about during discussions?

FAR 15.306(d) and (e) define the term *discussions* and prescribe rules for their conduct as follows:

> (d) Exchanges with offerors after establishment of the competitive range. Negotiations are exchanges, in either

a competitive or sole source environment, between the Government and offerors, that are undertaken with the intent of allowing the offeror to revise its proposal. These negotiations may include bargaining. Bargaining includes persuasion, alteration of assumptions and positions, give-and-take, and may apply to price, schedule, technical requirements, type of contract, or other terms of a proposed contract. When negotiations are conducted in a competitive acquisition, they take place after establishment of the competitive range and are called discussions.

(1) Discussions are tailored to each offeror's proposal, and shall be conducted by the contracting officer with each offeror within the competitive range.

(2) The primary objective of discussions is to maximize the Government's ability to obtain best value, based on the requirement and the evaluation factors set forth in the solicitation.

(3) At a minimum, the contracting officer shall, subject to paragraphs (d)(5) and (e) of this section and 15.307(a), indicate to, or discuss with, each offeror still being considered for award, deficiencies, significant weaknesses, and adverse past performance information to which the offeror has not yet had an opportunity to respond. The contracting officer is also encouraged to discuss other aspects of its proposal (such as cost, price, technical approach, past performance, and terms and conditions) that could, in the opinion of the contracting officer, be altered or explained to enhance materially the proposal's potential for award. However, the contracting officer is not required to discuss every area where the proposal could be improved. The scope and extent of discussions are a matter of contracting officer judgment.

(4) In discussing other aspects of the proposal, the Government may, in situations where the solicitation stated that evaluation credit would be given for technical solutions exceeding any mandatory minimums, negotiate

with offerors for increased performance beyond any mandatory minimums, and the Government may suggest to offerors that have exceeded any mandatory minimums (in ways that are not integral to the design), that their proposals would be more competitive if the excesses were removed and the offered price decreased.

(e) Limits on exchanges. Government personnel involved in the acquisition shall not engage in conduct that—

(1) Favors one offeror over another;

(2) Reveals an offeror's technical solution, including unique technology, innovative and unique uses of commercial items, or any information that would compromise an offeror's intellectual property to another offeror;

(3) Reveals an offeror's price without that offeror's permission. However, the contracting officer may inform an offeror that its price is considered by the Government to be too high, or too low, and reveal the results of the analysis supporting that conclusion. It is also permissible, at the Government's discretion, to indicate to all offerors the cost or price that the Government's price analysis, market research, and other reviews have identified as reasonable (41 U.S.C. 423(h)(1)(2));

(4) Reveals the names of individuals providing reference information about an offeror's past performance; or

(5) Knowingly furnishes source selection information in violation of 3.104 and 41 U.S.C. 423(h)(1)(2).

Thus, discussions are bargaining sessions in which offerors are given the chance to improve their proposals.

The heart of the discussions rule is in the first sentence of subparagraph (d)(3). The contracting officer must tell each offeror in the competitive range about deficiencies, significant weaknesses, and adverse past performance information to which it has not had a chance to respond.

GAO has expressed its requirements for discussions in several protest decisions, most definitively in *Department of the Navy—Reconsideration* (B-250158, May 28, 1993):

> As reflected in FAR § 15.610, CICA [the Competition in Contracting Act of 1984] effectively requires agencies to point out weaknesses, deficiencies or excesses in proposals necessary for an offeror to have a reasonable chance of being selected for award. . . .Also, while agencies generally must lead offerors into the areas of their proposals that require amplification or correction for them to have a reasonable chance of award, there is no obligation to afford all-encompassing discussions or to discuss every element of a technically acceptable competitive range proposal.

So, how should an agency go about conducting discussions? What contracting officers ought to do is disclose the agency's evaluation of each offeror's proposal by giving the offeror the complete evaluation report that pertains to its proposal and asking the offeror to point out any errors of fact or reasoning on the part of the evaluators. Second, the contracting officer should tell each offeror about changes that the agency would like the offeror to make in its offer, if any, without disclosing the contents of any other offers. If agencies would take these steps, they would eliminate any possibility of a sustained protest for failing to conduct meaningful discussions.

But for some reason contracting officers seem to worry more about saying too much than about saying too little, despite the fact that they are much more likely to lose a protest by saying too little. Under the current rules, there is no good reason to hold any information back from an offeror, since by protesting to GAO the offeror's lawyer can obtain a protective order and get every scrap of paper generated by the agency during proposal evaluation. Thus, the wisest and fairest course of action is to disclose the entire evaluation report and let the offeror point out errors in it or modify its proposal accordingly.

113. What is *technical leveling,* and what are the rules about it?

Technical leveling is an obsolete term that appeared in FAR 15.610(d) before the FAR Part 15 Rewrite; the rule read as follows:

> The contracting officer and other Government personnel involved shall not engage in technical leveling (i.e., helping an offeror to bring its proposal up to the level of other proposals through successive rounds of discussion, such as by pointing out weaknesses resulting from an offeror's lack of diligence, competence, or inventiveness in preparing the proposal).

Technical leveling was sometimes referred to as "coaching." The FAR Part 15 Rewrite eliminated the express prohibition against technical leveling. [See *Dynacs Engineering Company, Inc.* (B-284234; B-284234.2; B-2842343, March 17, 2000).]

The concept of technical leveling emerged in the 1960s, when aerospace defense firms complained about the way that the Department of Defense (DoD) was conducting source selections for weapon development programs. They claimed that DoD officials were providing offerors that had submitted weak proposals with information from better proposals (technical transfusion) to make the weaker ones "technically level" with the better ones, so that award could be made to the technically acceptable offeror with the lowest price. A December 1970 report by the Aerospace Industries Association described the problem this way:

> Existing source selection policy emphasizes that "... a manageable but competitive number of final proposals for the selection process" is assured. One of the techniques used to achieve this goal is to allow proposers the opportunity to correct deficiencies in their technical approach by having members of the proposal evaluation team engage in a technical discussion of purported deficiencies; this results in technical upgrading all or most proposals to the technically acceptable level. Technical transfusion is accomplished in one of two ways: (a) specific transfer of an idea or concept from one proposer to another or (b) by giving a government developed or owned idea to only some of the competitors. The end result of this technical leveling and technical transfusion is technical qualification of an adequate number of contractors for the final selection process. Two things happen as a result of this practice: (a) the initially lower rated technical proposals are essentially upgraded, and (b) contractors tend to protect their clever, inventive and unique concepts and ideas by only partial disclosure in initial proposals or by technical disclosure at a depth which is inadequate for proper evaluation. Most of the aerospace industry believes that this technical upgrading and technical transfusion is detrimental to the competitive process in that final technical negotiations tend to become an illegitimate cost auction since most bidders end with almost equal scores on their upgraded technical proposals.

(Aerospace Industries Association, *Essential Technical Steps and Related Uncertainties in DOD Weapon Systems Development, Phase IV Final Report,* December 1970, pp. 52–53.)

When the first edition of the FAR was published in September 1983, it prohibited technical leveling and technical transfusion. (Auctioning had been prohibited for many years prior to publication of the FAR.) The prohibition was regulatory, not statutory. Fear of technical leveling has led many contracting officers to be excessively cautious about what they say during discussions. This has resulted in sustained protests based on failure to conduct meaningful discussions. For example, in *Global Industries, Inc.* (B-270592.2, March 29, 1996), GAO sustained a protest because the agency had failed to conduct meaningful discussions. Specifically, the agency had not informed the protester about certain weaknesses in its proposal because it had feared that such discussions would have been technical leveling. GAO reported:

> [T]he agency maintains that any weaknesses with regard to the evaluation factor aesthetics, comfort and marketability were inappropriate topics for discussions in that such matters generally reflected the inventiveness of each offeror in the development of its products, and raising such issues would involve the agency in "product development." The agency maintains that if such weaknesses had been brought to Global's attention, the agency would have been required to discuss similar "product development" matters with other offerors, and that this would have constituted technical leveling.
>
> We first note that while technical leveling is defined by FAR § 15.610(d) as helping an offeror bring its proposal up to the level of other proposals "through successive rounds of discussions," Global had only a single round of discussions during which the agency's serious concerns were not identified. We also fail to see how labeling the concern a "product development" matter is of any consequence with respect to the question of whether discussions were required.

In *Department of the Navy—Reconsideration* (B-250158.4, May 28, 1993), GAO sustained a protest because the agency had not disclosed weaknesses in a proposal. In that case, GAO said:

> [I]n our view, the agency's limited technical discussions were not justified by concerns as to technical transfusion or technical leveling. . . .[T]echnical leveling was not an apparent concern since it only arises as an issue where, as a result of successive rounds of discussions, the agency

> helped an offeror to bring its proposal up to the level of the other proposals. Successive rounds of discussions were not contemplated here. Moreover, the weaknesses in Eldyne's proposal were not inherent in Eldyne's approach nor would they have involved extensive revision to resolve.

In *CBIS Fed., Inc.* [71 Comp. Gen. 319 (B-245844.2)], GAO held that technical leveling could not occur if there was only one round of discussions, saying:

> CBIS [the protester] bases a significant portion of its argument that the agency's discussions with Telesec constituted leveling on its view that leveling may occur at any point during discussions. The protester contends, for example, that a number of questions put to the awardee in the first round of discussions resulted in technical leveling. In our view, the concept of technical leveling is inapplicable to the first round, as by definition, leveling requires *repeated rounds* of discussions.

These cases are typical of those in which agencies or protesters have misconstrued the technical leveling rule. Part of the problem is the fact that FAR 15.610(d) associated technical leveling with "pointing out weaknesses." This led many agencies to believe that although they had to disclose *deficiencies* during discussions, they were prohibited from disclosing *weaknesses*.

The fact is that GAO has never sustained a protest about technical leveling. In fact, there has only been one decision by any tribunal in which a protest of technical leveling was sustained, and that was a one-time decision of the General Services Board of Contract Appeals (GSBCA) during the years in which it had jurisdiction over protests about information technology procurements. [See *Tidewater Consultants, Inc.*, GSBCA No. 8069-P, 85-3 BCA ¶ 18,387 (1985).]

FAR 15.610(d), in the pre-Rewrite edition of FAR Part 15, is an interesting example of how a poorly written rule has caused confusion, the adoption of ineffective procedures, and a large number of protests. Everyone whose job it is to write statutes and regulations should study the technical leveling rule and the body of litigation that it inspired. Fortunately, the prohibition against technical leveling was not statutory, and the FAR Part 15 Rewrite eliminated it.

114. What is *technical transfusion,* and what are the rules about it?

The term *technical transfusion* no longer appears in the FAR, having been eliminated by the FAR Part 15 Rewrite. Before the Rewrite, FAR 15.610(e) prohibited technical transfusion and warned that it might constitute a violation of the Procurement Integrity Act "to which civil and criminal penalties and administrative remedies apply." The term was defined in FAR 15.610(e)(1) as follows:

> Technical transfusion (i.e., Government disclosure of technical information pertaining to a proposal that results in improvement of a competing proposal)....

The prohibition against technical transfusion arose out of aerospace defense industry complaints about the way that Department of Defense officials conducted source selections for weapon development contracts. Technical transfusion was considered a technique to facilitate technical leveling, a practice to which they objected. The prohibition was one of several factors that led contracting officers to be conservative about what they disclosed to offerors during discussions.

Although the FAR no longer uses the term *technical transfusion,* FAR 15.306(e)(2) still effectively prohibits the practice, which it describes as an exchange of information that:

> Reveals an offeror's technical solution, including unique technology, innovative and unique uses of commercial items, or any information that would compromise an offeror's intellectual property to another offeror.

All government personnel should be aware that they are treading on dangerous ground whenever they disclose the contents of an offeror's proposal to anyone that is not on the government's evaluation team. Unlike technical leveling, technical transfusion may be a criminal act, depending on what information was "transfused." FAR 3.104-8 provides for criminal and civil penalties and administrative remedies for improper disclosure of contractor bid or proposal information. FAR 3.104-1 defines the term *contractor bid or proposal information* as follows:

> "Contractor bid or proposal information" means any of the following information submitted to a Federal agency as part of or in connection with a bid or proposal to enter into a Federal agency procurement contract, if that information has not been previously made available to the public or disclosed publicly:
>
> (1) Cost or pricing data (as defined by 10 U.S.C. 2306a(h) with respect to procurements subject to that section, and section 304A(h) of the Federal Property and Administrative Services Act of 1949 (41 U.S.C. 254b(h)), with respect to procurements subject to that section).
>
> (2) Indirect costs and direct labor rates.
>
> (3) Proprietary information about manufacturing processes, operations, or techniques marked by the contractor in accordance with applicable law or regulation.
>
> (4) Information marked by the contractor as "contractor bid or proposal information" in accordance with applicable law or regulation.
>
> (5) Information marked in accordance with 52.215-1(e).

Agency personnel should also be aware of the Trade Secrets Act (18 U.S.C. § 1905), which provides as follows:

Disclosure of confidential information generally

> Whoever, being an officer or employee of the United States or of any department or agency thereof, any person acting on behalf of the Office of Federal Housing Enterprise Oversight, or agent of the Department of Justice as defined in the Antitrust Civil Process Act (15 U.S.C. 1311-1314), publishes, divulges, discloses, or makes known in any manner or to any extent not authorized by law any information coming to him in the course of his employment or official duties or by reason of any examination or investigation made by, or return, report or record made to or filed with, such department or agency or officer or employee thereof, which information concerns or relates to the trade secrets, processes, operations, style of work, or apparatus, or to the identity, confidential statistical data, amount or source of any income, profits, losses, or expenditures of any person, firm, partnership, corporation, or association; or permits any income return or copy thereof or any book containing any abstract or particulars thereof to be seen or examined by any person except as provided by law; shall be fined under this title, or imprisoned not more than one year, or both; and shall be removed from office or employment.

In view of these laws and regulations, contracting officers should take steps to ensure that the information in proposals is safeguarded against improper disclosure.

115. What is *auctioning*, and what are the rules about it?

Auctioning is the practice of disclosing one offeror's price to another offeror in an effort to persuade the second offeror to lower its price, or telling an offeror a specific price that it must propose. The FAR once prohibited the practice. Prior to the FAR Part 15 Rewrite, FAR 15.610(e)(2) described auctioning techniques as follows:

> (i) Indicating to an offeror a cost or price that it must meet to obtain further consideration;
>
> (ii) Advising an offeror of its price standing relative to another offeror (however, it is permissible to inform an offeror that its cost or price is considered by the Government to be too high or unrealistic); and
>
> (iii) Otherwise furnishing information about other offerors' prices.

However, the term *auctioning* no longer appears in the FAR, and the practice is no longer strictly forbidden. Instead, FAR 15.306(e) provides as follows:

> Limits on exchanges. Government personnel involved in the acquisition shall not engage in conduct that...
>
> (3) Reveals an offeror's price without that offeror's permission. However, the contracting officer may inform an offeror that its price is considered by the Government to be too high, or too low, and reveal the results of the analysis supporting that conclusion. It is also permissible, at the Government's discretion, to indicate to all offerors the cost or price that the Government's price analysis, market research, and other reviews have identified as reasonable (41 U.S.C. 423(h)(1)(2))[.]

Thus, auctioning is permissible if the government gets offerors' permission to disclose their prices or if the government decides to tell offerors the price that it considers to be reasonable.

The practice has now gained acceptance in the form of "reverse auctions" or "online reverse auctions," sometime called "upside down" auctions. In this technique, the government discloses offerors' prices and invites the offerors to propose lower prices in head-to-head competition in accordance with a prescribed protocol until a time limit is reached. The technique has become popular worldwide, but it is also controversial. GAO has held the technique to be legal under the simplified acquisition procedures prescribed in FAR Part 13 and has said that the FAR neither recognizes nor prohibits the use of reverse auctions. See *MTB Group, Inc.* (B-295463, February 23, 2005). The technique appears to have been used mainly for the acquisition of goods, especially commodities, and some agencies claim to have achieved large savings through its use. Government-wide policy has not been issued concerning the use of reverse auctions, but some agencies have published internal policies and procedures.

116. When may offerors modify or revise their proposals?

The FAR makes a distinction between a *proposal modification* and a *proposal revision,* defining these terms in FAR 15.001 as follows:

> *Proposal modification* is a change made to a proposal before the solicitation closing date and time, or made in response to an amendment, or made to correct a mistake at any time before award.
>
> *Proposal revision* is a change to a proposal made after the solicitation closing date, at the request of or as allowed by a contracting officer, as the result of negotiations.

Once the date and time for the receipt of proposals has passed, proposal revisions are governed by FAR 15.306, *Exchanges with offerors after receipt of proposals,* and FAR 15.307, *Proposal revisions.* An analysis of those rules indicates that offerors may *revise* their proposals only during *discussions* and in response to the contracting officer's request for final proposal revisions, but not during *clarifications* or *communications*. FAR 15.307 provides as follows:

> (a) If an offeror's proposal is eliminated or otherwise removed from the competitive range, no further revisions to that offeror's proposal shall be accepted or considered.
>
> (b) The contracting officer may request or allow proposal revisions to clarify and document understandings reached during negotiations. At the conclusion of discussions, each offeror still in the competitive range shall be given an opportunity to submit a final proposal revision. The contracting officer is required to establish a common cut-off date only for receipt of final proposal revisions. Requests for final proposal revisions shall advise offerors that the final proposal revisions shall be in writing and that the Government intends to make award without obtaining further revisions.

FAR 15.001 indicates that if a contracting officer amends an RFP after the receipt of proposals, an offeror may *modify* its proposal in response. FAR 15.001 also indicates that an offeror may *modify* its proposal at any time to correct a mistake. It is clear that an offeror can correct all kinds of mistakes during discussions. However, FAR 15.306(a)(2) limits *clarifications* before award without discussions to the resolution of "minor or clerical errors." This language is confusing, because it seems unlikely that "minor or clerical errors" include all kinds of mistakes. Thus, it is unclear whether correction of more serious mistakes is permitted during clarification before award without discussions.

The rule in FAR 15.306(b)(3)(i) for *communications* refers the reader to FAR 14.407 with regard to "ambiguities in the proposal or other concerns (e.g., errors, omissions, or mistakes)." FAR Part 14 prescribes rules for sealed bidding. FAR 14.407 prescribes rules for dealing with mistakes in bids that are discovered both before and after award. FAR 14.407-2 allows the correction of apparent clerical mistakes at any time. FAR 14.407-3 describes how to deal with mistakes discovered after bids are opened, but before contract award. It provides in pertinent part as follows:

> (a) If a bidder requests permission to correct a mistake and clear and convincing evidence establishes both the existence of the mistake and the bid actually intended, the agency head may make a determination permitting the bidder to correct the mistake; provided, that if this correction would result in displacing one or more lower bids, such a determination shall not be made unless the existence of the mistake and the bid actually intended are ascertainable substantially from the invitation and the bid itself.
>
> (b) If—
>
> (1) A bidder requests permission to withdraw a bid rather than correct it;
>
> (2) The evidence is clear and convincing both as to the existence of a mistake and as to the bid actually intended; and
>
> (3) The bid, both as uncorrected and as corrected, is the lowest received, the agency head may make a determination to correct the bid and not permit its withdrawal.
>
> (c) If, under paragraph (a) or (b) of this subsection, (1) the evidence of a mistake is clear and convincing only as to the mistake but not as to the intended bid, or (2) the evidence reasonably supports the existence of a mistake but is not clear and convincing, an official above the contracting officer, unless otherwise provided by agency procedures, may make a determination permitting the bidder to withdraw the bid.
>
> (d) If the evidence does not warrant a determination under paragraph (a), (b), or (c) of this section, the agency head may make a determination that the bid be neither withdrawn nor corrected.

The remainder of FAR 14.407-3 describes the administrative procedure for investigating suspected or alleged mistakes in bids. These restrictions on the correction of mistakes during communications seem strange, because if an agency is conducting communications, it is because it intends to establish a competitive range and conduct discussions. If an agency suspects that an offeror has made a mistake but thinks that the proposal is sufficiently competitive to merit further consideration, it could include the offeror in the competitive range and let it correct the mistake during discussions.

117. What are the rules about final proposal revisions (best and final offers)?

FAR 15.307, *Proposal revisions,* reads as follows:

> (a) If an offeror's proposal is eliminated or otherwise removed from the competitive range, no further revisions to that offeror's proposal shall be accepted or considered.
>
> (b) The contracting officer may request or allow proposal revisions to clarify and document understandings reached during negotiations. At the conclusion of discussions, each offeror still in the competitive range shall be given an opportunity to submit a final proposal revision. The contracting officer is required to establish a common cut-off date only for receipt of final proposal revisions. Requests for final proposal revisions shall advise offerors that the final proposal revisions shall be in writing and that the Government intends to make award without obtaining further revisions.

In short, if an agency conducts discussions with offerors in a competitive range, then it must give each of those offerors at least one chance to revise its proposal in light of those discussions, except for any offerors that were eliminated from further consideration during the discussion process. Note that an agency may allow the offerors a chance to submit one or more revisions *during* discussions or limit them to a single, final proposal revision at the conclusion of discussions. No matter which approach it takes, once the agency has decided to close the discussions, it must give every offeror that is still in contention a chance to submit a *final* proposal revision, setting a common (i.e., same for all) date for submission and notifying the offerors that it is their last chance to make changes.

In the past, FAR 15.611(c) had discouraged contracting officers from reopening discussions after the submission of "best and final offers," but the references to reopening discussions were eliminated by the FAR Part 15 Rewrite. FAR 15.611(c) had required that if an agency did reopen discussions, it had to give the offerors still remaining in contention an opportunity to submit a second best and final offer. Since the FAR no longer contemplates the reopening of discussions, it does not mention the need for second final proposal revisions. However, it is likely that GAO would require an agency to solicit a second round of final proposal revisions if it reopened discussions.

PART VI

Making the Source Selection Decision

The questions in this part address the processes for and rules about selecting the contractor, including the analysis of nonprice/price tradeoffs. They also address notifications, debriefings, and protests.

118. How should the government make *tradeoffs* among proposals?

An agency will have to make *tradeoffs* when no offeror is best on all the evaluation factors, but one is better on some and another is better on others. A tradeoff involves giving up (trading off) some of one evaluation factor (e.g., price) to get more of another (e.g., quality). The best way to make tradeoffs is to compare the offerors in a series of pairs, identifying the differences between the offerors in each pair and deciding which represents the better value.

Consider the following simple example. Assume that a buyer is purchasing an automobile and is interested in only two factors, which the buyer considers to be equally important: gasoline mileage and the purchase price of the car. Table VI-1 displays the gasoline mileages and proposed firm-fixed-prices offered by six firms.

TABLE VI-1
SIMPLE TRADEOFF PROBLEM NO. 1

Offeror	*Miles per Gallon*	*Purchase Price*
A	15	$21,000
B	22	$29,000
C	18	$19,000
D	26	$31,000
E	31	$28,000
F	20	$23,000

The first step in the tradeoff process is to determine if any of the offerors is *dominated* by any of the others. An offeror is dominated if at least one other offeror is better on *all* factors, or is tied on some factors and better on all the others. In Table VI-1, Offeror C offers better gasoline mileage than Offeror A at a lower price. Thus, A is dominated by C, and the buyer should not give A further consideration. (Logically, since Offeror C is better than Offeror A, any offeror that is equal to or better than C will also be better than A.)

No other offeror is dominated, so now the buyer will have to make tradeoffs. Comparing Offeror B to Offeror C, the buyer sees that B offers better gasoline mileage but C offers a lower price. The question is whether the difference of four miles per gallon is worth the difference of $10,000. In this case, the determination is easy to make. The buyer is concerned about gasoline mileage as a source of operating cost; thus, to determine the benefit associated with the difference in gasoline mileage, the buyer simply has to convert gasoline mileage to dollars. The buyer plans to drive the car 75,000 miles and assumes that gasoline will sell for no more than $1.50 a gallon. Thus, the cost of gasoline is equal to: (75,000/22 miles per gallon) x $1.50. Using this formula, the buyer can easily see that choosing Offeror B would save only $1,135.50 over the operational life of the car. The difference in gasoline mileage is not worth the difference in price. Even if the price of gasoline increased to $3.00 per gallon, Offeror C would still be the better value.

So now the buyer compares Offeror C to Offeror D, and so on. Such comparisons show that Offeror C is the best value, even though it offered the lowest gasoline mileage among the nondominated offerors.

This example was simple because the buyer could convert the nonprice factor into dollars to measure the differences in benefits associated with the differences in gasoline mileage. It is rarely that easy. What about more complicated procurements? Consider the example in Table VI-2, a procurement for environmental cleanup services. The buyer is making the evaluation on the basis of two factors that he considers to be equally important: (1) experience, measured in terms of the number of similar projects performed by the offerors; and (2) proposed price.

TABLE VI-2
SIMPLE TRADEOFF PROBLEM NO. 2

Offeror	*Experience*	*Price*
A	12	$ 900,000
B	6	$ 875,000
C	1	$ 790,000
D	19	$ 995,000
E	13	$ 910,000
F	5	$ 914,000

Scanning the table, the buyer can see that Offeror F is dominated by Offerors A, B, and E, and so eliminates Offeror F from further consideration. No other offeror is dominated, so the buyer begins making paired comparisons. Comparing Offeror A to Offeror B, the buyer must decide whether experience gained from six additional projects is worth $25,000. This is a risk/price tradeoff, since the main value of experience is its predictive value. The buyer assumes that the more experience a firm has, the more it has learned and thus the more capable it is. But how much is the six-year difference worth? What is the measure of the benefit derived from the greater experience? The buyer cannot think of any reasonable way to convert experience into dollars, so this is a judgment call. The buyer must first decide whether the six-project difference in experience makes Offeror A a significantly lower risk than Offeror B; if so, the buyer must then decide whether the lower risk is worth $25,000.

In a real-life procurement of hazardous waste cleanup services, in which the evaluation factors were price and past performance and in which price was more important, a contracting officer had to choose between an offeror whose past performance was "very good" and whose price was $4,292,871.68, and an offeror whose past performance was "marginally acceptable" and whose price was $3,646,855.40. The contracting officer chose to pay the $646,016.28 price premium in order to take the lower risk. The lower priced offeror protested the decision to GAO. In *CORVAC, Inc.* (B-244766, November 13, 1991), GAO quoted the contracting officer's explanation for his tradeoff decision as follows:

> I believe that [the winning offeror's] proposal represents the optimal combination of performance and cost. The type of past performance problems experienced by [the losing offeror] could potentially cost the Government a lot more financially and otherwise than the price difference between the two offers. It is reasonable to expect from [the winner's] very good past performance that these types of problems will not occur...it is sometimes a false economy to make decisions solely on low initial price....

GAO denied the protest, saying:

> To the extent that CORVAC is challenging the agency's price/technical tradeoff, we note that agencies have discretion in determining the manner and extent to which they will make use of the technical and price evaluation results. Institute of Modern Procedures, Inc., B-236964, Jan. 23, 1990, 90-1 CPD ¶ 93. Technical and price trade-

> offs are permitted and the extent that one may be sacrificed for the other is governed by the test of rationality and consistency with the stated evaluation criteria. See Grey Advertising, Inc., 55 Comp. Gen. 1111 (1976), 76-1 CPD ¶ 325. We will accord due weight to the agency's judgment concerning the significance of the difference in technical merit of offers and whether the difference is sufficiently significant to outweigh the price difference.

In this case, the price premium was justified, even though price was the most important factor and the benefits of the better past performance were speculative, because the contract was for cleaning up hazardous waste, and a mistake could cost much more than the difference in the offerors' prices. Had the procurement been for janitorial services, the contracting officer's decision might have been different.

So far, our examples have been simple ones involving only two factors—price and one nonprice factor. Tradeoff analysis becomes more challenging when several nonprice factors are involved. Consider the example in Table VI-3, which represents the findings about proposals for leased office space that are based on several equally important evaluation factors.

TABLE VI-3

COMPLEX TRADEOFF PROBLEM

Offeror	*Location*	*Image*	*Size*	*Comfort*	*Parking*	*Annual Rent*
A	70	Exc	10,000	Exc	15	$30,000
B	20	Fair	10,250	Fair	12	$20,000
C	50	Sat	10,500	Fair	15	$25,000
D	40	Poor	8,000	Good	20	$15,000
E	90	Good	10,250	Good	15	$20,000
F	10	Poor	10,500	Fair	22	$17,000

In this case, there are five equally important nonprice factors; three are quantified, two are not. Location is measured in miles from the center of the city (the shorter the distance the better); size is measured in square feet of floorspace (the larger the floorspace the better); and parking is measured in number of reserved spaces in the building (the more spaces the better). Building image and comfort are summarized verbally (excellent, good, satisfactory, fair, and poor).

This is a complex problem in tradeoff analysis. The buyer will have to make tradeoffs among six factors to determine which offeror in any paired comparison is the best value. Note that none of the offerors is dominated. The analysis would be even more complex if the nonprice factors were not equally important. In this situation, numerical scoring could simplify the problem by converting the five nonprice measurements on different scales for location, image, size, comfort, and parking to scores on a 0- to 100-point scale, which serves as a kind of common denominator. This would make it easier to make initial comparisons and tradeoffs.

No source selection decision should be based on tradeoffs between scores and prices. Scores are merely analytical aids; source selection decisions must be based on tradeoffs between the actual nonprice factor differences and the prices. The key to making sound tradeoff analyses is to compare the offerors in series of pairs, identify the nonprice differences among the competing proposals, and then decide whether the benefits associated with the nonprice differences are worth the differences in the prices. The differences in the nonprice factors are not significant, per se; it is the benefits associated with the differences that matter.

FAR 15.308 says, "Although the rationale for the selection decision must be documented, that documentation need not quantify the tradeoffs that led to the decision." GAO has said that such tradeoffs are "governed by the test of rationality and consistency with the stated evaluation factors." The keys to success are systematic analysis and sound business reasoning. Numerous books and articles describe techniques for making these kinds of analyses. [See, for example, *Decision Analysis for Management Judgment,* 3d. ed., by Paul Goodwin and George Wright (Jossey-Bass, 2004); *Decision Analysis and Behavioral Research,* by Detlof von Winterfeldt and Ward Edwards (Cambridge: Cambridge University Press, 1986); and "Even Swaps: A Rational Method for Making Tradeoffs," by John S. Hammond, Ralph L. Keeney, and Howard Raiffa, in *Harvard Business Review,* March-April 1998.]

119. What are the limits on an agency's discretion when choosing the winner?

The extent of an agency's discretion to choose the winner of a source selection competition depends on which source selection process it uses and on the evaluation factors in the RFP. If an agency uses the lowest price technically acceptable source selection process described in FAR 15.101-2, then its discretion is limited to determining which proposals are acceptable and which are not; the award must go to the offeror who submitted the lowest priced technically acceptable proposal. Acceptability is a pass or fail determination, and agencies may exercise a reasonable amount of discretion when deciding whether or not a proposal is acceptable. In *GTS Duratek, Inc.* (B-280511.2; B-280511.3, October 19, 1998), GAO noted:

> The procuring agency is responsible for evaluating the data submitted by an offeror and ascertaining if they provide sufficient information to determine the acceptability of the offeror's services; we will disturb this technical determination only if it is shown to be unreasonable. Inframetrics, Inc., B-257400, Sept. 30, 1994, 94-2 CPD ¶ 138 at 3. While we do not make an independent determination of the merits of a technical proposal, the agency's judgment must have a rational basis and be consistent with the stated evaluation criteria. Pacific Consol. Indus., supra. Consistent with this requirement, an agency must document its technical determinations in sufficient detail to show they are not arbitrary. Id.

The extent of the agency's discretion to determine acceptability will depend on how acceptability is defined in the RFP. If acceptability is based on an objective matter such as weight (e.g., "to be acceptable, the device must weigh five pounds or less"), then the agency will have virtually no discretion; but if acceptability is based on a subjective matter such as "soundness of approach" (e.g., "to be acceptable, the offeror must propose a sound approach"), then the agency will have considerable discretion.

If an agency uses the tradeoff process described in FAR 15.101-1, then it has considerable discretion to select the winner. For example, in *LTR Training Systems, Inc.* (B-274996; B-274996.2, January 16, 1997), GAO stated:

> In a negotiated procurement, contracting officials have broad discretion in determining the manner and extent to which they will make use of technical and price evaluation results. TRW, Inc., 68 Comp. Gen. 511 (1989), 89-1 CPD ¶ 584. In reviewing an agency's source selection decision, we will examine the evaluation supporting that decision to ensure that the evaluation was reasonable and consistent with the stated evaluation criteria. Contel Fed. Sys., 71 Comp. Gen. 11 (1991), 91-2 CPD ¶ 325.

In *Ryan Associates, Inc.* (B-274194; B-274194.2; B-274194.3, November 26, 1996), GAO said:

> In a negotiated procurement, the government is not required to make award to the lowest-cost, technically acceptable offeror unless the RFP specifies that cost will be the determinative factor for award. General Servs. Eng'g, Inc., B-245458, Jan. 9, 1992, 92-1 CPD ¶ 44. Agency officials have broad discretion in determining the manner and extent to which they will make use of technical and cost evaluation results. Cost/technical tradeoffs may be made; the extent to which one may be sacrificed for the other is governed by the test of rationality and consistency with the established evaluation factors. Id.

So the limits of discretion are rationality and consistency with the evaluation factors in the RFP. Thus, in *Science and Engineering Services, Inc.* (B-276620, July 3, 1997), GAO said:

> Where as here, a solicitation provides that technical considerations are more important than cost, source selection officials have broad discretion in determining the manner in which they will make use of the technical and cost evaluation results in arriving at a source selection decision; such cost/technical tradeoffs are governed only by the test of rationality and consistency with the RFP's stated evaluation criteria. JB Indus., B-251118.2, Apr. 6, 1993, 93-1 CPD ¶ 297 at 7.

In *BE, Inc.; PAI Corporation* (B-277978; B-277978.2, December 16, 1997), GAO said:

> Even where cost or price is the least important evaluation factor, an agency may make award to an offeror with a lower-cost, lower-scored proposal if it determines that the cost premium involved in awarding to a higher-rated, higher-priced offeror is not justified. Southern Research, B-266360, Feb. 12, 1996, 96-1 CPD ¶ 65 at 3; Dayton T. Brown, Inc., B-229664, Mar. 30, 1988, 88-1 CPD ¶ 321 at 4-5.

A source selection authority's discretion is not limited by the findings or the recommendations of the agency's source selection evaluation board. In its decision in *Cessna Aircraft Company* (B-261953.5, February 5, 1996), GAO noted:

> Source selection officials in negotiated procurements are not bound by the recommendations or evaluation judgments of evaluators. Grey Advertising, Inc., 55 Comp. Gen. 1111 (1976), 76-1 CPD ¶ 325. Thus, source selection officials have broad discretion in determining the manner and extent to which they will make use of the technical and cost evaluation results, and their technical judgments are governed only by the tests of rationality and consistency with the stated evaluation criteria. Id.;

> Oklahoma Aerotronics, Inc.—Recon., B-237705.2, Mar. 28, 1990, 90-1 CPD ¶ 337. Source selection officials may properly question the conclusions reached by a technical evaluation panel, and, where those conclusions are not convincing or lack support, we see nothing improper with selection authorities requesting additional information from the evaluators in support of their ratings. See, e.g., Wyle Labs., Inc.; Latecoere Int'l., Inc., 69 Comp. Gen. 648 (1990), 90-2 CPD ¶ 107; Calspan Corp., B-255268, Feb. 22, 1994, 94-1 CPD ¶ 136; Latecoere Int'l., Inc.—Advisory Opinion, B-239113.3, Jan. 15, 1992, 92-1 CPD ¶ 70.

120. How do agencies award contracts?

An *award* is the act of accepting an offer. An agency awards a contract by notifying an offeror that it has accepted its offer. FAR 15.504 prescribes that process as follows:

> The contracting officer shall award a contract to the successful offeror by furnishing the executed contract or other notice of the award to that offeror.
>
> (a) If the award document includes information that is different than the latest signed proposal, as amended by the offeror's written correspondence, both the offeror and the contracting officer shall sign the contract award.
>
> (b) When an award is made to an offeror for less than all of the items that may be awarded and additional items are being withheld for subsequent award, each notice shall state that the Government may make subsequent awards on those additional items within the proposal acceptance period.
>
> (c) If the Optional Form (OF) 307, Contract Award, Standard Form (SF) 26, Award/Contract, or SF 33, Solicitation, Offer and Award, is not used to award the contract, the first page of the award document shall contain the Gov-

> ernment's acceptance statement from Block 15 of that form, exclusive of the Item 3 reference language, and shall contain the contracting officer's name, signature, and date. In addition, if the award document includes information that is different than the signed proposal, as amended by the offeror's written correspondence, the first page shall include the contractor's agreement statement from Block 14 of the OF 307 and the signature of the contractor's authorized representative.

As indicated by the introductory paragraph, there are two ways to award a contract. The first way requires the agency's contracting officer to prepare a complete contract document that reflects the terms of an offeror's proposal and of the agency's RFP, obtain the offeror's signature on two copies, sign both copies to indicate the government's acceptance, and send one of the two signed originals (often marked "duplicate original") to the offeror.

The second way to award a contract requires the contracting officer to sign the "award" portion of the government form under which the offeror submitted its offer [i.e., blocks 18 through 20 of Standard Form 26, *Award/Contract*; blocks 19 through 28 of Standard Form 33, *Solicitation, Offer, and Award*; blocks 29 through 31 of Standard Form 1442, *Solicitation, Offer, and Award (Construction, Alteration, or Repair)*; blocks 26 and 28 of Standard Form 1447, *Solicitation/Contract*; blocks 29 and 31 of Standard Form 1449, *Solicitation/Contract/Order for Commercial Items*; or block 15 of Optional Form 307, *Contract Award*] and send a copy to the contractor. The contracting officer can also notify an offeror of the acceptance of its offer by letter.

FAR Subpart 4.1, *Contract Execution*, prescribes the following rules for signing contracts:

> **4.101 Contracting officer's signature.**
>
> Only contracting officers shall sign contracts on behalf of the United States. The contracting officer's name and

official title shall be typed, stamped, or printed on the contract. The contracting officer normally signs the contract after it has been signed by the contractor. The contracting officer shall ensure that the signer(s) have authority to bind the contractor (see specific requirements in 4.102 of this subpart).

4.102 Contractor's signature.

(a) Individuals. A contract with an individual shall be signed by that individual. A contract with an individual doing business as a firm shall be signed by that individual, and the signature shall be followed by the individual's typed, stamped, or printed name and the words, "an individual doing business as ________" [insert name of firm].

(b) Partnerships. A contract with a partnership shall be signed in the partnership name. Before signing for the Government, the contracting officer shall obtain a list of all partners and ensure that the individual(s) signing for the partnership have authority to bind the partnership.

(c) Corporations. A contract with a corporation shall be signed in the corporate name, followed by the word "by" and the signature and title of the person authorized to sign. The contracting officer shall ensure that the person signing for the corporation has authority to bind the corporation.

(d) Joint venturers. A contract with joint venturers may involve any combination of individuals, partnerships, or corporations. The contract shall be signed by each participant in the joint venture in the manner prescribed in paragraphs (a) through (c) of this section for each type of participant. When a corporation is participating, the contracting officer shall verify that the corporation is authorized to participate in the joint venture.

(e) Agents. When an agent is to sign the contract, other than as stated in paragraphs (a) through (d) of this section, the agent's authorization to bind the principal must be established by evidence satisfactory to the contracting officer.

4.103 Contract clause.

The contracting officer shall insert the clause at 52.204-1, Approval of Contract, in solicitations and contracts if required by agency procedures.

The act of sending a duplicate original or a copy of the contract or the award document to the offeror is referred to as *distributing* the contract. FAR Subpart 4.2 prescribes the following rules for contract distribution:

4.201 Procedures.

Contracting officers shall distribute copies of contracts or modifications within 10 working days after execution by all parties. As a minimum, the contracting officer shall—

(a) Distribute simultaneously one signed copy or reproduction of the signed contract to the contractor and the paying office;

(b) When a contract is assigned to another office for contract administration (see Subpart 42.2), provide to that office—

(1) One copy or reproduction of the signed contract and of each modification; and

(2) A copy of the contract distribution list, showing those offices that should receive copies of modifications, and any changes to the list as they occur;

(c) Distribute one copy to each accounting and finance office (funding office) whose funds are cited in the contract;

(d) When the contract is not assigned for administration but contains a Cost Accounting Standards clause, provide one copy of the contract to the cognizant administrative contracting officer and mark the copy "For Cost Accounting Standards Administration Only" (see 30.601(b));

(e) Provide one copy of each contract or modification that requires audit service to the appropriate field audit office listed in the "Directory of Federal Contract Audit Offices" (copies of this directory can be ordered from the—

U.S. Government Printing Office
Superintendent of Document
Washington, DC 20402

referencing stock numbers 008-007-03189-9 and 008-007-03190-2 for Volumes I and II, respectively); and

(f) Provide copies of contracts and modifications to those organizations required to perform contract administration support functions (e.g., when manufacturing is performed at multiple sites, the contract administration office cognizant of each location).

4.202 Agency distribution requirements.

Agencies shall limit additional distribution requirements to the minimum necessary for proper performance of essential functions. When contracts are assigned for administration to a contract administration office located in an agency different from that of the contracting office (see Part 42), the two agencies shall agree on any necessary distribution in addition to that prescribed in 4.201 above.

Usually, it is the act of distributing the signed document to the offeror, rather than the act of signing the documents per se, that constitutes the award (i.e., acceptance of the offer).

The solicitation provision at FAR 52.215-1, *Instructions to Offerors—Competitive Acquisition,* paragraph 10, says:

> A written award or acceptance of proposal *mailed or otherwise furnished* to the successful offeror within the time specified in the proposal shall result in a binding contract without further action by either party.

[Italics added.]

FAR 52.212-1, *Evaluation—Commercial Items,* includes similar language for contracts for commercial items. Note that if the contract includes the clause at FAR 52.204-1, *Approval of Contract,* then the award (acceptance) will not be effective until approval has been granted by higher authority within the agency.

[For an in-depth discussion of the law about award of contracts/acceptance of offers, see John Cibinic, Jr., and Ralph C. Nash, Jr., *Formation of Government Contracts,* 3rd ed. (Washington, D.C.: The George Washington University Law School, 1998), pp. 224–237.]

121. When can the government reject all proposals and cancel the solicitation?

FAR 15.305(b) says, "The source selection authority may reject all proposals received in response to a solicitation, if doing so is in the best interests of the Government." Before the FAR Part 15 Rewrite, FAR 15.608(b) read as follows:

> All proposals received in response to a solicitation may be rejected if the agency head determines in writing that—
>
> (1) All otherwise acceptable proposals received are at unreasonable prices;

> (2) The proposals were not independently arrived at in open competition, were collusive, or were submitted in bad faith (see Subpart 3.3 for reports to be made to the Department of Justice);
>
> (3) A cost comparison as prescribed in OMB Circular A-76 and Subpart 7.3 shows that performance by the Government is more economical; or
>
> (4) For other reasons, cancellation is clearly in the Government's interests.
>
> (5) A violation or possible violation of section 27 of the Office of Federal Procurement Policy Act, as amended (41 U.S.C. 423), has occurred (see 3.104).

An agency should reject all proposals and cancel the solicitation only after carefully considering all of the practicable alternatives, since doing so will inconvenience and aggravate a lot of people. If an offeror protests an agency's decision to reject all proposals, the protester will have to show that the agency's decision was unreasonable.

In *R. & W. Flammann GmbH* (B-278486, February 4, 1998), GAO sustained a protest against an Air Force contracting officer's rejection of all proposals and cancellation of a solicitation for the painting of military family housing. The contracting officer had learned that someone in the government had leaked information about some of the offerors' prices after the receipt of proposals, so he decided to reject all offers and cancel the solicitation. The offeror who had the lowest prices protested. GAO decided that the contracting officer's decision was unreasonable, saying:

> Under FAR § 15.608(b)(4) (June 1997), a procuring agency may reject all proposals received in response to an RFP if cancellation is "clearly in the Government's interest." The determination that cancellation is clearly in the interest of the government must have a reasonable basis. Griffin Servs., Inc., B-237268 et al., June 14, 1990,

> 90-1 CPD ¶ 558 at 2. Here, we conclude that cancellation would be improper and that award should be made to Flammann on the basis of its low offer under the RFP. We agree that the contracting officer was warranted in being concerned that the integrity of this procurement might have been compromised, and that the matter required prompt investigation. However, the contracting officer's decision to cancel the solicitation without first determining that the "irregularities" actually did compromise an award under this RFP was not reasonable. While the agency asserts that the disclosure of prices detrimentally affected the integrity of the procurement, the contracting officer had no information that anyone benefited from, or was prejudiced by, the disclosure of the prices to the original low offeror and the original third low offeror, neither of whom was able to change its prices to benefit from this knowledge. Further, the contracting officer recognized that there was no evidence suggesting that Flammann was involved in any of the irregularities of concern to the agency. As noted above, Flammann's request for correction concerned errors which were clear from the RFP pricing pages submitted with its offer and were discoverable by the agency upon review of the offer without Flammann's request for correction. Clearly, the contracting officer had not developed facts to support the cancellation at the time he made the decision, and the record presented in this case does not provide that support.

In another case, *Tender Loving Care Ambulance & Ambulette Co. Inc.* (B-276571.2, July 17, 1997), the Army had issued a small business set-aside RFP for emergency medical technician services on an indefinite-delivery/indefinite-quantity basis. The Army received two proposals and awarded a contract. The losing offeror protested the winner's size status, and the U.S. Small Business Administration decided that the winner was not a small business and was ineligible to receive the award. Instead of awarding the contract to the loser, the Army canceled the RFP on the grounds that: (1) the estimate of services was inaccurate; (2) it had left a required clause out of the solicitation; and (3) the loser's prices were too high. The loser protested, but GAO decided that any one of those reasons was good enough and denied the protest.

122. When must an agency notify an offeror that it did not win the contract, and what information does it have to provide with the notification?

FAR 15.503 states the rules about notifications to unsuccessful offerors, as follows:

> **15.503 Notifications to unsuccessful offerors.**
>
> (a) *Preaward notices*—(1) *Preaward notices of exclusion from competitive range.* The contracting officer shall notify offerors promptly in writing when their proposals are excluded from the competitive range or otherwise eliminated from the competition. The notice shall state the basis for the determination and that a proposal revision will not be considered.
>
> (2) *Preaward notices for small business programs.* (i) In addition to the notice in paragraph (a)(1) of this section, the contracting officer shall notify each offeror in writing prior to award, upon completion of negotiations, determinations of responsibility, and, if necessary, the process in 19.304(d)—
>
> (A) When using a small business set-aside (see Subpart 19.5);
>
> (B) When a small disadvantaged business concern receives a benefit based on its disadvantaged status (see Subpart 19.11 and 19.1202) and is the apparently successful offeror;
>
> (C) When using the HUBZone procedures in 19.1305 or 19.1307; or

(D) When using the service-disabled veteran-owned small business procedures in 19.1405.

(ii) The notice shall state—

(A) The name and address of the apparently successful offeror;

(B) That the Government will not consider subsequent revisions of the offeror's proposal; and

(C) That no response is required unless a basis exists to challenge the small business size status, disadvantaged status, HUBZone, or service-disabled veteran-owned status of the apparently successful offeror.

(iii) The notice is not required when the contracting officer determines in writing that the urgency of the requirement necessitates award without delay or when the contract is entered into under the 8(a) program (see 19.805-2).

(b) *Postaward notices.* (1) Within 3 days after the date of contract award, the contracting officer shall provide written notification to each offeror whose proposal was in the competitive range but was not selected for award (10 U.S.C. 2305(b)(5) and 41 U.S.C. 253b(c)) or had not been previously notified under paragraph (a) of this section. The notice shall include—

(i) The number of offerors solicited;

(ii) The number of proposals received;

(iii) The name and address of each offeror receiving an award;

(iv) The items, quantities, and any stated unit prices of each award. If the number of items or other factors makes listing any stated unit prices impracticable at that time, only the total contract price need be furnished

> in the notice. However, the items, quantities, and any stated unit prices of each award shall be made publicly available, upon request; and
>
> (v) In general terms, the reason(s) the offeror's proposal was not accepted, unless the price information in paragraph (b)(1)(iv) of this section readily reveals the reason. In no event shall an offeror's cost breakdown, profit, overhead rates, trade secrets, manufacturing processes and techniques, or other confidential business information be disclosed to any other offeror.
>
> (2) Upon request, the contracting officer shall furnish the information described in paragraph (b)(1) of this section to unsuccessful offerors in solicitations using simplified acquisition procedures in Part 13.
>
> (3) Upon request, the contracting officer shall provide the information in paragraph (b)(1) of this section to unsuccessful offerors that received a preaward notice of exclusion from the competitive range.

There are several things to note about FAR 15.503. First, the rules for preaward notices and postaward notices are different. Second, the rules are different: (a) when a procurement has been set aside for small businesses; (b) when a small disadvantaged business receives a benefit based on its disadvantaged status; (c) when the agency is using HUBZone procedures; or (d) when the agency is using service-disabled veteran-owned procedures. Third, there are no strict time requirements for preaward notices, but agencies must make postaward notices within three days after the date of contract award. Fourth, the required contents of notices vary.

A ruling of the U.S. Court of Appeals for the Federal Circuit indicates that notwithstanding FAR 15.503(b)(iv), disclosure of the winning offeror's unit prices may violate the Trade Secrets Act. See: *McDonnell Douglas Corp. v. National Aeronautics and Space Administration*, 180 F.3d 303, June 25,

1999, U.S. Court of Appeals, D.C. Circuit. The Department of Justice has established a webpage to provide information and guidance about this issue at http://www.usdoj.gov/oip/foiapost/2002foiapost13.htm.

The preaward notice required by FAR 15.503(a)(1) is intended to stop unsuccessful offerors from spending bid and proposal money as soon as possible after an agency has decided that those offerors have no chance of winning the contract—that is, once they have been eliminated from the competitive range "or otherwise eliminated." The FAR requires that the contracting officer notify them "promptly," but otherwise establishes no deadline. A preaward notice must explain the basis for a determination to eliminate an offer, but the FAR does not require that the notice explain in detail. Many contracting officers dread having to issue this notice, because they fear that a losing offeror will protest its exclusion. Even if the agency's decision is sound, a protest at this point in the process will place a serious administrative burden on the agency.

The preaward notice required by FAR 15.503(a)(2) is intended to give the losers a chance to challenge the winner's claim that it is a small business concern when a procurement is conducted in accordance with one of the small business programs in FAR Part 19. (See FAR 19.302, *Protesting a small business representation*.) According to FAR 19.302(d)(1), a loser must protest the winner's size status by the close of the fifth business day following the day it receives the preaward notice. Thus, the key piece of information in this notice is the name and address of the winning offeror.

The postaward notice to unsuccessful offerors is a matter of simple courtesy, but it gives losing offerors a chance to question the agency's source selection decision. The way that a contracting officer words this notice can affect an unsuccessful offeror's decision about whether or not to file a protest. Unfortunately, many contracting officers do not appreciate the emotional impact that such a notice can have on a company's managers and employees, especially if the procurement is large or important to the company's fortunes, or if the source selection process has been long and costly. Contracting officers must consider how the tone and content of the notice will affect its reception by persons whose futures might be affected by the source selection decision.

123. What is a *debriefing*?

A *debriefing* is an explanation of the government's evaluation of an offeror's proposal. Although the term *debriefing* suggests a face-to-face meeting, a debriefing can take the form of a meeting, a letter, or a telephone conversation. FAR 15.505 states that an offeror that has been eliminated from the competition before an agency has selected the winning offeror may request a debriefing before award. FAR 15.506 states that other offerors, including the winner of the competition, may request a debriefing after award.

124. What are the rules about debriefings?

The rules about debriefings are in FAR 15.505, *Preaward debriefing of offerors,* and 15.506, *Postaward debriefing of offerors,* which read as follows:

> **15.505 Preaward debriefing of offerors.**
>
> Offerors excluded from the competitive range or otherwise excluded from the competition before award may request a debriefing before award (10 U.S.C. 2305(b)(6)(A) and 41 U.S.C. 253b(f) - (h)).
>
> (a)(1) The offeror may request a preaward debriefing by submitting a written request for debriefing to the con-

tracting officer within 3 days after receipt of the notice of exclusion from the competition.

(2) At the offeror's request, this debriefing may be delayed until after award. If the debriefing is delayed until after award, it shall include all information normally provided in a postaward debriefing (see 15.506(d)). Debriefings delayed pursuant to this paragraph could affect the timeliness of any protest filed subsequent to the debriefing.

(3) If the offeror does not submit a timely request, the offeror need not be given either a preaward or a postaward debriefing. Offerors are entitled to no more than one debriefing for each proposal.

(b) The contracting officer shall make every effort to debrief the unsuccessful offeror as soon as practicable, but may refuse the request for a debriefing if, for compelling reasons, it is not in the best interests of the Government to conduct a debriefing at that time. The rationale for delaying the debriefing shall be documented in the contract file. If the contracting officer delays the debriefing, it shall be provided no later than the time postaward debriefings are provided under 15.506. In that event, the contracting officer shall include the information at 15.506(d) in the debriefing.

(c) Debriefings may be done orally, in writing, or by any other method acceptable to the contracting officer.

(d) The contracting officer should normally chair any debriefing session held. Individuals who conducted the evaluations shall provide support.

(e) At a minimum, preaward debriefings shall include—

(1) The agency's evaluation of significant elements in the offeror's proposal;

(2) A summary of the rationale for eliminating the offeror from the competition; and

(3) Reasonable responses to relevant questions about whether source selection procedures contained in the solicitation, applicable regulations, and other applicable authorities were followed in the process of eliminating the offeror from the competition.

(f) Preaward debriefings shall not disclose—

(1) The number of offerors;

(2) The identity of other offerors;

(3) The content of other offerors' proposals;

(4) The ranking of other offerors;

(5) The evaluation of other offerors; or

(6) Any of the information prohibited in 15.506(e).

(g) An official summary of the debriefing shall be included in the contract file.

15.506 Postaward debriefing of offerors.

(a)(1) An offeror, upon its written request received by the agency within 3 days after the date on which that offeror has received notification of contract award in accordance with 15.503(b), shall be debriefed and furnished the basis for the selection decision and contract award.

(2) To the maximum extent practicable, the debriefing should occur within 5 days after receipt of the written request. Offerors that requested a postaward debriefing in lieu of a preaward debriefing, or whose debriefing was delayed for compelling reasons beyond contract award, also should be debriefed within this time period.

(3) An offeror that was notified of exclusion from the competition (see 15.505(a)), but failed to submit a timely request, is not entitled to a debriefing.

(4)(i) Untimely debriefing requests may be accommodated.

(ii) Government accommodation of a request for delayed debriefing pursuant to 15.505(a)(2), or any untimely debriefing request, does not automatically extend the deadlines for filing protests. Debriefings delayed pursuant to 15.505(a)(2) could affect the timeliness of any protest filed subsequent to the debriefing.

(b) Debriefings of successful and unsuccessful offerors may be done orally, in writing, or by any other method acceptable to the contracting officer.

(c) The contracting officer should normally chair any debriefing session held. Individuals who conducted the evaluations shall provide support.

(d) At a minimum, the debriefing information shall include—

(1) The Government's evaluation of the significant weaknesses or deficiencies in the offeror's proposal, if applicable;

(2) The overall evaluated cost or price (including unit prices) and technical rating, if applicable, of the successful offeror and the debriefed offeror, and past performance information on the debriefed offeror;

(3) The overall ranking of all offerors, when any ranking was developed by the agency during the source selection;

(4) A summary of the rationale for award;

(5) For acquisitions of commercial items, the make and model of the item to be delivered by the successful offeror; and

(6) Reasonable responses to relevant questions about whether source selection procedures contained in the

> solicitation, applicable regulations, and other applicable authorities were followed.
>
> (e) The debriefing shall not include point-by-point comparisons of the debriefed offeror's proposal with those of other offerors. Moreover, the debriefing shall not reveal any information prohibited from disclosure by 24.202 or exempt from release under the Freedom of Information Act (5 U.S.C. 552) including—
>
> (1) Trade secrets;
>
> (2) Privileged or confidential manufacturing processes and techniques;
>
> (3) Commercial and financial information that is privileged or confidential, including cost breakdowns, profit, indirect cost rates, and similar information; and
>
> (4) The names of individuals providing reference information about an offeror's past performance.
>
> (f) An official summary of the debriefing shall be included in the contract file.

These rules are reasonably straightforward. The content of preaward debriefings is understandably restricted because the source selection process is still underway, and confidentiality is essential. Thus, during a preaward debriefing, the agency must explain its evaluation of the offeror's proposal, but it must not provide any information about any of the other offerors, including their number or identity. During a postaward debriefing, the agency must not only explain its evaluation of the offeror's proposal, but it must also reveal how the offeror ranked in comparison to the other offerors and explain its "rationale" for the award decision. It must not disclose any confidential information in any other offeror's proposal.

The tricky part about giving a debriefing is understanding the psychology of the process. The government personnel giving the debriefing know that they are facing a disappointed and perhaps hostile party, and they may feel on the defensive about their evaluation and apprehensive about saying something that will prompt a protest. The offeror's representatives may be stunned and even angry after having gone through a demanding process of anticipation, presolicitation and preproposal conferences, solicitation analysis, solicitation amendments, proposal preparation, periods of what seemed like endless waiting, discussions, preparation of revised proposals followed by more waiting, and then the blow of receiving a notice to an unsuccessful offeror. Any reticence or lack of success on the part of the government personnel in explaining their agency's findings may fuel suspicions that the process was unfair or even rigged in favor of the eventual winner.

Openness within the limits established by FAR 15.506(e) is the key to a successful debriefing (assuming that the agency conducted a sound evaluation). Contracting officers would do well to remember that an offeror can obtain any information withheld from it during a debriefing by hiring an attorney to file a protest. Withholding information may prompt a protest designed to obtain it through other means. Thus, the best course of action is to disclose and explain all the information generated by the agency during the evaluation of the offeror's proposal and to invite the offeror to point out errors of fact or reasoning, or findings that are inconsistent with the evaluation factors for award. An attitude of openness, confidence, and a reasonable amount of sympathy on the part of an agency's personnel shows that they have nothing to hide or fear. If an offeror does discover a defect in the agency's evaluation process or conclusions, early discovery during a debriefing can save the agency time and embarrassment by giving it a chance to take corrective action on its own initiative.

While FAR 15.505(a)(3) and 15.506(a)(3) allow the government to refuse an untimely request for a debriefing, FAR 15.506(a)(4) says that agencies may accommodate untimely requests, and doing so may prevent a protest. Also, while FAR 15.505(b) allows an agency to refuse requests for preaward debriefings, doing so may prompt a protest; it is best to provide the debriefing as soon as possible. In that way, if the agency discovers that it did make a mistake, it can take corrective action without having to retrace its steps in the source selection process. And even though FAR 15.506(a)(1) allows agencies to delay postaward debriefings, agencies should not do so without good reason and should fully explain any delay to the requesting offeror.

Finally, FAR 15.506(d)(2) requires disclosure of the winner's unit prices during a debriefing. However, in 1999, the United States Court of Appeals for the District of Columbia Circuit ruled that while a contractor's total price may be disclosed to the public, the disclosure of "line item pricing information" may violate the Trade Secrets Act. See *McDonnell Douglas Corporation v. National Aeronautics and Space Administration*, 180 F.3d 303, June 25, 1999. Since violation of the Trade Secrets Act is a federal crime, government personnel should consult with their agency's attorney before releasing any offeror's prices to any other offeror during a debriefing. The Department of Justice provides information and guidance about this issue at http://www.usdoj.gov/oip/foiapost/2002foiapost13.htm.

125. What is a *protest*, and what are the rules about filing protests?

FAR 33.101 defines the term *protest* as follows:

> "Protest" means a written objection by an interested party to any of the following:
>
> (1) A solicitation or other request by an agency for offers for a contract for the procurement of property or services.

> (2) The cancellation of the solicitation or other request.
>
> (3) An award or proposed award of the contract.
>
> (4) A termination or cancellation of an award of the contract, if the written objection contains an allegation that the termination or cancellation is based in whole or in part on improprieties concerning the award of the contract.

A protest may be filed with the agency conducting the procurement, GAO, or the U.S. Court of Federal Claims. Most protests are filed with agencies and with GAO. FAR 33.103 includes guidance and procedures for protests to agencies; FAR 33.104 includes guidance and procedures for protests to GAO. In addition, GAO has published its own rules about filing protests; these are in Title 4 of the Code of Federal Regulations (C.F.R.), Part 21. The Court of Federal Claims has established its own rules for filing protests, which are lawsuits rather than administrative proceedings; the FAR does not include guidance on protests to the Court.

Perhaps the most important protest rule has to do with the deadline for filing a protest. The FAR does not establish deadlines. GAO has established deadlines in its bid protest regulations at 4 C.F.R. 21.2, *Time for Filing*, as follows:

> (a)(1) Protests based upon alleged improprieties in a solicitation which are apparent prior to bid opening or the time set for receipt of initial proposals shall be filed prior to bid opening or the time set for receipt of initial proposals. In procurements where proposals are requested, alleged improprieties which do not exist in the initial solicitation but which are subsequently incorporated into the solicitation must be protested not later than the next closing time for receipt of proposals following the incorporation.
>
> (2) Protests other than those covered by paragraph (a)(1) of this section shall be filed not later than 10 days af-

ter the basis of protest is known or should have been known (whichever is earlier), with the exception of protests challenging a procurement conducted on the basis of competitive proposals under which a debriefing is requested and, when requested, is required. In such cases, with respect to any protest basis which is known or should have been known either before or as a result of the debriefing, the initial protest shall not be filed before the debriefing date offered to the protester, but shall be filed not later than 10 days after the date on which the debriefing is held.

(3) If a timely agency-level protest was previously filed, any subsequent protest to GAO filed within 10 days of actual or constructive knowledge of initial adverse agency action will be considered, provided the agency-level protest was filed in accordance with paragraphs (a)(1) and (a)(2) of this section, unless the contracting agency imposes a more stringent time for filing, in which case the agency's time for filing will control. In cases where an alleged impropriety in a solicitation is timely protested to a contracting agency, any subsequent protest to GAO will be considered timely if filed within the 10-day period provided by this paragraph, even if filed after bid opening or the closing time for receipt of proposals.

(b) Protests untimely on their face may be dismissed. A protester shall include in its protest all information establishing the timeliness of the protest; a protester will not be permitted to introduce for the first time in a request for reconsideration information necessary to establish that the protest was timely.

(c) GAO, for good cause shown, or where it determines that a protest raises issues significant to the procurement system, may consider an untimely protest.

Instances in which GAO invokes the "issues significant to the procurement system" exception to the timeliness rules are exceedingly rare. Research indicates that GAO has invoked that rule on few occasions in the nearly ten-year period 1995 through July 2005. It did so in 1999, in the matter of *Pyxis Corporation* (B-282469; B-282469.2, July 15, 1999). GAO explained its action as follows:

> Our review of the chronology of the protest leads us to conclude that Pyxis failed to assert the bid protest ground concerning the ordering of non-FSS items in a timely fashion....
>
> Nevertheless, we will consider this issue pursuant to the significant issue exception to our timeliness rules. 4 C.F.R. § 21.2(c). We do so in view of the conflict in this area of the law between the Court of Federal Claims' ATA decision and our prior decisions, the resolution of which is of importance to the procurement community. Moreover, the issue itself—the rules governing the ordering of non-FSS items in connection with an FSS buy—is one that we consider of widespread interest to the procurement system.

GAO invoked the exception once again in 2001, in the matter of *The Finlen Complex* (B-288280, October 10, 2001). GAO explained its reluctance to invoke the significant issue exception in *Peacock, Myers & Adams* (B-279327, March 24, 1998), as follows:

> While our timeliness rules may seem harsh in some cases, they reflect the dual requirements of giving all parties a fair opportunity to present their cases and resolving protests expeditiously without disrupting or delaying the procurement process. Mea d Data Cent., supra. Application of the timeliness requirement here establishes a readily discernible rule, which results in fair and equal treatment of all protesters. Peacock asserts that we should consider this case under our significant issue exception to our timeliness requirements. 4 C.F.R. § 21.2(c). However, we will not consider the merits of an untimely protest by invoking the significant issue exception unless the protest raises an issue of first impression or one that would be of widespread interest to the procurement community.

In other decisions, GAO has said that it rarely invokes the significant issue exception because doing so would render its timeliness rules meaningless. [See *Merck & Co., Inc.* (B-248655, May 19, 1992).]

126. Who can file a protest?

The FAR does not say who can file a protest. FAR 33.102(a) says that agencies "shall consider all protests. . . ." GAO will consider protests only from *interested parties*, which FAR 33.101 defines as follows:

> "Interested party for the purpose of filing a protest," as used in this subpart, means an actual or prospective offeror whose direct economic interest would be affected by the award of a contract or by the failure to award a contract.

GAO uses the same definition in its bid protest regulations [4 C.F.R. 21.0(a)] and has elaborated on it in numerous protest decisions. For example, in *Continental Service Company* (B-274531, December 17, 1996), GAO said:

> Under the bid protest provisions of the Competition in Contracting Act of 1984, 31 U.S.C. §§ 3551-3556 (1994), as amended by Pub. L. No. 104-106, §§ 4321(d), 5501, 5603, 110 Stat. 186, 674, 698, 700 (1996), only an "interested party" may protest a federal procurement. That is, a protester must be an actual or prospective offeror whose direct economic interest would be affected by the award of a contract or the failure to award a contract. Bid Protest Regulations, section 21.0(a), 61 Fed. Reg. 39,042 (July 26, 1996) (to be codified at 4 C.F.R. § 21.0(a)). Determining whether a party is interested involves consideration of a variety of factors, including the nature of issues raised, the benefit of relief sought by the protester, and the party's status in relation to the procurement. Black Hills Refuse Serv., 67 Comp. Gen. 261 (1988), 88-1

> CPD ¶ 151. A protester is not an interested party where it would not be in line for contract award were its protest to be sustained.

In other words, to be an *interested party*, a protester would have to be in a position to win the contract if its protest were sustained.

The rules about who may file protests with the Court of Federal Claims are more complicated. For a comprehensive legal analysis of those rules, see Ralph C. Nash, Jr., John Cibinic, Jr., and Karen O'Brien, *Competitive Negotiation: The Source Selection Process, 2d ed.* (Washington, D.C.: The George Washington University Law School, 1999), pp. 863–891.

127. When does an agency have to delay contract award or suspend contract performance because of a protest?

Rules that require agencies to delay contract award or suspend contract performance upon receipt of a protest are often referred to as "CICA stay" rules—"CICA" referring to the Competition in Contracting Act of 1984, and "stay" being the legal term for an order to stop some action.

CICA STAYS BASED ON PROTESTS FILED WITH THE AGENCY

An agency must delay award if it receives a protest before award; it must suspend performance of a contract that has already been awarded if it receives a protest (1) within ten days after the contract has been awarded, or (2) within five days after the date on which it offered to provide a debriefing in response to a timely request for a debriefing, whichever is later. FAR 2.101 says that *day* means calendar day. FAR 33.103(f) provides as follows with respect to protests filed with the agency:

Action upon receipt of protest. (1) Upon receipt of a protest before award, a contract may not be awarded, pending agency resolution of the protest, unless contract award is justified, in writing, for urgent and compelling reasons or is determined, in writing, to be in the best interest of the Government. Such justification or determination shall be approved at a level above the contracting officer, or by another official pursuant to agency procedures.

(2) If award is withheld pending agency resolution of the protest, the contracting officer will inform the offerors whose offers might become eligible for award of the contract. If appropriate, the offerors should be requested, before expiration of the time for acceptance of their offers, to extend the time for acceptance to avoid the need for resolicitation. In the event of failure to obtain such extension of offers, consideration should be given to proceeding with award pursuant to subparagraph (f)(1) of this section.

(3) Upon receipt of a protest within 10 days after contract award or within 5 days after a debriefing date offered to the protester under a timely debriefing request in accordance with 15.505 or 15.506, whichever is later, the contracting officer shall immediately suspend performance, pending resolution of the protest within the agency, including any review by an independent higher level official, unless continued performance is justified, in writing, for urgent and compelling reasons or is determined, in writing, to be in the best interest of the Government. Such justification or determination shall be approved at a level above the contracting officer, or by another official pursuant to agency procedures.

(4) Pursuing an agency protest does not extend the time for obtaining a stay at GAO. Agencies may include, as part of the agency protest process, a voluntary suspension period when agency protests are denied and the protester subsequently files at GAO.

CICA STAYS BASED ON PROTESTS FILED WITH GAO

An agency must delay award of a contract if it receives notice of a protest from GAO before award; it must suspend performance of a contract that has already been awarded if it receives notice of a protest from GAO (1) within ten days after contract award, or (2) within five days after the date on which it offered to provide a debriefing in response to a timely request for a debriefing, whichever is later. FAR 33.104(f) addresses protests filed with GAO before award as follows:

> (b) *Protests before award.* (1) When the agency has received notice from the GAO of a protest filed directly with the GAO, a contract may not be awarded unless authorized, in accordance with agency procedures, by the head of the contracting activity, on a nondelegable basis, upon a written finding that—
>
> (i) Urgent and compelling circumstances which significantly affect the interest of the United States will not permit awaiting the decision of the GAO; and
>
> (ii) Award is likely to occur within 30 days of the written finding.
>
> (2) A contract award shall not be authorized until the agency has notified the GAO of the finding in paragraph (b)(1) of this section.
>
> (3) When a protest against the making of an award is received and award will be withheld pending disposition of the protest, the contracting officer should inform the offerors whose offers might become eligible for award of the protest. If appropriate, those offerors should be requested, before expiration of the time for acceptance of their offer, to extend the time for acceptance to avoid the need for resolicitation. In the event of failure to obtain

> such extensions of offers, consideration should be given to proceeding under subparagraph (b)(1) of this section.

Note that the CICA stay takes effect on the date the agency receives a notice of the protest from GAO—not on the date the protester files the protest or notifies the agency that it has filed a protest.

FAR 33.104(c) and (d) address protests filed with GAO after award, and provide as follows:

> (c) *Protests after award.* (1) When the agency receives notice of a protest from the GAO within 10 days after contract award or within 5 days after a debriefing date offered to the protester for any debriefing that is required by 15.505 or 15.506, whichever is later, the contracting officer shall immediately suspend performance or terminate the awarded contract, except as provided in subparagraphs (c)(2) and (3) of this section.
>
> (2) In accordance with agency procedures, the head of the contracting activity may, on a nondelegable basis, authorize contract performance, notwithstanding the protest, upon a written finding that—
>
> (i) Contract performance will be in the best interests of the United States; or
>
> (ii) Urgent and compelling circumstances that significantly affect the interests of the United States will not permit waiting for the GAO's decision.
>
> (3) Contract performance shall not be authorized until the agency has notified the GAO of the finding in paragraph (c)(2) of this section.
>
> (4) When it is decided to suspend performance or terminate the awarded contract, the contracting officer should attempt to negotiate a mutual agreement on a no-cost basis.

> (5) When the agency receives notice of a protest filed with the GAO after the dates contained in subparagraph (c)(1), the contracting officer need not suspend contract performance or terminate the awarded contract unless the contracting officer believes that an award may be invalidated and a delay in receiving the supplies or services is not prejudicial to the Government's interest.
>
> (d) *Findings and notice.* If the decision is to proceed with contract award, or continue contract performance under paragraphs (b) or (c) of this section, the contracting officer shall include the written findings or other required documentation in the file. The contracting officer also shall give written notice of the decision to the protester and other interested parties.

Note that the determination of whether or not a CICA stay takes effect is based on the date the agency receives a notice of the protest from GAO. However, FAR 33.102(d) provides as follows:

> Protest likely after award. The contracting officer may stay performance of a contract within the time period contained in subparagraph 33.104(c)(1) if the contracting officer makes a written determination that—
>
> (1) A protest is likely to be filed; and
>
> (2) Delay of performance is, under the circumstances, in the best interests of the United States.

Proceeding with an award in the face of a protest in accordance with FAR 33.104(b)(1) is called "overriding a CICA stay." Agencies do override CICA stays, but not very often.

A key consideration in these rules is the effect of the timing of debriefings. If an unsuccessful offeror requests a debriefing within three days after the date it receives a notification of its elimination from the competition before award, or within three days after the date it receives a notification of contract award, then its request for a debriefing is timely. If the contracting officer delays the debriefing date, then he or she is extending the offeror's protest deadline further into the period of contract performance. Thus, it may not pay to postpone a debriefing.

Suppose that a contract is awarded on September 1. The contracting officer sends a notice to unsuccessful offerors by certified mail, return receipt requested, which Offeror X receives on September 3. The clock has now begun to run on the CICA stay deadline. The contracting officer receives the offeror's request for a postaward debriefing on September 5, within the three-day deadline in FAR 15.506(a)(1). At this point, the CICA stay deadline clock is still running toward September 13; but the contracting officer offers to conduct the debriefing on September 15. The effect of this decision is to extend the CICA stay deadline until September 20, the fifth day after the debriefing date offered. [See 4 C.F.R. 20.2(c)(2) and FAR 33.104(c)(1).] Had the contracting officer offered to conduct the debriefing on or before September 8, it would not have affected the original deadline.

The same rule applies to an offeror that has been eliminated from the competition before award. Suppose that Offeror Y is eliminated from the competitive range before award, requests a debriefing within three days after the date on which it receives the notification, and the contracting officer decides to postpone the debriefing until after award. The contracting officer has extended the CICA stay deadline to the fifth day after the date on which he or she offered to conduct the debriefing.

Note that if an agency delays a debriefing, the postaward CICA stay deadline extension in FAR 33.104(c)(1) is to *five* days after the date on which the agency offered to conduct the debriefing, but the *protest filing deadline* extension in 4 C.F.R. 20.2(c)(2) is to *ten* days after that date.

128. What does it take to win a protest?

To win a protest, the protester must show that the agency violated statute or regulation, made a decision that was inconsistent with the terms of its RFP, or made an unreasonable decision, and that the agency's action was prejudicial to the interests of the protester. If the protester can prove that the agency violated statute or regulation, or that its decision was inconsistent with the terms of the RFP or was unreasonable, but cannot show that the agency's action was prejudicial to the protester's interests, then GAO will not sustain the protest. In its decision in *Scientific and Commercial Systems Corporation; Omni Corporation* (B-283160; B-283160.2; B-283160.3; B-283160.4; B-283160.5, October 14, 1999), GAO found:

> Competitive prejudice is an essential element of every viable protest. Diverco, Inc., B-259734, Apr. 21, 1995, 95-1 CPD ¶ 209 at 3. Our Office will not sustain a protest unless the protester demonstrates a reasonable possibility that it was prejudiced by the agency's actions, that is, unless the protester demonstrates that, but for the agency's actions, it would have had a substantial chance of receiving the award. McDonald-Bradley, B-270126, Feb. 8, 1996, 96-1 CPD ¶ 54 at 3; see Statistica, Inc. v. Christopher, 102 F.3d 1577, 1581 (Fed. Cir. 1996).

The federal courts apply the same standard. In *Statistica, Inc. v. Christopher* [102 F.3d 1577, 1581 (1996)], the U.S. Court of Appeals for the Federal Circuit determined:

> A protester must show not simply a significant error in the procurement process, but also that the error was prejudicial, if it is to prevail in a bid protest. See Data Gen. Corp. v. Johnson, 78 F.3d 1556, 1562 (Fed. Cir. 1996) (citing cases). To establish competitive prejudice, a protester must demonstrate that but for the alleged error, there was a "'substantial chance that [it] would receive an award—that it was within the zone of active consideration.'" CACI, Inc.-Fed. v. United States, 719 F.2d 1567,

1574-75 (Fed. Cir. 1983) (quoting Morgan Bus. Assocs., Inc. v. United States, 619 F.2d 892, 896 (Ct. Cl. 1980)) (emphasis added).

In Data General, this court said that "the appropriate standard is that, to establish prejudice, a protester must show that, had it not been for the alleged error in the procurement process, there was a reasonable likelihood that the protester would have been awarded the contract." 78 F.3d at 1562 (emphasis added).

Appendix A

Competitive Processes in Government Contracting: The FAR Part 15 Process Model and Process Inefficiency

Vernon J. Edwards

Boiled down to its essence, choosing a contractor in a competitive acquisition is a matter of information processing. The decisionmaker collects information about alternative choices (competing firms), assesses each alternative on the basis of specified criteria (evaluation factors), and then compares each alternative to the others on the basis of those assessments in order to rank them and determine which is best. The process is essentially the same no matter what method of contracting is used: ordering against a General Services Administration (GSA) multiple award schedule contract, simplified acquisition, sealed bidding, negotiation, or "fair opportunity" under a multiple award delivery or task order contract.

When planning a competitive acquisition, agency acquisition personnel must design a process for getting information about the alternatives, assessing each alternative, and com-

---

This article was first published online in slightly different form at *Where in Federal Contracting?* (www.wifcon.com) in 2003. It discusses inefficiencies in the use of FAR Part 15 Competitive Negotiated Procedures. It expands upon topics discussed in Questions 12, 13, 14, 16, 37, 38, and 94. © 2005 by Vernon J. Edwards.

paring the alternatives in order to determine which is best. In developing their process they must take into account their objectives for process quality, schedule, and costs. They must consider the attributes of a good decision, the time available to make it, and the human and technological resources (e.g., computers and decision support software) at their disposal. Presumably, they want to minimize their transaction costs by making the best decision they can in the shortest reasonable time and using no more of their agency's resources than absolutely necessary. They also should want to economize on the demands made on the competing firms, so as to not make government business unattractive to the best firms by making it too costly and time-consuming.

A review of protest decisions by the U.S. Government Accountability Office (GAO) and the literature on government contracting suggests that some agencies fail to design efficient competitive processes because they follow a poor process model. That model has evolved over the course of 50 years in connection with source selections conducted under Federal Acquisition Regulation (FAR) Part 15, Contracting by Negotiation, and its predecessors.[1] I shall refer to this model as the FAR Part 15 Process Model.

THE FAR PART 15 PROCESS MODEL

The FAR has never prescribed a step-by-step process for conducting a source selection; instead, it has prescribed rules governing the design of source selection processes. The current rules in the FAR cover organizing for source selection (§ 15.303); preparing and issuing requests for proposals and amendments thereto (§§ 15.203, 15.204, 15.205, 15.206, 15.209 and 15.304); exchanging information with prospec-

[1] The FAR took effect on April 1, 1984. Before the FAR, the rules for "procurement by negotiation" were in the Defense Acquisition Regulation, Section III, and the Federal Procurement Regulation, Section III.

tive and actual offerors (§§ 15.201, 15.306 and 15.307); submitting, receiving, handling, modifying, and revising proposals (§§ 15.207 and 15.208); evaluating proposals (§ 15.305); and making the selection decision (§ 15.308). FAR § 15.100 expressly states that it describes only some of the processes and techniques that agencies may use to conduct a source selection.

Nevertheless, by the end of the 1950s a model process had emerged within the federal procurement bureaucracy that has been passed down to succeeding generations of acquisition personnel through word of mouth, on-the-job training, and classroom instruction.[2] The main steps of that process model are set forth in Table 1.

Table 1. The FAR Part 15 Process Model

Step	*Action*
1	Agency issues a request for proposals that solicits complete proposals from all competitors.
2	Agency receives competing proposals.
3	Agency convenes a panel or set of panels to evaluate the competing proposals.
4	Panels evaluate all proposals on the basis of the complete set of evaluation factors for awards.
5	Panels report their findings to the decisionmaker in writing.

continues

[2] The process at its most elaborate is described in considerable detail in *TFX Contract Investigation, Hearings before the Permanent Subcommittee on Investigations, Committee on Government Operations, United States Senate, 88th Congress, First Session,* Part 1 (1963). See, especially, the testimony of Col. Charles A. Gayle and Mr. Robert Emmett Dunne, pp. 41–80. See, too, the description of "system source selection" in: Art, R.J., *The TFX Decision: McNamara and the Military* (Boston: Little, Brown & Company, 1968), pp. 56–62.

Table 1. continued

Step	*Action*
6	Decisionmaker either: (a) selects the contractor or (b) establishes a "competitive range" that includes all of the most highly rated competitors.[3]
7	Agency negotiates ("conducts discussions") with the remaining competitors.
8	Agency asks remaining competitors to submit final proposal revisions.
9	Agency receives final proposal revisions.
10	Agency convenes panels to evaluate final proposal revisions.
11	Panels evaluate all final proposal revisions.
12	Panels report their findings to the decisionmaker in writing.
13	Decisionmaker selects the contractor.
14	Decisionmaker announces the award decision.

This process model has two key characteristics: (1) every competitor is required to submit a complete proposal at the outset of the competition that addresses all of the evaluation factors for award, and (2) the agency conducts negotiations with more than one firm. The significance of these two characteristics lies in the effect that they have on the amount of information that a competitor must prepare and submit and that an agency must process in order to make a source selection decision, and on the time and resources required to prepare and process that information.

Soliciting Complete Proposals from All Competitors. The first key characteristic of the FAR Part 15 Process Model is that all competitors must submit complete proposals at the outset of the competition. Suppose that an agency plans to select the contractor on the basis of (a) technical approach;

[3] Before the FAR Part 15 Rewrite took effect on January 1, 1998, the rule for establishing the competitive range had been to include all offerors that had a reasonable chance of being selected for award and those whose chances were in doubt. At present, the rule in FAR § 15.306(c)(1) generally requires inclusion of "all of the most highly rated proposals."

(b) management plan; (c) experience; (d) past performance; (e) small, small disadvantaged, and woman-owned small businesses subcontracting plan; and (f) price. Under the FAR Part 15 Process Model the agency will require all the competitors to submit information pertinent to all of those factors at the outset. It will require every competitor to submit (1) a technical proposal; (2) a management proposal; (3) information about its experience; (4) information about its past performance; (5) its plan for small, small disadvantaged, and women-owned small business subcontracting; and (6) prices and supporting price information. As a consequence of this approach, the evaluation panel must assess every competitor on the basis of all of that information.

As a general rule, the more information that an evaluation panel must process, the more time and/or personnel that it will need in order to process it, and the more information that the decisionmaker will have to consider when he or she compares the competitors to determine which is best. It is generally not too difficult to process complete proposal information received from two to five competitors, depending on the amount of information solicited, and this approach saves time by having complete proposals ready at hand for the evaluators at the outset of the competition and avoiding the need to pause while awaiting successive submissions. But it can be a challenge to process complete information from 10 competitors. And the challenge can be great when an agency receives proposals from 15 or more competitors. In extreme cases, the challenge can even be overwhelming.

Thus, in at least some cases, the process would be more efficient if agencies limited the amount of information that the competitors must submit initially, and thus the amount of information that the evaluators must process and the decisionmaker must consider, so long as the limitations are consistent with good decisionmaking practices. One way to do that is to limit the number of evaluation factors. Another way to do it is to apply the evaluation factors in phases in order to progressively narrow the competitive field, asking the competitors in each phase to submit only the information needed in that phase. In this way an agency could initially ask for limited information, eliminate some competitors on that basis, and carry fewer competitors into subsequent phases in which more detailed and voluminous information is obtained and processed. This type of phased evaluation process is sometimes referred to as "down-select."[4]

Negotiations with Multiple Competitors. Another source of information processing costs is conducting negotiations (discussions) with more than one firm. Although the FAR permits agencies to award contracts on the basis of initial offers without negotiations (discussions), agencies sometimes establish a competitive range consisting of more than one competitor, negotiate with them all, and then solicit competitive final proposal revisions from them.[5] The evaluation panel must then evaluate those revisions and report their assessments to the decisionmaker.

FAR § 15.306(c)(1) states that when establishing a competitive range an agency must include "all of the most highly rated proposals." The more proposals included in the competitive range, the more information that the agency will have to process and the more time and resources will be used

---

[4] See the definition in Nash, R. et al., *The Government Contracts Reference Book,* 2d ed. (Washington, D.C.: The George Washington University Law School, 1998), p. 200; "Innovative Procurement Procedures: The Nuclear Regulatory Commission's Test Program," in *The Nash & Cibinic Report,* February 2000, 14 N&CR ¶ 9; and "Postscript: Innovative Procurement Procedures," in *The Nash & Cibinic Report,* October 2000, 14 N&CR ¶ 53. See: Edwards, V., *Source Selection Answer Book* (Vienna, VA: Management Concepts, 2000), pp. 215–219, for a discussion of the distinction between source selection downselect and programmatic downselect.

[5] Most RFPs include the boilerplate language in FAR § 52.215-1 to the effect that the agency intends to award without discussions. I do not know of any source of statistics for how often the government actually does award without discussions.

in the source selection process. In the explanatory statement that accompanied the *Federal Register* publication of the FAR Part 15 Rewrite, the FAR Council stated:

> We also note that comments received from Government agencies indicate that award is nearly always made to one of the three most highly rated offerors in the competitive range... . The incidence of award to an offeror other than one of the three such proposals is so small that it does not support keeping any business, particularly a small business with limited bid and proposal resources, in a competition that the business has virtually no chance of winning.[6]

FAR § 15.306(c)(2) states that in the interests of efficiency agencies may include fewer than "all" of the most highly rated proposals in the competitive range if they include a notice of that possibility in the RFP. Agencies may also establish a competitive range that includes only one offeror.[7] Historically, GAO has been skeptical when an agency has established a competitive range consisting of only one offeror and has said that it will subject such decisions to close scrutiny if it receives a protest in that regard. However, there is evidence that it has backed away from that stance since the FAR Part 15 Rewrite took effect on January 1, 1998.[8] In sum, the regulations provide plenty of latitude to keep the number in the competitive range small; it seems that there is little reason to include more than three in most circumstances.

Aside from the information processing costs associated with negotiating with more than one competitor, there is some evidence that negotiating with more than one firm during a source selection does not produce a true meeting of

---

[6] 62 *Fed. Reg.* 51224, 51226 and 51228 (1977).

[7] See, e.g.: *SOS Interpreting, Ltd.*, B-287505, June 12, 2001.

[8] See: "Competitive Range of One: Is There Special Scrutiny?" in *The Nash & Cibinic Report*, November 1999, 13 N&CR ¶ 61.

the minds. A government RFP is a very complicated business document. An RFP for a non-commercial item fixed-price contract in excess of $100,000 routinely contains more than 80 standard FAR clauses, and many specifications and statements of work are poorly written. Competitors must often read RFPs and prepare their proposals in haste and without an opportunity to sit down one-on-one with the government to go through the RFP to ensure a common understanding of the solicitation's terms. In order to reach a true meeting of the minds, the parties should fully discuss all terms and conditions in an effort to ensure that they understand them in the same way.

However, contracting officers have long been cautious to the point of being non-communicative when negotiating with more than one firm, due largely to concerns about fairness and improper disclosure of proposal information, but perhaps also due to the pressures of time. The record of board and court decisions suggests that when conducting competitive procurements agencies do not always discuss the specification or statement of work and the contract clauses in sufficient detail to reach a true meeting of the minds. Negotiations are too often limited to "deficiencies" and "weaknesses" in proposals, apparently based on the assumption that the parties share a common understanding of other terms and conditions. All too often, it is only after contract award that the parties learn that they have different ideas about their respective rights and obligations.[9] Thus, competitive negotiations are sometimes ineffective in producing a meeting of the minds. Although the FAR permits one-on-one negotiations between the government and the successful competitor after selection, but before award, such negotiations are not contemplated in the FAR Part 15 Pro-

---

[9] For a classic example of a "competitively negotiated" procurement failing to produce a meeting of the minds, see: *Omni Corporation v. U.S.*, 41 Fed. Cl. 585 (1998).

cess Model, and there is little evidence that agencies make much use of that technique to ensure that the parties really agree on the contract terms.[10]

THE FAR PART 15 PROCESS MODEL IN ACTION

Having considered the two key characteristics of the FAR Part 15 Process Model—(1) solicitation of complete proposals from every offeror at the outset of the competition and (2) negotiation with multiple competitors—I will now consider three examples of the model in action in which it has resulted in competitive process inefficiencies. I will describe its application to a source selection under FAR Part 15, to a GSA multiple award schedule, and to an acquisition conducted under FAR Part 13, simplified acquisition procedures. I will also discuss its application when providing contractors under multiple award task order contracts a fair opportunity to be considered.

Competitive Negotiation (Source Selection) Under FAR Part 15. Consider the case of the Department of Commerce's 1999 procurement for the award of governmentwide acquisition contracts for its Commerce Information Technology Solutions program (COMMITS). That procurement was the subject of a protest that was sustained by the U.S. General Accounting Office.[11] The agency's solicitation described only three evaluation factors: (1) past performance, (2) team com-

---

[10] The Department of Defense FAR Supplement (DFARS) formerly had included "Four-Step" procedures that expressly allowed for one-on-one negotiations after selection, but before award. However, on October 14, 1998, after the publication of the FAR Part 15 Rewrite, DOD announced that it was dropping those procedures from the DFARS because "FAR 15.101, Best value continuum, clearly allows such source selection procedures." See: 63 Fed. Reg. 55040 (1998).

[11] *Kathpal Technologies, Inc.; Computer & Hi-Tech Management, Inc.*, B-283137.3; B-283137.4; B-283137.5; B-283137.6, December 30, 1999.

position, and (3) price. Past performance was comprised of two subfactors, (a) quality recognition/certifications and (b) past performance management. The competitors were to present some of the information about the second subfactor, past performance management—described as the tools and techniques used in previous work and the results obtained—in a one-hour oral presentation. The RFP stated that the agency intended to give each competitor an opportunity to make an oral presentation.

The agency was surprised to receive more than 200 proposals, and so it decided to narrow the field by eliminating some on the basis of their competitiveness. Here is how GAO described the winnowing process:

> In performing this review, the SSEB chairs assigned letter ratings (from A+ to C–) under the two past performance subfactors and either a "+" or "–" under the team composition factor. Agency Report, exh. 4A, Memorandum for SSA concerning Clarification and Streamlining of Proposal Evaluation Guide and Processes 1 (May 28, 1999). No narrative explanations for these ratings were prepared, as was originally contemplated by the proposal evaluation guide. Id.; Agency's Post-Hearing Comments at 2. An initial screening matrix was prepared for each functional area that ranked offerors according to their relative ratings under the QRC subfactor; this document also noted each offeror's rating under the PPM subfactor and team composition factor and each offeror's average loaded hourly labor rate. Hearing exh. 1, Initial Screening Evaluation. The contracting officer reviewed the offerors' average loaded labor rates for realism and reasonableness; all of the offerors' average rates were determined to be reasonable. Declaration of Contracting Officer, Oct. 25, 1999, at 7; Agency's Post-Hearing Comments at 5.
>
> For each functional area, the SSEB chairs recommended, based only upon the offerors' QRC subfactor ratings, a cut-off that would provide for a "sufficient, high-quality competition." Agency Report, exh. 8, Source Selection

> Report, ¶ 4.0. As an example, for the ISE functional area, the agency received 125 proposals and 25 proposals were rated as B+ or better under the QRC subfactor. Hearing exh. 1, Initial Screening Evaluation. The SSEB chairs briefed the two SSAs (who were acting jointly) concerning the results of the initial screening and recommended to the SSAs that only those offerors that received a B+ or higher under the QRC subfactor be permitted to make an oral presentation. Although the SSEB chairs informed the SSAs of the significance of the letter ratings, there was no discussion of the specifics underlying each firm's rating. Hearing Testimony of SSEB Co-Chair. The SSAs agreed with the SSEB's recommendations. Id. No documentation was prepared memorializing the SSAs' consideration of, or decision to, limit the competition to those offers that were highest rated under the QRC subfactor. Id. Price was not considered in determining which offerors would be invited to make an oral presentation. Id.; Declaration of Contracting Officer, Oct. 25, 1999, at 5; Declaration of SSEB Co-Chair, Oct. 21, 1999, at 5.
>
> Kathpal's and CHM's proposals under the ISE area received B ratings under the QRC subfactor, and, on that basis, the protesters were not invited to make oral presentations.

Footnotes omitted. The agency apparently applied this process to more than 200 proposals.

Kathpal and Computer & Hi-Tech Management protested that by using this procedure to eliminate them, the agency had violated the terms of the RFP, because they had not been permitted to make oral presentations as promised. GAO sustained the protest on the grounds that (a) the agency did not really evaluate price, which must be evaluated in every source selection, and (b) the agency did not let the protesters make oral presentations, which it had promised it would do. GAO said that the agency could have amended the RFP to permit phased evaluation and progressive narrowing of the field of competitors:

> Once it realized how many firms were interested in competing, the agency could have elected to amend the solicitation to eliminate the oral presentation (and perhaps even one of the evaluation factors or subfactors) from the initial evaluation.

Thus, agencies may evaluate proposals in phases, and had the agency in this case planned for a phased evaluation and described that process in its RFP, or provided in the RFP for phased evaluation as a contingency procedure, its process would have been more efficient and there might not have been a protest, or the protest would have been denied.[12] Two hundred proposals is, of course, an unusually large number, but even if the number is only 15, a well-designed, phased evaluation process that quickly reduces the number to between three and five would be more efficient than the FAR Part 15 Process Model, and save time and resources for both the government and some of the competitors. In many cases the number could almost certainly be reduced simply by comparing prices before considering any other factors and eliminating competitors whose prices are too high.[13]

It stands to reason that if agencies can economize on their own information processing costs by evaluating competitors in phases and progressively narrowing the field, then they can economize on competitors' bid and proposal costs by soliciting proposal information in phases, asking for detailed

---

[12] See: "A Contingency Procedure for Source Selection," in *The Nash & Cibinic Report,* May 2000, 14 N&CR ¶ 25. It appears from the Dept. of Commerce's COMMITS website that 56 contracts were awarded in the COMMITS source selection. Both of the protesters are included among the vendors.

[13] This was actually done by a contracting officer with the U.S. Customs Service in a 1999 procurement, with the result that the number of offerors was reduced from more than 30 to less than 15 in a single day on the basis of price. There was no protest, and several of the offerors who were eliminated thanked the contracting office for saving their time and money. See: "A Contingency Procedure for Source Selection," in *The Nash & Cibinic Report,* May 2000, 14 N&CR ¶ 25.

and voluminous information only from those competitors who survive the early phases of the winnowing process. In an acquisition in which an agency anticipates receiving a large number of proposals, phased solicitation and evaluation could make for a more efficient, less time-consuming, and more economical competitive process.

Orders Against GSA Schedules. Whatever the advantages and disadvantages of the FAR Part 15 Process Model, it is understandable that agencies follow it when conducting source selections under FAR Part 15. What is remarkable and more difficult to understand is why they sometimes follow it when the rules in FAR Part 15 do not apply, e.g., when selecting a contractor for placement of an order against a GSA multiple award schedule and when conducting simplified acquisitions.

In the past few years, GAO has decided several protests in which agencies followed the FAR Part 15 Process Model when using GSA multiple award schedules.[14] FAR 8.404(b)(2) prescribes procedures for placing orders against GSA schedules in excess of the micro-purchase threshold ($2,500) but within the maximum order threshold. Agencies need only review catalogs or pricelists of at least three schedule contractors and select the one that they think represents the best value.[15] At its website, the GSA prescribes special proce-

[14] See, e.g.: *OMNIPLEX World Services Corporation,* B-291105, November 6, 2002; *KPMG Consulting LLP,* B-290716, September 23, 2002; *Avalon Integrated Services Corporation,* B-290185, July 1, 2002; *Uniband, Inc.,* B-289305, February 8, 2002; *OSI Collection Services, Inc.*; and *C.B. Accounts, Inc.,* B-286597.3, June 12, 2001.

[15] Defense agencies may no longer follow the procedures in FAR § 8.404(b), but must follow special procedures in Defense FAR Supplement § 208.404-70, which requires them to solicit offers either from a sufficient number of GSA schedule contractors to obtain three offers or all GSA schedule contractors on a schedule.

dures for ordering services that require a statement of work.[16] Those procedures are as follows:

> (a) When ordering services, ordering offices shall—
>
> (1) Prepare a Request (Request for Quote or other communication tool):
>
> (i) A statement of work (a performance-based statement of work is preferred) that outlines, at a minimum, the work to be performed, location of work, period of performance, deliverable schedule, applicable standards, acceptance criteria, and any special requirements (i.e., security clearances, travel, special knowledge, etc.) should be prepared.
>
> (ii) The request should include the statement of work and request the contractors to submit either a firm-fixed price or a ceiling price to provide the services outlined in the statement of work. A firm-fixed price order shall be requested, unless the ordering office makes a determination that it is not possible at the time of placing the order to estimate accurately the extent or duration of the work or to anticipate cost with any reasonable degree of confidence. When such a determination is made, a labor hour or time-and-materials quote may be requested. The firm-fixed price shall be based on the prices in the schedule contract and shall consider the mix of labor categories and level of effort required to perform the services described in the statement of work. The firm-fixed price of the order should also include any travel costs or other direct charges related to performance of the services ordered, unless the order provides for reimbursement of travel costs at the rates provided in the Federal Travel or Joint Travel Regulations. A ceiling price must be established for labor-hour and time-and-materials orders.

[16] http://www.gsa.gov/Portal/content/offerings_content.jsp?contentOID=116992&contentType=1004.

(iii) The request may ask the contractors, if necessary or appropriate, to submit a project plan for performing the task, and information on the contractor's experience and/or past performance performing similar tasks.

(iv) The request shall notify the contractors what basis will be used for selecting the contractor to receive the order. The notice shall include the basis for determining whether the contractors are technically qualified and provide an explanation regarding the intended use of any experience and/or past performance information in determining technical qualification of responses.

(2) Transmit the Request to Contractors: Based upon an initial evaluation of catalogs and price lists, the ordering office should identify the contractors that appear to offer the best value (considering the scope of services offered, pricing and other factors such as contractors' locations, as appropriate) and transmit the request as follows:

(i) The request shall be provided to at least three (3) contractors if the proposed order is estimated to exceed the micro-purchase threshold, but not exceed the maximum order threshold.

(ii) For proposed orders exceeding the maximum order threshold, the request shall be provided to an appropriate number of additional contractors that offer services that will meet the agency's needs.

(iii) In addition, the request shall be provided to any contractor who specifically requests a copy of the request for the proposed order.

(iv) Ordering offices should strive to minimize the contractors' costs associated with responding to requests for quotes for specific orders. Requests should be tailored to the minimum level necessary for adequate evaluation and selection for order placement. Oral presentations should be considered, when possible.

> (3) Evaluate Responses and Select the Contractor to Receive the Order: After responses have been evaluated against the factors identified in the request, the order should be placed with the schedule contractor that represents the best value. (See FAR 8.404)

Those procedures do not require issuance of the RFQ to all schedule contractors, the establishment of a competitive range, or negotiations with all offerors within the competitive range—rules in FAR Part 15 that are not applicable to the selection of a contractor under a GSA multiple award schedule. Yet we know that agencies have sometimes followed the FAR Part 15 Process Model even when FAR Part 15 did not apply to the acquisition.

In its decision in the matter of *Labat-Anderson, Inc.*, GAO describes a procurement in which the Immigration and Naturalization Service (INS) sought to award a blanket purchase agreement for direct mail and records management services against GSA's multiple award schedule for document management services and products.[17] The agency issued a request for quotations on June 26, 2000.[18] The RFQ asked quoters to submit extensive technical and price information. GAO describes the agency's scheme as follows:

> Offerors were required to submit separate technical and price proposals for evaluation by a technical evaluation committee (TEC) and a business evaluation committee (BEC), respectively. Proposals were to clearly demonstrate the offeror's understanding of the overall and specific requirements of the proposed BPA, and any proposal in which material information requested was not furnished or where indirect or incomplete answers or information

[17] *Labat-Anderson, Inc.,* B-287081; B-287081.2; B-287081.3, April 16, 2001. See, too, *Labat-Anderson, Inc. v. United States,* 50 Fed. Cl. 99 (2001).

[18] For information about the use of BPAs with GSA schedules, go to: http://www.gsa.gov/Portal/content/offerings_content.jsp?contentOID=116431&contentType=1004.

were provided might be considered unacceptable. RFQ ¶ 3.4. Offerors were required to submit both hard and electronic copies of their proposals. RFP ¶ 3.4.9.

Award was to be made to the offeror whose proposal represented the best value to the government based on three evaluation factors: technical approach, past performance, and price. The technical approach and past performance factors were equally weighted, and the two combined were significantly more important than price. RFQ ¶ 3.3. Of the two equally important technical approach subfactors, estimating model and management, only the former is at issue here.

Offerors were required to submit an estimating model that stated the underlying assumptions and constraints of their method for accomplishing the work under orders issued against the BPA, state the statistical basis for their estimates, and explain how they derived their technical approach from the analysis of the SOW and multiple years of workload data supplied by INS. Offerors were required to explain, illustrate, and explicate their model showing how the workload associated with each of the many forms processed under the program built to a model for the technical approach to operating each service center and the direct mail program as a whole; failure to do so was to be taken as a lack of understanding of the technical requirement and a deficient technical approach. RFQ ¶ 3.6.1.1. The RFQ listed specific criteria under which INS planned to evaluate this estimating model to assess the contractor's ability to provide the required services. RFQ ¶ 4.2.1. Under one criterion, offerors were required to show how using the INS estimates of forecasted demand and their own allocation and employment of labor assets using available data would result in an appropriately-sized workforce. Under another criterion, offerors were required to explain their methods and rationale for allocating labor among the functional areas (such as filing, mailroom operations, and data entry), given the forecasted demand. Id. INS's "estimates of forecasted demand" were based upon the 1999 historical

> workload data. Amendment No. 1 at Question and Answer (Q&A) Nos. 22, 29; RFQ Pricing Tables; RFQ attach. 9, reports C, D.
>
> Offerors were required to submit price proposals that included three sections relevant to this protest. First, offerors were to provide an explanation of pricing that described all assumptions made and constraints affecting price, as well as the offeror's price proposal methodology. Second, offerors were to complete electronic pricing tables in accordance with specific instructions. These pricing tables, which were to serve as the mechanism by which INS ordered services under the BPA, were built upon INS's estimates of forecasted demand. Third, offerors were to provide a priced version of the estimating model developed in their technical proposals. The models submitted for both the technical and price proposals were required to be the same except that the model submitted for the technical proposal could not contain any labor rates or prices. Offerors were required to "electronically link" the priced estimating model to the pricing tables in a manner that would allow INS to see how their proposed price was determined. RFQ ¶ 3.6.3.3.
>
> Price was to be evaluated for price reasonableness and cost realism, as well as total evaluated price. INS was to conduct its price analysis using one or more of the techniques specified in Federal Acquisition Regulation (FAR) § 15.404-1(b), and its cost realism analysis in accordance with FAR § 15.404- 1(d). INS might also reject any proposal that was unreasonable or materially unbalanced as to prices for basic and follow-on year quantities. The RFQ defined an unbalanced proposal as one that incorporated prices significantly less than cost for some items and/or prices that are significantly overstated for other items. RFQ ¶ 4.2.3.

The agency established an evaluation board that included a source selection advisory council, a technical evaluation panel, and a business evaluation committee. It received four proposals on August 7, 2000, completed the initial evaluations on August 26, established a competitive range, conducted discussions with three offerors, and received final proposal revisions on October 3. It then eliminated another offeror and reopened discussions with the remaining two. It amended the RFQ and received another round of final proposal revisions on November 2, 2000. It awarded the BPA (an ordering agreement, not an order) against the GSA schedule contract on January 3, 2001, six months after it had issued its RFQ. The loser protested, and GAO denied the protest on April 16, 2001; the protest decision is 16 pages long.

In deciding the protest, GAO made the following comments:

> As a preliminary matter, the RFQ stated that INS intended to issue a BPA against the vendor's GSA FSS contract. Accordingly, the provisions of FAR Subpart 8.4 apply here. Those provisions anticipate that agencies will review vendors' federal supply schedules and place an order directly with the schedule contractor that can provide the supplies or services that represent the best value and meet the government's needs. FAR § 8.404(b)(2); *Digital Sys. Group, Inc.*, B-286931, B-286931.2, Mar. 7, 2001, 2001 CPD ¶ __ at 6. Where, as here, the agency intends to use the vendors' responses as the basis of a detailed technical evaluation and price/technical tradeoff, it may elect, as INS did here, to use an approach that is like a competition in a negotiated procurement. Where an agency takes such an approach, and a protest is filed, we will review the agency's actions to ensure that the evaluation was reasonable and consistent with the terms of the solicitation. *COMARK Fed. Sys.*, B-278343, B-278343.2, Jan. 20, 1998, 98-1 CPD ¶ 34 at 4-5. This RFQ specifically stated that the source evaluation was to be conducted and selection made in accordance with the guidelines set forth in the FAR, and set forth specific procedures for the evaluation of proposals. Accordingly, while the provisions of FAR Part 15, which govern contracting by negotiation, do not directly apply, *Computer Prods., Inc.*, B-284702, May 24, 2000, 2000 CPD ¶ 95 at 4, we analyze

> Labat's contentions by the standards applied to negotiated procurements. *Digital Sys. Group, Inc., supra.*

Footnote omitted.

When ordering under a GSA schedule, why follow the FAR Part 15 Process Model, and thus submit to judgment under the case law appertaining thereto, when the FAR and the GSA permit the use of simpler competitive procedures? Why issue a request for quotations that requires that all competitors prepare extensive technical and price proposals? Why establish a complex evaluation organization? Why determine a competitive range? Why conduct two rounds of discussions and final proposal revisions? Why take *six months* to award *an ordering agreement*? Contracts were already established, and full and open competition had already been obtained.[19] It was just a matter of choosing from among the contractors. Why not, instead, just issue a statement of work, ask for quotes and experience and past performance information, pick a contractor, and then negotiate the terms of the BPA one-on-one, including final pricing formulas? One can find several cases like *Labat-Anderson* among the decisions of GAO.

Simplified Acquisitions. Some agencies follow the FAR Part 15 Process Model even when conducting simplified acquisitions. Agencies can use the simplified acquisition procedures described in FAR Part 13 to award contracts valued at up to $100,000, and up to $5 million for contracts for commercial items. Yet there are several cases on record of agencies using the FAR Part 15 Process Model to conduct such procurements.[20]

---

[19] FAR §§ 6.102(d)(3) and 8.404(a)(1).

[20] See, e.g.: *Kathryn Huddleston and Associates, Ltd.*, B-289453, March 11, 2002 and *Universal Building Maintenance, Inc.*, B-282456, July 15, 1999.

In its protest decision in the matter of *Finlen Complex, Inc.*, GAO describes an Army procurement of meals, lodging, and transportation for military service applicants coming to the military entrance processing station (MEPS) in Butte, Montana.[21] The Army wanted to establish a requirements contract with a local hotel to obtain those services. Since the procurement was for a commercial item valued at less than $5 million, the Army decided to use simplified acquisition procedures as permitted by FAR § 13.500(a).

The contracting officer issued a request for proposals, which GAO described as follows:

> The RFP here—issued to implement a procurement described on the solicitation's cover sheet as a "commercial acquisition, using simplified acquisition procedures"—anticipated award of a fixed-price, indefinite-quantity requirements contract, for a base period followed by four 1-year options, to the offeror whose proposal was considered most advantageous to the government. RFP at 28. The RFP advised that offers would "be evaluated on facility quality, food and transportation proposal, facility location, quality control, past performance and price factors." Id. The RFP also advised that the "technical/quality factors [would be] more important than cost or price." Id. Otherwise, the RFP was silent on the relative weight of the non-price evaluation factors. The RFP was also silent on the role in the selection decision of any non-price evaluation factor other than past performance. As for the role of past performance, the solicitation set forth considerable detail, including how the agency would use the past performance assessment, and what it would consider. (Although not disclosed to potential offerors, the relative weights set for this procurement were: facility quality, 30 percent; food and transportation, 25 percent; facility location, 20 percent; quality control, 20 percent;

---

[21] *Finlen Complex, Inc.*, B-288280, October 10, 2001; see the commentary on Finlen in "Complicating Simplified Acquisition Procedures: A New Twist," in *The Nash & Cibinic Report,* January 2002, 16 N&CR ¶ 2.

> and past performance, 5 percent. Agency Report (AR), Tab G.)

The agency received proposals from six hotels. It established a three-member team, which evaluated the proposals and wrote 85 pages of notes and a consensus report. The contracting officer's representative then wrote a decision document for the contracting officer's signature. The incumbent contractor protested, and GAO sustained the protest.

The protester argued that the selection decision was unfair because the solicitation was misleading about the relative importance of the evaluation factors, making past performance seem much more important than it really was. The Army countered by saying that the RFP was silent about the relative importance of the factors and that FAR §§ 12.602(a) and 13.106-1(a) say that agencies are not required to disclose the relative importance of evaluation factors in acquisitions of commercial items when using simplified acquisition procedures. GAO sustained the protest anyway, saying:

> With respect to the Army's contention that since this solicitation, on its face, is identified as a commercial item procurement using simplified acquisition procedures, no further analysis is needed, we disagree. We look to the substance of an agency's actions, rather than the form. In our view, the labeling of a procurement as "simplified" does not absolve the agency from its obligation to treat vendors fairly. See *COMARK Fed. Sys.*, B-278343, B-278343.2, Jan. 20, 1998, 98-1 CPD ¶ 34 at 4-5 (agency's use of a negotiated procurement approach, rather than a simple Federal Supply Schedule purchase, triggered requirement to provide for a fair and equitable competition).
>
> While there is no dispute here that the procurement of meals and locally available hotel rooms for MEPS applicants appears to fall squarely within the reach of a "commercial item," as that term is defined at FAR §

2.101, there is little about the procedures used in this procurement that can reasonably be called simplified. For example, the agency elected to use a request for proposal format that requires the commercial offerors here—hotels, specifically—to prepare proposals addressing five non-price evaluation factors, including one factor, quality control, for which offerors had to develop and submit a unique quality control plan requiring contracting officer approval of plan changes throughout the life of the contract. Upon receipt of offers, agency personnel conducted a full-scale evaluation, inspected offerors' premises, developed consensus scores, and made a written selection recommendation to the MEPS commander, who, in turn, recommended a selection decision to the contracting officer, who, in turn, made and documented the selection.

Despite the "simplified" label, this procurement is very similar to any other negotiated acquisition conducted under the rules set forth in FAR Part 15. Those rules require that when offerors are asked to prepare detailed proposals, those offerors must be advised of the weight of all factors and significant subfactors that will affect the contract award. FAR § 15.304(d). When our Office asked the Army to address why it would want to withhold this basic information from offerors preparing proposals, the agency answered "that revealing the relative importance of factors may result in offerors skewing their proposals to the more important factors." Agency Supp. Report at 7. In addition, the Army argued that revealing the relative weight of factors in the solicitation would hinder the agency's ability to change the weight of those factors during the course of its evaluation. Id. In our view, neither of these considerations is appropriate under the circumstances of this, or any other, procurement, nor are they advisable for the integrity of the public procurement process.

We recognize that CICA exempts solicitations in procurements using simplified procedures from the requirement that the relative importance of evaluation factors be dis-

> closed. 10 U.S.C. § 2305(a)(2). Moreover, we are sensitive to the fact that the thrust of FAR parts 12 and 13 is to avoid the use of procedures that constrict and complicate the acquisition process, and that FAR §§ 12.602(a) and 13.106-1(a)(2) do not, on their face, limit a contracting officer's discretion to disclose, or not disclose, the relative weight of evaluation criteria in a commercial item procurement conducted using simplified procedures. Nonetheless, basic principles of fair play are a touchstone of the federal procurement system, and those principles bound even broad grants of agency discretion. See Intellectual Properties, Inc., supra... .
>
> Here, where the agency required the commercial offerors to prepare detailed proposals addressing unique government requirements, withholding the relative weight of evaluation factors denied the offerors one of the basic tools used to develop the written, detailed proposals called for in the solicitation.

In short, calling an acquisition "simplified" does not make it so; it is not what you say you are doing that counts, it is what you actually do. Why did the Army prepare and issue an RFP, require competing hotels to prepare and submit written proposals, establish an evaluation board, and have that board prepare 85 pages of notes and an evaluation report? None of that is required by FAR Part 13.

A search of an American Automobile Club (AAA) website yielded a list of ten hotels in Butte, Montana. Why not have the MEPS commander prepare a checklist based on its requirements for food, lodging and transportation and then have one or two members of the detachment visit all ten hotels in Butte and complete a checklist for each? This could be done in one or two days. Why not then have the MEPS commander send to the contracting officer the names of three hotels that meet the MEPS's needs and with which they would be willing to do business? The contracting officer could then contact the three hotel managers, fax or e-mail a copy of the RFQ to each of them, and ask them to fax or e-mail price quotes. Based on the price quotes, the contracting officer, in consultation with the MEPS commander, could pick the hotel that represents the best value and negotiate an agreement on contract terms and conditions. The entire contractor selection process and negotiation could have been completed in a week or two.

The "Fair Opportunity" Process Under Multiple Award Delivery and Task Order Contracts. FAR § 16.505(b)(1) requires that when placing orders against multiple award delivery and task order contracts, agencies must provide each awardee a "fair opportunity to be considered" for each order in excess of $2,500. FAR § 16.505(b)(1)(ii) expressly states that the source selection procedures in FAR Subpart 15.3 do not apply to this process.[22] The fair opportunity process is not subject to protest, so there are no GAO decisions that illustrate the use of the FAR Part 15 Process Model therein. Nevertheless, there is considerable anecdotal and documentary evidence that some agencies have been conducting what are essentially mini-source selections when giving awardees a fair opportunity. Some industry associations have complained about the bid and proposal costs associated with such processes.[23] And some agencies have published formal guidance for providing a fair opportunity

---

[22] See, too: Defense FAR Supplement § 216.505-70 for special rules applicable to Defense agencies. That regulation also expressly states that FAR Subpart 15.3 does not apply.

[23] See: Professional Services Council, *Issue Paper: Task Order Contracts,* in which the following comment appears: "Frequently, the government requires extensive proposals for individual delivery/task orders, rather than the simple, low cost, process envisioned by the legislative drafters and regulatory designers. Some agencies require 50% or more of the effort of a full proposal. This adds costs and administrative burden for the contractor and the government." The paper may be found at the Council's website: http://www.pscouncil.org/westand/task_order.htm. See, too: Carlson, T., "The Tyranny of Multiple-Award Indefinite Delivery/Indefinite Quantity Contracts," available at http://www.tacarlson.com/documents/tyranny_of contracts.pdf.

process that reflects the FAR Part 15 Process Model. See, for example, the guidance issued by the National Institutes of Health, Information Technology Acquisition and Assessment Center: *Chief Information Officer-Solutions and Partners 2 Innovations (CIO-SP2i) Task Order Guidelines* (March 2001).[24] That guidance provides for the solicitation of complete task order proposals from all awardees and even "discussions" with multiple awardees prior to the award of the task order.

Again, the question must be asked: Why follow the FAR Part 15 Process Model when the FAR permits the use of a much simpler and more efficient process? Why ask for complete proposals from all awardees when FAR § 16.505(b)(1) does not require that this be done? And why conduct discussions with more than one contractor? Surely, there must be a simpler way to choose a contractor from among firms that have already been evaluated and awarded a contract, a way that is less costly and time-consuming for both the government and the contractors.

SOME BEST PRACTICES IN COMPETITIVE PROCESS DESIGN

One of an acquisition team's most important tasks is designing efficient competitive processes. While the FAR Part 15 Process Model is suitable for many acquisitions that fall under FAR Part 15, it is a cumbersome, time-consuming, and costly procedure to use when there are numerous competitors, and an unnecessarily complex procedure to use when ordering from GSA schedules, making simplified acquisitions, or giving offerors a fair opportunity to be considered under multiple-award deliver and task order contracts. Not even the new DOD procedures for ordering services under GSA schedules and task order contracts require contracting officers to follow the FAR Part 15 Process Model.[25]

---

[24] Available at: http://www.lmsi-nw.com/cio-sp2/task_guidelines/CIOSP2Guidelines.htm#_Toc512250729.

[25] See DFARS §§ 208.404-70 and 216.505-70.

As indicated by GAO's *Kathpal* decision, even when conducting a FAR Part 15 source selection there is no need to require complete proposal information from every competitor at the outset or to evaluate every offeror based on every evaluation factor. Agencies may solicit proposal information and evaluate the competitors in phases, progressively narrowing the competitive field based on limited information and obtaining detailed and voluminous information from only a few.

Acquisition personnel should design their competitive processes to comply with statute and regulation, to yield good decisions, and to economize on agency transaction costs and competitor bid and proposal costs. Acquisition personnel should not follow the FAR Part 15 Process Model without first considering alternative processes; instead, when appropriate, they should innovate to develop more efficient processes. In that regard, consider the following guiding principle of the Federal Acquisition System, as set forth in FAR § 1.102-4(e):

> The FAR outlines procurement policies and procedures that are used by members of the Acquisition Team. If a policy or procedure, or a particular strategy or practice, is in the best interest of the Government and is not specifically addressed in the FAR, nor prohibited by law (statute or case law), Executive order or other regulation, Government members of the Team should not assume it is prohibited. Rather, absence of direction should be interpreted as permitting the Team to innovate and use sound business judgment that is otherwise consistent with law and within the limits of their authority. Contracting officers should take the lead in encouraging business process innovations and ensuring that business decisions are sound.

Some best practices in competitive process design include the following:

- **Limit the number of evaluation factors.** It is the number of evaluation factors that determines the amount of information that must be obtained from competitors and processed by the government in order to reach a decision. Therefore, use no more evaluation factors than absolutely necessary and only those factors on which the differences among offerors are likely to be more than trivial.[26]

- **Limit the amount of proposal information required from competitors.** As a general rule, and especially when acquiring services, do not make offerors write technical or management expositions (narratives) describing how they will do the work or how they will organize, or specially-prepared quality assurance and safety plans, etc. Such writings are time-consuming and costly to prepare and to evaluate, but they do not necessarily demonstrate a firm's ability to perform, and usually are not binding in any meaningful sense. Moreover, incorporating such writings into a contract is inconsistent with performance-based service contracting policy. If agency technical personnel want to obtain first-hand insights into how well the competitors understand the work, require oral presentations *instead of* written technical or management proposals.[27]

---

[26] See: Edwards, V., *Source Selection Answer Book* (Vienna, VA: Management Concepts, 2000), pp. 79–83; "Streamlining Source Selection by Improving the Quality of Evaluation Factors," in *The Nash & Cibinic Report,* October 1994, 8 N&CR ¶ 10; "Postscript: Streamlining Source Selection by Improving the Quality of Evaluation Factors," in *The Nash & Cibinic Report,* December 1994, 8 N&CR ¶ 72; and, "Selecting the Evaluation Factors in Best Value Source Selection," in *The Nash & Cibinic Report,* June 1996, 10 N&CR ¶ 32.

[27] See: "The Status of Technical, Management, and Cost Proposals: Are They Part of a Negotiated Contract?" in *The Nash & Cibinic Report,* July 1993, 7 N&CR ¶ 37; "The Technical Proposal: Is it Fish or Fowl?" in *The Nash & Cibinic Report,* May 1997, 11 N&CR ¶ 22; "Postscript: The Technical Proposal," in *The Nash & Cibinic Report,* January 1998, 12 N&CR

- **Use the FAR Part 15 Process Model in source selections only when it is most effective.** When conducting source selections under FAR Part 15, use the FAR Part 15 Process Model when five or fewer proposals are expected and when obtaining complete proposals from all offerors at the outset of the competition will save time.

- **Consider phased submission of information and proposal evaluation.** When conducting source selections under FAR Part 15, and when there is a realistic likelihood of receiving more than five proposals, consider soliciting proposal information and evaluating proposals in phases. Alternatively, consider planning to use phased evaluation as a contingency procedure.[28]

- **Do not follow the FAR Part 15 Process Model when ordering from GSA schedules.** When using GSA's special ordering procedures for services that require a statement of work, do not follow the FAR Part 15 Process Model, and do not use FAR Part 15 terminology (e.g., "competitive range" or "discussions") or refer to FAR Part 15 in the RFQ. Non-Defense agencies should conduct market research, select at least three contractors to solicit based on experience, past performance, and perhaps an informal interview, provide those firms with a statement of work by fax or e-mail and ask for price quotes, then choose one firm with which to negotiate the terms of the order or blanket purchase agreement.

¶ 4; "Postscript II: The Technical Proposal," in *The Nash & Cibinic Report,* May 1998, 12 N&CR ¶ 28; "Postscript III: The Technical Proposal," in *The Nash & Cibinic Report,* August 1998, 12 N&CR ¶ 45; and Edwards, V., *Source Selection Answer Book* (Vienna, VA: Management Concepts, 2000), pp. 230–238.

[28] See: "A Contingency Procedure for Source Selection," in *The Nash & Cibinic Report,* May 2000, 14 N&CR ¶ 25, and Edwards, V., *Source Selection Answer Book* (Vienna, VA: Management Concepts, 2000), pp. 215–219 and 226–229.

Defense agencies complying with DFARS § 208.404-70 and expecting a large number of responses to their "fair notice of intent" should request limited information (experience, past performance, and price quote) at the outset of the competition and progressively narrow the competitive field before asking for more detailed proposal information. Except in unusual circumstances, pick one contractor and then negotiate the details of the order or blanket purchase agreement one-on-one; do not establish a competitive range, negotiate with more than one firm at a time, or solicit revised proposals from more than one competitor.

- **Do not follow the FAR Part 15 Process Model when making simplified acquisitions.** When using simplified acquisition procedures to buy complex supplies or services worth in excess of $25,000 and for which a synopsis must be published, and if planning to ask for more information than just a price quote, either: (a) select one firm for one-on-one negotiations based on experience, past performance, and a price quote and then negotiate to agreement on details; or (b) narrow the field of competitors on the basis of experience, past performance, and a price quote before asking for more detailed proposal information, providing a specification or statement of work and clauses for price quote development by fax or e-mail. Do not use FAR Part 15 terminology or refer to FAR Part 15 in the RFQ. Do not establish a competitive range, negotiate with more than one firm at a time, or solicit revised quotes or offers from more than one competitor.

- **Do not follow the FAR Part 15 Process Model when giving contractors under a multiple award delivery or task order contract a fair opportunity to be considered.** Maintain a dossier on each contractor reflecting its performance under task orders and any special qualifications that it may have demonstrated during

> performance. When the time comes to issue an order, send a draft of the order to each contractor and ask for a price quotation. Choose one contractor for one-on-one negotiations based on its past performance, its price quote, and, if appropriate, its special qualifications. Negotiate the details of the order with that contractor. If you cannot reach a satisfactory agreement, then go back and choose one of the other contractors for negotiation. Do not solicit complete proposals from every contractor, establish a competitive range, negotiate with more than one contractor at a time, or solicit revised quotes or offers from more than one contractor.

Our government is heavily dependent upon contractors to do work that is not inherently governmental, and it is going to become even more so in the future. This means that effective acquisition management is crucial to good government. In turn, the design of efficient competitive processes is essential to effective acquisition management, especially in this era of urgent needs and ever more limited staff resources. While the FAR Part 15 Process Model works well in many circumstances, it is not always the most efficient process and thus does not always reflect best practice. Acquisition professionals must innovate when designing competitive processes in order to economize on government transaction costs and contractor bid and proposal costs and obtain best value efficiently and within a reasonable amount of time.

Appendix B

The Relative Importance of Source Selection Evaluation Factors: Analysis of a Misunderstood Rule

Vernon J. Edwards

A former student recently brought to my attention the Comptroller General's protest decision in *CardioMetrix*, Comp. Gen. Dec. B-258108, 94-2 CPD ¶ 191. Reading the decision caused me to reflect on the fact that one of the most misunderstood rules in the Federal Acquisition Regulation is the rule that requires the disclosure of the "relative importance" of source selection evaluation factors. The rule appears in FAR 15.605(d)(1), which reads, in part, as follows:

> At a minimum, the solicitation shall clearly state the significant evaluation factors, such as cost or price, cost or price-related factors, past performance and other non-cost or non-price-related factors, and any significant subfactors, that will be considered in making the source selection, and their relative importance (see FAR 15.406-5(c)). The solicitation shall inform offerors of minimum requirements that apply to particular evaluation factors and significant subfactors. Further, the solicitation shall

---

This material *from The Nash & Cibinic Report* (July 1996) is reproduced with the permission of the publisher, Thomson West. Further use without the permission of the publisher is prohibited. For additional information or to subscribe, call 1-800-344-5009 or visit http://www.west.thomson.com. *The Nash & Cibinic Report* is now available on Westlaw. Visit http://www.westlaw.com.

state whether all evaluation factors other than cost or price, when combined, are—

(i) Significantly more important than cost or price;

(ii) Approximately equal to cost or price; or

(iii) Significantly less important than cost or price.

FAR 15.605(d)(2) goes on to state that the solicitation may elaborate on the relative importance of the evaluation factors and subfactors and that it may describe relative importance by means of "numerical weights," which, if used, need not be disclosed to the prospective offerors.

THE PROBLEM

The problem with the FAR provision quoted above is that it is ambiguous. Something is more or less important than something else with regard to some purpose or end. In relation to what end is one evaluation factor more important than another? There are at least two possible interpretations of FAR 15.605(d)(1). The first is that one evaluation factor is more important than another to the determination of the winner of the competition. The second is that one evaluation factor is more important than another to the satisfaction of an agency's procurement objectives. When asked to choose which of these interpretations reflects the meaning of FAR 15.605(d)(1), most persons select the first—relative importance to the determination of the winner. However, when it issues the solicitation, the Government does not and cannot know which evaluation factor will ultimately have the most influence on the selection of the winner.

To illustrate: Assume that in a source selection an agency will use numerical scoring (including numerical scoring of price) and that the solicitation will state that non-price factors are three times as important as price. Assume that the evaluation factors are fully and clearly defined attributes of proposals. The agency will score proposals on a 0 to 100–point scale, 100 being best, and will allot 75 points to non-price factors and 25 points to price. Assume that factor scores are well-defined functions of proposal factor performance, meaning that differences in factor scores will reflect substantive differences in the competing proposals. Assume that the outcome of the evaluation and scoring of proposals is as follows:

Offeror	Non-Price Score	Price Score	Total Score
A	70	19	89
B	70	25	95
C	70	14	84

The non-price factor scores indicate that evaluators determined that there were no substantive differences in the offerors' technical proposals. The marginal differences in the offerors' total scores are entirely the result of the differences in their prices. The selection of the winning offeror will be based entirely on the differences in the offerors' prices. Therefore, price will be the most important factor in determining the winner. Is this inconsistent with the statement of relative importance in the solicitation?

In a source selection in which there are two or more evaluation factors, the selection of the winner is based on the marginal differences in the competing offerors' non-price factor scores and prices. In the usual case, the Government makes a series of paired comparisons between the competing offerors, trading off the differences in the non-price factor strengths and weaknesses and the proposed prices. If in any comparison an offeror has both the higher non-price factor score (better combination of strengths and weaknesses) and the lower price, then that offeror is the better value. If an offeror has the higher non-price factor score and the higher price, then the Government must decide if the offeror's marginal non-price superiority is worth the marginal difference in price. If it is, then the higher-scored, higher-priced offeror is the better value. If it is not, then the lower-scored, lower-priced offeror is the better value. The importance of any factor to the determination of the winner depends on the marginal differences between the offerors. (For an analysis of the protest decisions in this regard, see Nash & Cibinic, *Competitive Negotiation: The Source Selection Process* at 500–505 (Geo. Wash. Univ. 1993).)

Assume another procurement where an agency has chosen product quality, past performance, qualifications of key personnel, and price as its evaluation factors. Assume that the agency will score each offeror on each factor, including price, on a 0 to 100–point scale, adjust the raw score by a weighting factor, and then add the weighted scores to determine which offeror is best overall. Product quality is considered the most important factor and is assigned an importance weight of .40. Offeror past performance, qualifications of key personnel, and price are each weighted .20. The solicitation states that product quality is the most important factor and that past performance, key personnel, and price are less important but equally important to one another. The unweighted (raw) factor scores of the four offerors are as follows:

Offeror	Product Quality	Past Performance	Key Personnel	Price
A	86	60	79	100
B	88	70	81	90
C	82	80	75	95
D	84	90	81	90

The weighted factor scores and total weighted scores are as follows:

Offeror	Product Quality	Past Performance	Key Personnel	Price	Total Weighted Score
A	34.4	12	15.8	20	82.2
B	35.2	14	16.2	18	83.4
C	32.8	16	15	19	82.8
D	33.6	18	16.2	18	85.8

Offeror D received the highest total weighted score despite the fact that it received the third highest score on product quality, the factor that the solicitation stated would be most important. Offeror B received the second highest total weighted score and the highest score on product quality. In comparing Offeror D to Offeror B, it is obvious that D's advantage over B is due entirely to its better past performance. Past performance is only one-half as important as product quality. Thus, past performance will be the most important factor in determining which offeror received the highest total weighted score. If the scores reflect substantive differences among the competing proposals, then D should win the competition. Note that Offeror A received the lowest total weighted score, notwithstanding the fact that it received the second highest score on the most important factor.

This illustration demonstrates that the Government cannot know what the marginal differences in the offerors' scores will be until the scoring is complete. It thus demonstrates that the Government cannot know at the outset which factor will be most important to—i.e., have the greatest influence on—the award decision until it has scored the proposals. All that the Government can state before the proposals have been scored is its relative degree of preference for each of the factors, which should reflect its sense of the importance of each factor to the satisfaction of the Government's procurement objectives.

THE IMPORTANCE OF RELATIVE IMPORTANCE

The FAR does not say why solicitations should state the relative importance of the evaluation factors. However, one obvious reason is to provide offerors with guidance about what the Government wants so that they can prepare their proposals accordingly. During proposal preparation offerors may find themselves faced with the choice of offering more quality at a higher price or less quality at a lower price. The only way to make an intelligent choice is to ask the customer which it prefers—higher quality or lower price. This is what any salesperson would do. To answer the question intelligently, the customer should determine what is the margin of additional quality and how much more it will cost. The customer can then decide if the margin of additional quality is worth the margin of additional cost. In general, we can expect that the strength of a customer's preference for a given margin of additional quality will decrease as the margin of additional cost increases.

Many Government agencies have recognized this reality and state in their requests for proposals that while non-price factors are more important than price, as the offerors become more equal in non-price merit the importance of price to the source selection decision will increase. This technique has been called "variable weighting." (See Nash & Cibinic, supra, at 211–219.) However, it is important to recognize that, as demonstrated above, this will be true whether the RFP says so or not. Moreover, the opposite is also true. As prices approach equality, the relative importance of non-price factors to the source selection decision will increase. It is also true of the relative importance of non-price subfactors.

In the open market, many buyers and sellers continuously exchange information about product or service non-price factors and prices in a highly informal process, making tradeoffs and continuously adjusting their desires and offerings throughout that process. But in Government source selection, communications between the buyer and the sellers are constrained by rules and a high order of process formality. In the absence of open communications, each offeror must try to guess what combination of non-price factors and price will win the contract, without knowledge of its competitors' plans. Many combinations are possible. The customer usually will not know in advance what they are, much less which ones actually will be offered. At best, a Government agency usually can provide little more than highly general guidance about its preferences.

As has been demonstrated above, even if the Government scores all factors numerically, including price, and discloses the numerical scoring system and the factor weights, the prospective offerors cannot know the ultimate impact that any factor will have on the source selection decision because this depends on the marginal differences among the competing offerors on each of the factors. Even if an offeror knows that it can offer the best possible combination of non-price factors, it cannot know its chances of winning without knowing the margin of difference between it and its closest competitor on those factors and the margin of difference in their prices. At any given margin of superiority in the non-price factors, the greater the margin of difference in prices the lower the probability that the superior, higher-priced offeror will win the contract. With perfect knowledge of its competitors' plans, an offeror could adjust its offer of non-price factors, its offer of price, or both to improve its chances for success. But that information will not be available unless someone violates the Procurement Integrity Act.

If the purpose of stating the relative importance of the factors is to provide offerors with general guidance about how to make tradeoffs during proposal preparation, then what sense does it make to state the relative importance of factors like past performance and experience? Presumably, an offeror cannot change its history of past performance and experience. Offerors do not "propose" their past performance or experience in any meaningful sense of the word. Arguably, an offeror could reduce its price to compensate for its poor past performance or lack of experience. But would this make the offeror a better risk or a worse one? Perhaps, if a solicitation states that past performance and experience are highly important, an offeror with a poor record of past performance or little experience will decide not to submit a proposal.

"EQUAL" IMPORTANCE

What does it mean to say that two factors are equally important? There are at least two possible meanings. One possible meaning is that the Government requires a specific level of performance on each of two factors and that an offer of an extra amount of one factor will not compensate for an insufficient amount of the other. The factors are equally important in the sense that an offeror must propose some specific or minimum amount of both.

A second possible interpretation of "equally important" is that the Government is indifferent to a choice between some additional amount of one factor or some additional amount of another. Either offer would receive the same score as the other. However, while this may be true for some specific combination of factor measurements, it is highly unlikely that it would be true for all possible combinations of factor measurements. Thus, in making tradeoffs between proposals of guns and butter, the Government may be indifferent to a choice between an additional six guns or an additional 20 pounds of butter. However, it is unlikely that the Government would be similarly indifferent to all possible alternatives of additional guns or butter.

To illustrate: Suppose that a solicitation states that the evaluation factors are technical approach, key personnel, and price. The solicitation also states that technical approach and key personnel are equally important and that, together, they are more important than price. The solicitation further states that the Government will score technical approach and key personnel by allocating a maximum of 50 points to each, but that it will not assign a score to price. Suppose that the Government receives two proposals, and that after evaluation the results are as follows:

Offeror	Technical Approach	Key Personnel	Price
A	50	20	$1,100,000
B	20	50	$1,000,000

Based on these results, and assuming that both offerors have met all minimum requirements, the Government should choose Offeror B. Since technical approach and key personnel are equally important, it should not matter to the Government which of the technical approach/key personnel alternatives it chooses. Price is the only real discriminating factor and will determine the winner. Given this result, price is the most important factor to the selection outcome. If either technical approach or key personnel was more important, then the Government would have to make a tradeoff between one offeror's marginal superiority on the most important factor and the marginal difference in the offerors' prices.

But assume that the factors are equally important and that the results of the evaluation were as follows:

Offeror	Technical Approach	Key Personnel	Price
A	50	30	$1,100,000
B	30	40	$1,000,000

How will the statement that technical approach and key personnel are equally important in this scenario affect the source selection decision? Will it mean that A's 20-point advantage in technical approach is offset by B's 10-point advantage in key personnel, with the result that B will win based on its lower price?

It is unlikely that the Government would be indifferent with regard to the choice of technical approach/key personnel alternatives in this scenario. It is more likely that the marginal difference in technical approach would be more influential in the selection of the winner than the marginal difference in key personnel. The two factors may have been equally important in terms of the Government's objectives, but not in terms of their influence on the source selection decision. Technical approach and key personnel would be equally important to the outcome of the competition only under a very limited set of circumstances: either when all offerors receive the same scores for the two factors or when they receive offsetting scores that sum to the same total score.

In the *CardioMetrix* decision, the Comptroller General reported that an Internal Revenue Service solicitation had stated that "the [g]overnment is more concerned with obtaining superior technical features than with making an award at the lowest overall price to the [g]overnment." The RFP stated that technical factors would be scored on a scale of 100 points and that price would not be scored. The RFP also stated that the Government "will not make an award at a significantly higher price . . . to achieve slightly superior technical features." The protester complained that this scheme eliminated price as an evaluation factor.

Although he denied the protest, the Comptroller concluded that the statement in the RFP that the Government was more concerned with technical superiority than with award at the lowest price did not amount to a sufficiently clear indication of the relative importance of the evaluation factors. Consequently, he ruled that the proper interpretation of the RFP was that technical factors and price were equally important. This conclusion is contrary to the plain meaning of the words in the RFP and to logic.

In this procurement the Government certainly was not, in general, indifferent to tradeoffs between technical superiority and price, although it may have been indifferent to tradeoffs between specific measures of technical superiority and price. It is clear from the language of the RFP that the Government considered technical factors to be more important than price up to a point. The Government gave prospective offerors the best advice that it could give in the absence of perfect advance knowledge about the offers that it would receive. That advice was that if forced to make a choice of offering either greater technical quality at a higher price or lower technical quality at a lower price, offerors should keep in mind the Government's general preference for technical superiority. But offerors should also be mindful of the competition. As the margin of difference in price for a given margin of difference in technical quality increased, the Government's degree of preference for that given margin of technical quality would decrease. Apparently, however, the Comptroller would have found a simple sentence to the effect that technical factors would be more important than price to have been clearer. Either the Comptroller is confused about the meaning of "equal importance," or he needs to explain his interpretation to the rest of us.

SOME SUGGESTIONS

In the preceding discussion I have assumed that the evaluation factors are fully and clearly defined attributes and that the scores are well-defined functions of specific measurements or ratings of proposal factor performance. However, I have found that in practice most evaluation factors—especially factors like "soundness of approach," "understanding of the problem," and "proposed organization"—are usually not fully and clearly defined and that scores (whether numerical or adjectival) are not well-defined functions of specific levels of proposal factor performance. Thus, in practice, solicitation statements about the relative importance of evaluation factors are extremely vague. They communicate very little useful information to prospective offerors. In any event, even when the Government communicates its preferences as clearly as possible, the kind of information that offerors would like to have and that usually is available to them in open market transactions (Who are my competitors? What are the features of their products and services? How do those products and services differ from mine? What are their prices? What are the preferences of consumers?) usually is unavailable to them in a Government procurement.

Government contracting and technical personnel must understand these concepts and problems to fashion language for solicitations that communicates the most helpful information about its procurement objectives and factor tradeoff preferences. Offerors must understand these concepts and problems to avoid being confused by statements such as "The evaluation factors are listed below in descending order of importance," and "Quality is weighted 50 percent, Past Performance is weighted 25 percent, and Price is weighted 25 percent" (percent of what?).

The FAR Council can clear up some of this misunderstanding during its rewrite of FAR Part 15 by directing that agencies state the relative importance of the evaluation factors to the achievement of their procurement objectives. But regardless of whether the FAR Council clarifies the meaning of the FAR, solicitations should make it clear that statements of relative importance of the evaluation factors indicate their relative importance to the Government's objectives and not their relative influence on the source selection decision. The Comptroller General should make its protest decisions accordingly.

Readers of this article who would like a more thorough discussion of these concepts should obtain a copy of *Decision Analysis and Behavioral Research* (Cambridge Univ. Press 1986) by Detlof von Winterfeldt and Ward Edwards and read Chapter 8. The research on which that book is based was supported, in part, by the U.S. Office of Naval Research.

A less comprehensive but less technical discussion appears in *Decision Analysis for Management Judgment* (John Wiley & Sons 1991) by Paul Goodwin and George Wright on pages 19–21 and 25–26.

APPENDIX C

Streamlining Source Selection by Improving the Quality of Evaluation Factors

Vernon J. Edwards

Almost everyone involved with Government contracting can tell a horror story about a "best value" source selection that involved the development of a lengthy and costly proposal, about a source selection that took two years to complete, and about a protest that delayed an important project and increased its costs. Legislators, policymakers, and acquisition managers are currently looking for ways to "streamline" the source selection process. I would suggest that the single most effective thing acquisition managers can do to streamline the best value source selection process is to improve their choices of evaluation factors for award.

TYPICAL RFPS—AN ESSAY-WRITING CONTEST

Consider the typical Request for Proposals (RFP). It includes a statement of work or specification that describes the Government's requirements as well as its preferred contract

---

This material from *The Nash & Cibinic Report* (October 1994) is reproduced with the permission of the publisher, Thomson West. Further use without the permission of the publisher is prohibited. For additional information or to subscribe, call 1-800-344-5009 or visit www.west.thomson.com. *The Nash & Cibinic Report* is now available on Westlaw. Visit www.westlaw.com.

terms and conditions. It also includes evaluation factors for award like "understanding of the problem," "soundness of approach," or "quality of the management plan." Such RFPs usually instruct offerors to read the statement of work or specification and then to propose a plan or "approach" to doing the work, but caution offerors that approaches that depart from the terms of the RFP may result in rejection of the proposal.

For example, a current RFP for task order "advisory and assistance services" includes a statement of work that describes about 14 generic tasks and subtasks, such as "[a]dvise and assist the [agency's] Executive Committee on the updating and/or development and implementation of a new [total quality management (TQM)] plan," and "[d]esign and facilitate a wide variety of structured activities . . . for the purpose of organizational improvement." The RFP states that technical factors will comprise 80% of the total evaluation weight and lists four equally important technical factors: (1) company background and experience, (2) technical and management approach, (3) personnel qualifications, and (4) plans for use of outside resources. The RFP goes on to state that technical proposals must contain "detailed explanations of proposed approaches to performing and accomplishing the work . . . and a specific outline of the actual tasks proposed to be performed in order to complete the work." The RFP warns: "Repeating the work statement without elaborating on the specific tasks to be performed is unacceptable."

In response, offerors will probably submit lengthy technical proposals because of the weight assigned to technical factors, the vagueness of the tasks in the statement of work, and the warning that offerors must submit an elaborate response or risk rejection. (The RFP did not include a proposal page limitation.) The proposals will be expensive to produce, to read, and to evaluate. How much of this is necessary?

RFPs typically include two broad categories of "technical" or "management" evaluation factors. The first category relates to factual matters about offeror capability and includes such factors as experience, past performance, key personnel qualifications, capability of facilities, and product specifications. The second category relates to offerors' descriptions, promises, or predictions about what they will do, achieve, or deliver in the future. It includes descriptions of their plans, procedures, "design concepts," and promises or predictions about their performance or the performance of their products. This category includes such factors as "understanding the problem," "soundness of approach," and "merits of the proposed design."

It is in response to the second category of factors that offerors must write lengthy proposals, especially when an RFP combines those factors with instructions to provide detailed explanations and warnings not to repeat the work statement without elaboration. These factors relate to assertions about future events, which are not verifiable. To respond to the first category of factors, an offeror should report facts. But to respond to the second category of factors, the offeror must invent something to say.

When an RFP includes a complete description of the Government's requirements and terms and conditions, the evaluation factors constitute little more than a test of the offerors' knowledge and rhetorical skill. The offerors' technical and management proposals will play little or no role in contract formation. They will simply provide information for the Government to use in evaluating and comparing the offerors. The Government assumes that the technical and management proposals will indicate the offerors' relative capabilities and prospects for success. Thus, RFPs that include such factors effectively compel offerors to compete in essay-writing contests. Source selection decisions based on these criteria too often reflect the ability of an offeror to write a good essay rather than its ability to do the work. (For a classic example, see *SMS Data Products Group, Inc., GSBCA 8589-P,* 87-1 BCA ¶ 19496, 1986 BPD ¶ 206.) The reaction of competent contractors to such requirements is entirely predictable. See an article in the proceedings of the fifth annual conference of the Association of Proposal Management Professionals, which was held in Washington, D.C., suggesting that companies develop reusable "plans" and "TQM blurbs" as a means of winning these essay-writing contests.

An offeror's assertions—predictions, plans, and promises—about the future in a proposal are not reliable bases upon which to judge its capability and prospects for success for several reasons. First, the proposal may reflect the knowledge and writing skill of consultants and proposal writers rather than the performance capability of the offeror. Second, even if the offeror did write the proposal, the ability to promise, plan, or predict does not demonstrate the ability to execute. Third, a plan is merely a statement of intentions, made without perfect knowledge about the future. The future is rarely as we hope or expect it to be, and most projects do not proceed as planned. The ability to write a good plan does not demonstrate the ability to respond effectively to unanticipated contingencies. Fourth, the Government may lack the expertise to evaluate proposed plans and designs. Indeed, as users rather than designers, Government personnel may not be able reliably to predict project success based on a performance plan or predict product or system mission performance based on a conceptual design. Requirements to write proposals in response to factors in the second category increase the cost and time of source selection. But the claim that such proposals are essential to sound source selection decision-making is dubious. Government agencies can streamline the source selection process by omitting this second category of factors.

ILLUSORY BENEFITS OF BAFOS

Agencies further increase the cost and time of source selection when they conduct discussions to tell offerors what they do not like (deficiencies) about their assertions, plans, conceptual designs, or predictions and then ask them to revise and resubmit them as best and final offers (BAFOs). (Agencies are telling offerors: "You flunked the first essay exam, but we'll give you a chance to take it again.") The BAFO procedure may add little of value because assertions, plans, predictions, and conceptual designs may not mean much. Moreover, the procedure may encourage offerors to reduce prices or costs and fees excessively in a desperate attempt to win the contract. The procedure's benefits may thus be doubly illusory. The BAFO may not only add nothing of value, it may plant the seeds of conflict and poor performance.

RFPS FOR RESEARCH AND DEVELOPMENT

What about large research and development contracts (or design-build construction contracts)? Many would argue that solicitations for such programs should request proposals that include detailed—albeit preliminary or "conceptual"—design information (e.g., problem definition, feasibility, functional flow, requirements allocation, tradeoff, and other analyses), systems engineering plans, configuration management plans, and so forth. Such proposals often contain thousands of pages, cost millions of dollars to produce, and require months to study and evaluate. Certainly, tradition weighs in heavily on the side of those who argue the need for such proposals.

But one must wonder how many of the large systems that have been fielded by the National Aeronautics and Space Administration, the Department of Defense, and other agencies are significantly different from the design concept in the winning proposal. The relationship between the winning concept and the final product is often distant because the initial statement of Government requirements tends to be vague or ambiguous, incomplete, and tentative and because the factors that drive and constrain those requirements are often highly dynamic. The plans and proposed designs solicited by RFPs are, in fact, sales presentations. They are designed to persuade the Government that the offeror has the capability to succeed. They are the answers to essay questions.

Here are three propositions, offered in response to those who argue for the need for detailed technical proposals for research and development programs:

(1) In selecting a system development contractor, the Government is entering into a partnership that is established on the basis of a developmental capability and an expectation of success.

(2) Proposed project plans and preliminary designs will count for little in the long run because initial statements of requirements are usually vague or ambiguous, incomplete, and tentative, and because the factors that drive and constrain requirements will change during the course of development. Therefore, they are not the most reliable bases for predicting success in research and development procurements.

(3) Contractor experience, past performance, and key personnel qualifications are far more reliable indicators of developmental capability and predictors of success than factors such as "soundness of approach" or "merits of proposed design."

The larger and more complex the system, and the longer the period of development, the greater the force of these propositions.

RETHINKING EVALUATION FACTORS

The most reliable indicators of an offeror's capability and prospects for success are its record of experience, its reputation for past performance, and the qualifications of its key personnel. Add price or estimated cost and fee, and you have all the best-value evaluation factors most agencies will ever need to select a contractor. For supply contracts, the Government may need to include a factor relating to verification of product specifications. Facility capability and capacity also may be important. Omitting essay contest factors and associated proposal preparation instructions will eliminate the cost and time associated with the preparation, evaluation, discussion, and revision of lengthy technical and management proposals. (For an excellent example of an effective, streamlined procurement, see *CORVAC, Inc.*, Comp. Gen. Dec. B-244766, 91-2 CPD ¶ 454, a protest involving a procurement for hazardous waste processing in which the only evaluation factors were price and past performance.)

By rethinking their ideas about evaluation factors for award, acquisition managers can reduce the time and cost associated with best-value source selection. Better evaluation factors will improve the quality of competition in Government contracting and benefit both Government and industry. Beneficial change can come without new legislation, new policy, or rewriting the Federal Acquisition Regulation.

APPENDIX D

The Level of Confidence Assessment Rating Technique: A Tool for Source Selection

Vernon J. Edwards

In its decision in the protest of *Colmek Systems Engineering*, Comp. Gen. Dec. B-291931.2, July 9, 2003, the U.S. Government Accountability Office (GAO) described how the Department of the Navy used a technique called Level of Confidence Assessment Rating (LOCAR) to evaluate offers in an acquisition for the initial production, delivery, and support of underwater imaging systems. The systems are used to search for, detect, locate, and classify mines and other underwater explosives. Only two firms submitted proposals for what was to be a ten-year, fixed-price and cost-reimbursement, indefinite-delivery-indefinite-quantity contract. The protestor had proposed a price/cost of $6,743,935; the firm that was selected had proposed a price/cost of $8,613,493. The agency selected the higher-price firm. GAO denied the protest.

This article was first published online in slightly different form at *Where in Federal Contracting?* (www.wifcon.com) in 2004. It provides a detailed explanation of the Level of Confidence Assessment Rating (LOCAR) technique for source selection, which is discussed in Question 37, *What is the Fast Track/LOCAR source selection procedure?* Copyright © 2005 by Vernon J. Edwards.

Here is how GAO described the Navy's source selection process:

> Source selection was to be determined using a specified methodology. The first step was to determine the "promised value" which, in this procurement, was the total point score awarded under the technical approach factor. RFP S: M.II.(1). The second step was to assign a level of confidence assessment rating (LOCAR) to each offeror's capability (including relevant experience and past performance) using a scale indicating the degree of confidence the Navy had in the firm's ability to succeed. RFP S: M.II.(2). The third step was to determine the Navy's level of confidence and expected value associated with each offeror. The level of confidence was a subjective rating that would reflect the degree to which the Navy believed an offeror was likely to keep the promises it made in its offer. The expected value was to be ascertained by multiplying the promised value by the LOCAR and was to be expressed in terms of a percentage. RFP S: M.II.(3). To determine which offeror represented the best value to the government, the Navy was to make a series of paired comparisons among the offerors, trading off the differences in the non-price factors against the difference in most probable price between the offerors. If the offeror with the higher expected value had the higher price, the Navy had to decide whether the margin of higher expected value (that is, the greater prospects for success) was worth the higher price. RFP S: M.II.
>
> The solicitation stated that the Navy planned to award the contract on the basis of initial proposals, without conducting discussions. RFP S: M.I. As a result, offerors were told that their proposals should contain their best terms from a technical, cost/price, relevant experience and past performance standpoint. If considered necessary by the contracting officer, however, discussions would be conducted only with those offerors determined to have a reasonable chance for award. Id.

Footnote omitted.

The LOCAR technique was first described in 1994 in a monograph published by The George Washington University Law School's Government Contracts Program: *How to Evaluate Past Performance: A Best-Value Approach.* GAO first mentioned the LOCAR technique in its decision in the matter of *Moore Medical Corporation,* Comp. Gen. Dec. B-261758, October 26, 1995 (protest denied), which was about an acquisition of surgical supplies by the Department of Veterans Affairs. Since 1995, the technique has been used by a number of agencies in addition to the Navy and the Department of Veterans Affairs, including the Social Security Administration (facility management services), the Department of Energy (nuclear fuel facility design, construction, operation, and maintenance), the Department of the Treasury (mobile x-ray services), the Department of the Army (demilitarization of ammunition), and the Environmental Protection Agency (technical services). (Attachment 2 is a list of GAO decisions that mention the LOCAR technique.) This article will describe the LOCAR technique and explain how to use it in source selections conducted pursuant to Federal Acquisition Regulation (FAR) Part 15.

The LOCAR technique is a form of risk assessment that is coupled with a scoring mechanism. The underlying assumption of the LOCAR technique is that the selection of any contractor entails some risk, because one can never be certain what result an offeror will produce if selected for contract award; accordingly, agencies must try to determine how much value they think they would actually receive from each offeror and compare offerors on the basis of expected value rather than promised value. When using the technique an agency (1) determines the value of the promises that each offeror has made; (2) determines how much confidence it has that each offeror will keep its promises; (3) adjusts its assessments of each offeror's promised value on the basis of its level of confidence in the offeror, converting *promised value* to *expected value*; and (4) considers its assessment of each offeror's *expected value* when making nonprice/price tradeoffs in order to determine which offeror represents the best value.

The LOCAR technique employs numerical scoring. Since many acquisition practitioners are wary about the use of numerical scoring in source selection, a few words about numerical scoring are appropriate at this time. The LOCAR technique is a framework for thinking, not a formula for decision making. It uses numerals as shorthand for substantive verbal descriptions of an offeror and its proposal. When employing the LOCAR technique in a source selection, the source selection authority uses the scores to order his or her thinking *initially*, but makes the source selection decision based on the documented advantages and disadvantages of the competing offerors and their proposals. The LOCAR technique is a device for thinking about a problem of choice. A LOCAR is a product of subjective judgment; it is not a precise measurement of an objective reality. Everyone who uses or plans to use the LOCAR technique must understand that it is just a device and that tradeoffs and source selection decisions must be made, explained, and justified on the basis of the documented pros and cons of the competing offerors and their proposals, and not the LOCAR scores. Those who work for organizations that forbid the use of numerical scores, or who cannot overcome their aversion to the use of numerals, can still use the LOCAR technique, but must use words or other symbolic devices (e.g., color ratings) instead of numbers. See Attachment 1 for the LOCAR numerical scale and possible adjectival substitutes.

AN OVERVIEW OF THE LOCAR TECHNIQUE

In overview, the LOCAR technique includes the following steps:

1. First, the evaluators assess the nonprice promises in each of the competing offers based on the stated evalu-

ation factors for award and give each offer a numerical score on a scale of 0 to 100 points (or an adjectival rating) to summarize their assessment of the offer's value. This score is called the *promised value score.*

2. Second, the evaluators assess each offeror's capability based on the factors stated in the RFP, including experience and past performance and any other factors that bear on the offeror's *ability* to perform. The evaluators write descriptions of their assessment findings but do not assign numerical scores.

3. Third, the evaluators meet and talk to reach a consensus about how much confidence they have in each offeror that it will keep its promises, based on their assessments of the offeror's capabilities, and they give each offeror a LOCAR, which is a numerical score on a decimal scale of between 0 and 1. (See Attachment 1.) The higher the evaluators' confidence in the offeror, the higher the rating. Thus, a LOCAR of .1 would indicate that the evaluators have very little confidence in an offeror; a LOCAR of .9 would indicate a very high level of confidence; and a LOCAR of .5 would indicate that the evaluators think the likelihood that the offeror will keep its promises is 50-50.

4. Finally, the evaluators multiply the *promised value* score by the LOCAR to produce the *expected value* score. For example, if an offeror has a promised value score of 90 points and a LOCAR of .8, its expected value score would be 72 (90 x .8 = 72); if an offeror has a promised value score of 100 and a LOCAR of .5, its expected value score would be 50.

The source selection authority then compares the offerors to each other based on their expected values and prices in order to *initially* rank them from best to worst. He or she then compares the offerors in a series of pairs based on the detailed evaluation documentation, making tradeoffs as necessary in order to identify the offeror that represents the best value. The table below illustrates what such a comparison might look like.

Offeror	Promised Value	LOCAR	Expected Value	Price
A	98	.6	59 (58.8)	$1,000,000
B	87	.9	78 (78.3)	$1,100,000

Note that Offeror A initially seems to offer a better value than Offeror B, but that after development and application of the LOCAR, Offeror B seems to be the better value on the basis of the evaluators' higher confidence in its ability to keep its promises. It is up to the source selection authority to decide what to do on the basis of this information.

ESSENTIAL BACKGROUND: OFFERS AND INFORMATION

When evaluating proposals in a source selection, agencies evaluate two things: the offerors and the offers that they make. There are two general categories of evaluation factors: offer factors and offeror capability factors. The offer factors pertain to what the offeror promises to do or deliver; the offeror capability factors pertain to the offeror's ability, as a firm, to keep its promises.

Every *proposal* submitted in response to a government request for proposals consists of two main parts: (1) an offer and (2) information about the offeror. The offer is a set of promises that become binding upon acceptance by the government. It consists of nonprice promises about the product or service that the offeror will deliver or render, and a promise either to do the work for a stated price or to try to do the work within an estimated cost and for a stated fee. The information about the offeror includes its certifications and representations, and information about its experience, past performance, management policies and procedures, key personnel, and prospective subcontractors, etc.

When an agency prepares an RFP it must decide what kind of offers (promises) it wants from offerors. The simplest offer is a promise to comply with the specification or statement of work and the contract clauses in the RFP. A more complex offer might include offeror-specific promises about service performance levels and product attributes. So-called "technical" and "management" proposals—in which offerors describe their "approach" to doing this or that—may or may not be promises from a legal standpoint; they may be nothing more than estimates, opinions, predictions, statements of business policy, or statements of contingent intention. As such, they might tell an agency something about an offeror's knowledge and ability, but they do not promise to do any specific thing or to do anything in a specific way. It is therefore important for the contracting officer to determine whether such technical and management proposals, if required, are to be offers (promises) or merely information that reveals the offerors' capabilities. The RFP proposal preparation instructions and descriptions of the evaluation factors for award must be written accordingly, and all members of the evaluation team must be properly informed, so that they know whether they are reading promises or just information.

THE PROPOSAL EVALUATION PROCESS IN GENERAL

In order to evaluate an offer (promises), an agency must do three things: first, it must determine what the offer says; second, it must determine how good or how bad the offer is in terms of the specified evaluation factors; and third, it must determine how well the offer compares to competing offers. Before performing the third step the agency should consciously decide how credible the offer is. It must ask itself: Do we think that if we accept this offer we will we get what we are being promised at the proposed price or the estimated cost and proposed fee? This is a matter of subjective probability assessment.

The credibility of an offer depends in part on what we know about the firm that made it. An offer that would be credible if it came from one firm might not be credible if it came from another. For example, an offer to do complicated and difficult work might be credible if made by a firm that has successfully performed that kind of work many times, but it might not be credible if made by a firm that has never done that kind of work. Thus, when performing the second step in an evaluation—determining how good or how bad the offer is in terms of the specified evaluation factors for award—an agency must ponder the possible difference between *promised value* and *expected value*. An offer might *promise* great value, but when considered in light of its source its expected value might be less, perhaps much less.

AN ILLUSTRATION OF THE LOCAR TECHNIQUE

Suppose that an agency issued an RFP for services. The RFP described the services and included a complete set of contract clauses. The services were complex in nature and would have to be performed under moderately difficult conditions. The RFP instructed offerors to promise that they would perform in accordance with the Government's terms and to propose a firm-fixed-price. It also instructed them to (1) submit specified information about their experience doing the kind of work described by the RFP, (2) furnish the names of references that would provide information about their past performance, and (3) provide information about certain of their key personnel. The RFP stated that the agency would award the contract without discussions, but that it reserved the right to conduct discussions if in the Government's interests to do so.

The RFP said that the agency would select the contractor on the basis of: (a) the acceptability of the offer; (b) the offeror's experience and past performance, (c) the qualifications of its key personnel; and (d) the reasonableness of its proposed price. The RFP said that the nonprice factors, when combined, would be significantly more important than price. It said that offer acceptability was the most important nonprice factor and that acceptability would be evaluated on a pass or fail basis. Experience was the second most important nonprice factor. Past performance and key personnel were equally important and together constituted the third most important nonprice factors. The RFP said that the agency would compare the offerors and make nonprice/price tradeoffs on the basis of the expected value of their offers, and that in order to determine expected value the agency would develop a LOCAR for each offeror, based on what it learned about the offeror's experience, past performance, and key personnel.

The RFP said that an offer would be acceptable on a pass or fail basis if it manifested the offeror's assent to the terms of the model contract without exception or condition. It said that acceptable offers would be given a score of 100 points and that unacceptable offers would be given a score of 0 points, and that this score would be considered the "promised value" of the offer.

The RFP said that the agency would assess each offeror's experience on the basis of the number of jobs it had performed in which it had done similar work under similar conditions. It said that when evaluating past performance the agency would assess the quality of the work that the offeror had done based on the statements of its references and on other information that the agency could obtain from other sources. It said that key personnel would be evaluated on the basis of experience, reputation, and formal education, in that order.

The RFP also said that the agency would assign to each offeror a LOCAR decimal rating on a scale of between 0 and 1. The LOCAR was to be based on the agency's subjective assessment of the offeror's experience, past performance, and key personnel. A LOCAR of 0 would indicate that the agency had no confidence in the offeror and believed that it would probably fail to keep one or more of its promises and thus would perform unsatisfactorily. A LOCAR of 1 would indicate that the agency had complete confidence in the offeror and believed that if given the contract the offeror would keep all of its promises and perform satisfactorily. A LOCAR of .5 would indicate that the agency thought that the chances were 50-50 that the offeror would either keep its promises or not. The RFP said that the agency would not assign either a 0 or a 1, since such scores would indicate absolute certainty, but would assign a LOCAR of between .1 and .9.

Finally, the RFP said that the agency would determine the expected value of each offer by multiplying its promised value by the assigned LOCAR. Thus, if an offeror submitted an acceptable proposal and received a LOCAR of .7, its expected value would be 70 (100 x .7 = 70). The RFP said that the agency would *initially* compare the offers to each other and rank them on the basis of expected value and price; however, it said that the source selection authority would use the LOCAR and the expected value score only as aids to decisionmaking analysis, and would base the selection decision on the documented pros and cons of the offerors and their offers.

The agency received four proposals in response to its RFP. The contracting officer immediately checked the offerors' certifications and representations and checked their offers for completeness, compliance with the proposal preparation instructions, and for any exceptions or conditions with respect to the solicitation's terms. He found that one offeror (Offeror B) had taken exception to the warranty of services clause and that its offer was, therefore, unacceptable. He wrote a memorandum for record describing his findings and set the offer aside. It would not be considered further, since it could be made acceptable only through discussions, and the agency did not plan to conduct discussions. If the agency changed its mind and decided to conduct discussions, the contracting officer would re-examine the proposal and determine whether or not to include it in the competitive range.

The contracting officer convened the agency evaluation board and instructed them to assess the offerors' experience, past performance, and key personnel. The evaluation board contacted the references provided by the offerors and did some independent investigating by contacting state licensing officials and boards and by searching the Federal Procurement Data Center, the Internet, and LexisNexis®. The board wrote one memorandum for record for each offeror describing their findings. Once this work had been done the summary results were as follows:

Offeror	Offer	Experience	Past Performance	Key Personnel	Price
A	100	1 similar job	Excellent	Good	$15,430,000
B	0*	10 similar jobs	Very good	Excellent	$15,700,000
C	100	7 similar jobs	Excellent	Very Good	$15,590,000
D	100	None	No record	Excellent	$15,420,000

*Offeror B took exception to the warranty of services clause.

In order to develop LOCARs the contracting officer assembled the evaluation board and proceeded on an offeror-by-offeror basis, asking each of them to review the findings about each offeror's experience, past performance, and key personnel. He then asked them: Based on the information you have reviewed, would you say that the offeror is (a) more likely to succeed than to fail, (b) more likely to fail than to succeed, or that (c) it is a toss-up between success and failure? He explained that "to succeed" did not mean to perform perfectly or superlatively, but to perform acceptably, so that the agency would be willing to do business with the firm again. He also explained that "to fail" did not mean complete failure or default, but that performance is less than fully satisfactory and that the agency would be unwilling to do business with the firm again. For Offeror A there was a consensus that it was more likely to succeed, so the contracting officer then asked: Do you think that the offeror is closer to certain success or to a toss-up? Closer to certain success would mean a LOCAR of .8 or .9; closer to a toss-up would mean a LOCAR of .6 or .7. The vote was split on this question, but most evaluators favored closer to a toss-up. The contracting officer encouraged discussion and exchanges of views in order to reach a consensus of .65.

Proceeding in this way, conducting votes and encouraging discussion and debate, the contracting officer led the evaluators to a consensus about a LOCAR for each offeror. In one or two cases the group decided that they needed more information, and the contracting officer sought clarification from an offeror in accordance with FAR 15.306(a) or obtained additional information from other sources. The contracting officer made sure that everyone understood that LOCAR development was subjective, that a LOCAR was merely shorthand for a set of opinions, and that a LOCAR did not represent any objective reality.

Based on its assessments of the offerors' experience, past performance, and key personnel, the agency assigned the following LOCARS and expected values:

Offeror	Promised Value	LOCAR	Expected Value
A	100	.65	65
B	0	N/A	N/A
C	100	.9	90
D	100	.5	50

In assigning a LOCAR of .65 to Offeror A, the evaluators decided that the offeror's one similar contract was only very limited experience with the complex and moderately difficult work that the offeror would have to perform. They thought that Offeror A was more likely to succeed than to fail, but did not feel confident that it was highly likely to succeed.

After consulting with the source selection authority, the contracting officer instructed the evaluators not to assign a LOCAR to Offeror B, because its offer was unacceptable and the only way it could be made acceptable would be through discussions. The contracting officer and the source selection authority agreed that Offeror B did not have any advantages over the other offerors that would warrant the conduct of discussions to improve its proposal.

The evaluators assigned a LOCAR of .9 to Offeror C based on its extensive experience, its very good past performance, and the qualities of its key personnel, which had been with the firm for many years.

Finally, the evaluators assigned a LOCAR of .5 to Offeror D. Since the offeror had no record of past performance the agency did not take its past performance into account in developing the LOCAR. Although it proposed excellent key personnel, those persons were new to the firm, and the evaluators decided that in light of the firm's lack of any experience and the newness of its key personnel, its chances of success were, at best, 50-50.

The contracting officer wrote a memorandum for record about the deliberations concerning each offeror in order to document the basis for its assigned LOCAR and expected value. He also wrote a memorandum for record that summarized the overall findings of the evaluation board and presented it to the source selection authority along with the other documentation. The summary findings were as follows:

Offeror	Promised Value	LOCAR	Expected Value	Proposed Price
A	100	.65	65	$15,430,000
C	100	.9	90	$15,590,000
D	100	.5	50	$15,420,000

The source selection authority used the summary findings to make initial comparisons among the offerors. She then referred to the detailed findings of the board and the record of the LOCAR deliberations to confirm or adjust her initial comparisons, made tradeoffs, and selected Offeror C. In comparing Offeror A to Offeror C, the source selection authority decided that Offeror C was the better value. Offeror C's more extensive experience and better staff made C a better risk and worth the $60,000 price premium, since marginal performance could cost the agency much more than $60,000. Comparing Offeror C to Offeror D, the source selection authority decided that Offeror C's much more extensive experience outweighed Offeror D's slightly better staff and that it was worth the $80,000 difference to get the benefit of that experience. The source selection authority made notes of the tradeoffs she made and the reasons for her selection decision and instructed the contracting officer to make the award. The contracting officer used the source selection authority's notes to prepare a memorandum for record documenting her tradeoff analysis and the bases for her decision, obtained her approval of the memorandum, and proceeded to make the award.

In this illustration the LOCAR helped the agency to understand the relationship among the offers it received and the capabilities of the offerors. The LOCAR was not essential to the decisionmaking process and did not determine the outcome of the source selection, but it helped to structure the process by providing a mechanism for integrating the various findings about the offers and the offerors' capabilities.

ANOTHER ILLUSTRATION

In the last illustration all offerors made identical offers of services, except for their proposed prices, and the agency evaluated the offers only for acceptability, on a pass or fail basis. What if an agency asks offerors to propose offeror-unique products that might have varying degrees of value depending on the product attributes?

Suppose that an agency issued an RFP that requested offers for a commercial product that would perform a certain function. The RFP specified certain product performance attributes, such as reliability measured in mean time between failures and maintainability measured in mean time to repair, and minimum levels of performance for each such attribute. The RFP said that the agency would determine best value based on (a) the acceptability of offers, (b) the relative extent to which the offered products met or exceeded the minimum performance level for each of the specified performance attributes, (c) the offeror's relative production experience and past performance, (d) the agency's subjective level of confidence that the offeror would keep its promises about quality and delivery, and (e) price.

The RFP said that the agency would select the contractor on the basis of: (a) the acceptability of its offer, (b) the extent to which its proposed product exceeded minimum performance requirements, (c) the offeror's relative production experience and past performance, and (d) the reasonableness of its proposed price. The RFP said that the nonprice factors were equally important and that, when combined, they would be significantly more important than price. The RFP said that the agency would compare the offerors and make nonprice/price tradeoffs on the basis of the expected value of their offers, and that in order to determine expected value the agency would develop a LOCAR for each offeror, based on what it learned about the offeror's experience, past performance, and key personnel.

The RFP said that the agency would evaluate offer acceptability on a pass or fail basis. It said that the evaluation of acceptability would be based on the offeror's assent to the specifications and contract clauses without exception or condition, and on its express promise to meet all minimum product requirements. It said that the agency would further evaluate acceptable offers to the extent that they promised to exceed specified minimum product requirements. The RFP said that the agency would compare the offerors and make nonprice/price tradeoffs on the basis of the expected value of their offers, and that in order to determine expected value the agency would develop a LOCAR for each offeror based on what it learned about the offeror's production experience and past performance. It said that the agency intended to make an award without discussions but reserved the right to conduct discussions if it would be in the government's best interests.

The RFP said that an unacceptable offer would receive 0 points and would not be evaluated further, unless the source selection authority decided that it would be in the government's best interests to conduct discussions. Acceptable offers would receive 50 points. The RFP said that acceptable offers could receive up to 50 additional points based on the extent to which they promised that their products would exceed the specified minimum levels of performance. It said that an offer's total score for offer acceptability and exceeding the minimum levels of performance would be considered the offer's *promised value*. The RFP also said that the evaluators would assign to each offeror a LOCAR on a scale of between 0 and 1, based on their assessment of the offeror's production experience and past performance, and that the evaluators would determine the *expected value* of each offer by multiplying its promised value by the assigned LOCAR. The RFP said that the agency would not assign either a 0 or a 1, since such scores would indicate absolute certainty, but would assign a LOCAR of between .1 and .9. Finally, the RFP said that the source selection authority would use the expected value score as an aid to decisionmaking analysis but that he would select the contractor on the basis of the evaluators' substantively documented findings about product quality and offeror capability.

The agency received five offers, and the contracting officer examined each to determine whether or not it was acceptable. Four offers were acceptable, and she assigned 50 points to each of them. One offer was unacceptable because it took exception to a minimum requirement, so the contracting officer set it aside. Three of the acceptable offers promised performance in excess of the minimum requirements, so she sent them to the evaluation board's technical panel for assessment. The evaluators considered each offer based on the promised levels of performance and the technical credibility of the promises and scored them accordingly. Meanwhile, an offeror capability evaluation panel assessed each offeror's production experience and past performance. The results of this initial phase of the evaluation were as follows:

Offeror	Offer Acceptability	Performance in Excess of Minimums	Promised Value	Production Experience	Past Performance	Unit Price
A	50	45	95	Slight	Good	$185,000
B	50	0	50	Extensive	Excellent	$145,000
C	0	Not evaluated	0	Not evaluated	Not evaluated	$180,000
D	50	25	75	Good	Fair-Poor	$170,000
D	50	20	70	Very Good	Very Good	$175,000

The contracting officer convened a joint meeting of the technical panel and the offeror capability evaluation panel in order to develop a LOCAR. They considered one offeror at a time.

The panel assigned a LOCAR of .6 to Offeror A. While its past performance was good, it had produced and sold only a few units and had not yet achieved the production rate that would be necessary in order to meet the contract delivery requirements, which raised a question in the evaluators' minds about its ability to maintain product quality at a higher production rate. The few customers for the product liked it and said delivery had been timely, but also said that they had not been using it very long. They said that the product did malfunction occasionally but that warranty service was good.

The panel assigned Offeror B a LOCAR of .9. Its product had been in production for more than three years and at a rate that was more than enough to meet the contract delivery requirements while maintaining quality. Its customers liked the product, said that delivery had been timely, and said that warranty service, though rarely needed, was excellent.

The panel assigned Offeror D a LOCAR of .4. The offeror had produced a significant number of units and at a rate high enough to meet the contract delivery requirements, but its customers said that while the product was good when it worked, it malfunctioned in troublesome ways too often, despite the offeror's test data, and that while product delivery had been timely, warranty service was slow and not always effective on the first visit. Most of its customers said that they would not buy the product again, despite its advertised performance.

The panel assigned Offeror E a LOCAR of .8. It had produced a large number of units at a production rate adequate to meet contract delivery requirements. Its customers liked the product very much, said delivery had been timely, and said that malfunctions were infrequent. They said that when they did call for warranty service it was occasionally slow, but always effective on the first try, and that the company was working hard to respond more quickly.

After developing the LOCARs and determining each offeror's expected value, the results were as follows:

Offeror	Total Promised Value	LOCAR	Expected Value	Unit Price
A	95	.6	57	$185,000
B	50	.9	45	$145,000
C	0	N/A	N/A	$180,000
D	75	.4	30	$170,000
E	70	.8	56	$175,000

The contracting officer wrote a memorandum for record for each offeror, which explained the basis for the offeror's LOCAR. He then collected the documentation prepared by the technical evaluation panel and the offeror capability evaluation panel and submitted the package to the source selection authority for consideration. The source selection authority compared the offerors to each other in a series of pairs to rank them from best to worst. First, he ranked them on the basis of their expected value scores and prices. His initial impression was that Offeror E was the best value. He then considered the detailed information contained in the evaluation documentation.

Comparing Offeror A to Offeror B, the source selection authority decided that Offeror A was the better value, mainly because of its product performance. He decided that the additional technical performance would be worth the $40,000 difference in unit price, since it would mean that the product would have a longer service life for his agency. He was willing to take the risk posed by Offeror A's slight production experience, thinking that its evident desire to make its product a success would motivate it to maintain product quality at higher production rates.

Comparing Offeror A to Offeror D, he decided that Offeror A was the better value, since its product had more technical promise and its past performance was better. Although Offeror A did not have as much production experience as Offeror D and had a higher price, he felt that Offeror D's poor quality and warranty service made it a greater risk, and he was willing to pay $15,000 to avoid that risk.

However, after comparing Offeror A to Offeror E, he decided that Offeror E was the better value. Although Offeror E's product did not have as much technical promise as Offeror A's, it was good enough to meet the agency's needs for the foreseeable future, and the product's very good reputation, the offeror's good and improving warranty service, and its lower price made it the better value.

The source selection authority also compared Offeror E to Offerors B and D. The choice boiled down to a tradeoff between the expectation of better product capability from Offeror E against Offeror B's slightly better past performance and its lower price, since Offeror D's fair-poor past performance put it out of the running. The source selection authority was still inclined toward Offeror E but decided to consult with the contracting officer and evaluation board before making a decision. After the consultation, the source selection authority selected Offeror E and notified the contracting officer accordingly.

The contracting officer and the evaluation board suggested to the source selection authority that the agency hold discussions to see if Offeror A could be persuaded to lower its price. The source selection authority assented, and the contracting officer established a competitive range that included only Offerors A and E. The contracting officer, the source selection authority, and the evaluation board agreed that Offeror B was at too much of a technical disadvantage to have any real chance of selection; Offeror C's product would have to be modified extensively to enable it to meet all of the minimum performance requirements, and there would be no test data to confirm the performance of its new design before contract award; and Offeror D's past performance was not good enough.

During discussions with Offeror A the contracting officer asked for a price reduction of "at least" five percent. She also asked for a description of what the offeror could and would do to maintain product quality at higher production rates, and for specific reliability and warranty service targets coupled with stipulated price reductions for failing to meet the targets. During discussions with Offeror E the contracting officer asked for the offeror's best possible price, and also asked for reliability and warranty service targets coupled with stipulated price reductions for failing to meet the targets. The contracting officer then asked both offerors for final proposal revisions, telling them that the source selection authority would consider their reliability targets and target price reduction packages along with the other evaluation factors in making his decision. She said that the source selection authority would consider performance in excess of minimums, production experience, past performance, the reliability packages, and price to be equal in importance.

Offeror A's revised price was $179,000, and it offered a package of reliability and warranty service targets with price reductions for failure to meet targets. Offeror E's revised price was $173,000 and also came with a package of reliability and warranty service targets and target failure price reductions. The evaluators reconsidered the promised value scores based on the reliability targets and decided not to change the scores or the LOCARs. The source selection authority considered the offerors' unchanged expected values and their reliability and warranty service target packages and, after consultation with the contracting officer and the evaluation board, decided that Offeror E was still the better value based mainly on its better production experience and lower price. The contracting officer awarded the contract to Offeror E at the source selection authority's direction.

In both of the above illustrations the LOCAR technique helped the evaluation boards to integrate their assessments of the offerors' promises and capabilities, and it provided the source selection authority with both a framework and a focus for tradeoff analysis and decisionmaking. However, in neither case did the LOCAR determine the outcome of the competition. It served only as an analytical device.

THE NATURE AND FUNCTION OF THE LOCAR

A LOCAR is not a score for an offeror's capability; it is not an expression of the value of an offeror's experience, past performance, or key personnel, etc. A LOCAR is an expression of an agency's confidence in an offeror, based on the agency's assessment of certain qualities of the offeror as an organization—the nature, depth, and breadth of its experience; the quality of its past performance; the qualifications of its key employees, etc. A LOCAR of .6 to .9 indicates that an agency is confident that an offeror will do well in terms of its promises if given the contract. A LOCAR of .1 to .4 indicates that an agency is not confident that the offeror will do well. A LOCAR of .5 indicates that the agency thinks the offeror is equally likely to do well or poorly—it is a 50-50 toss-up.

The function of the LOCAR technique is to help an agency to think about how an offeror's capability affects the value of its offer, i.e., its promises. The LOCAR technique requires the evaluators to contemplate the significance of their assessments of an offeror's capability and to ponder what those assessments might mean in terms of the promises the offeror has made. In order to develop a LOCAR the evaluators must consider the offeror's capabilities and ask themselves: What might this mean for the future? Based on what we know about this firm, what are the chances that we'll actually get what it has promised?

OFFERORS WITHOUT A RECORD OF PAST PERFORMANCE

Since past performance is a capability factor that contributes to LOCAR development, what if an offeror has no record of past performance? How should this affect a LOCAR? FAR 15.305(a)(2)(iv) says:

> In the case of an offeror without a record of past performance or for whom information on past performance is not available, the offeror may not be evaluated favorably or unfavorably on past performance.

A LOCAR is not a score for past performance, per se. It is an expression of an agency's confidence in an offeror, based in part on its past performance and on other capability factors. If past performance is the only capability factor, and if an offeror has no record of past performance, then the only LOCAR that an agency could logically give to the offeror would be .5, which would signify that the agency thinks performance might be either satisfactory or unsatisfactory. However, when evaluating an offeror's capability, it is best not to limit the assessment to past performance. At a minimum, a capability assessment should be based upon both experience and past performance, with experience being an assessment of *what* and *how much* work the offeror has done and past performance being an assessment of *how well* the offeror did its work. If an offeror has had no experience with the kind of work that it would have to perform under a contract, then an agency should take that into consideration when developing a LOCAR; however, with no record of past performance the agency cannot assess performance quality. Thus, the lack of a record of past performance should not affect the development of the LOCAR, but a lack of experience should affect the LOCAR.

THE LOCAR DEVELOPMENT PROCESS

The best way to develop a LOCAR is through discussion and debate among the evaluators leading to a consensus. After the evaluators have assessed the offerors' capabilities based on the factors identified in the solicitation, someone, perhaps the contracting officer, should lead the evaluators in a series of meetings, one for each offeror, in order to develop a LOCAR for each offeror.

The leader should begin by asking the evaluators to individually review the findings about the offeror's capabilities. This can be done either before the meeting or at its start, depending on the volume of the evaluation documentation. After the evaluators have familiarized themselves with the findings, the leader should ask them to individually place the offeror into one of three categories: (a) more likely to succeed than to fail, (b) more likely to fail than to succeed, or (c) equally likely to succeed or to fail. The leader should instruct the participants that "success" means satisfactory performance, not flawless or superlative performance, and that "failure" means unsatisfactory performance, but not necessarily default. The leader should instruct the participants not to assign any LOCAR number at this point, because once a person has settled on a number in his or her own mind it becomes harder to keep an open mind, and the discussion focuses prematurely on which number to assign, which makes achievement of a consensus more difficult.

Once all of the evaluators have placed the offeror into one of the three LOCAR categories, the leader should tally the results and determine whether or not there is a categorical consensus. If there is no consensus the leader should encourage the participants to discuss the evaluation findings and exchange views. After a reasonable amount of discussion the leader should ask the evaluators to again individually place the offeror into a category. If there is still a wide disparity of views after the second categorization, then there is a serious problem that must be resolved before any progress can be made. The contracting officer and the leader of the evaluation team should meet to discuss what to do next.

Assuming that the evaluators agree, more or less, on the category in which the offeror belongs—for instance, a significant majority believe that the offeror is more likely to succeed than to fail, and one or two evaluators think that the chances are 50-50—the leader should ask those who placed the offeror in the more-likely-to-succeed category to decide whether they think that the offeror is closer to certain success or to 50-50. (If the majority believes that the offeror is more likely to fail than to succeed, the leader should ask whether the offeror is closer to 50-50 or to certain failure.) Again, the leader should instruct the participants not to choose a number, but to select a category. Those who think that the offeror is closer to 50-50 presumably would assign a LOCAR of either .6 or a .7. Those who think that the offeror is closer to certain success presumably would assign a LOCAR of .8 or .9. When each participant has placed the offeror in a category the leader should again tally the results and encourage discussion and debate to arrive at a consensus. Only when a categorical consensus has been achieved should the leader permit the group to try to settle on a specific LOCAR number. As a matter of convention, do not assign a LOCAR of 0 or 1, since those numbers signify absolute certainty; assign a number in the range of .1 to .9. Compromises can be reached by settling on midpoints, such a .65 or .85. The leader should encourage group discussion until there is a general consensus (though perhaps not a perfect agreement).

A good leader should be able to lead a small group to a consensus about the first offeror within two hours. Each succeeding case will require less time as the group becomes more familiar and comfortable with the process. The leader should be on the lookout for participant fatigue or participant alienation, which might lead to a hasty or false consensus. Take a break at the first sign of group fatigue; take a break and try to solve problems of participant alienation at the first sign of it.

The LOCAR technique is an approach to thinking about the value of an offer. Various agencies have used it successfully in various ways for almost ten years. Its usefulness lies in the process of LOCAR development, during which the evaluators think about their confidence in an offeror's promises from the standpoint of their knowledge about and assessment of the offeror's capabilities, and exchange views. The result is that the source selection authority bases his or her decision on *expected value*, rather than mere *promised value*. Commitment to the process is the key to using the LOCAR technique effectively.

Attachment A

THE LOCAR SCALE

1.0 Success is certain (complete confidence)
0.9
0.8
0.7
0.6
0.5 Success and failure are equally likely
0.4
0.3
0.2
0.1
0.0 Failure is certain (no confidence)

"Success" means that the contractor performs satisfactorily but not flawlessly or in a superlative manner.

"Failure" means that the customer was not satisfied with the contractor's performance, not that the contractor failed completely or defaulted.

Those forbidden or unwilling to use numerals can use an adjectival scale. While awkward to use, such a scale can be made to work. Examples include:

Highly confident
Very confident
More confident
Confident
Somewhat confident
50-50
Somewhat unconfident
Unconfident
More unconfident
Very unconfident
Highly unconfident

Confident++++
Confident+++
Confident++
Confident+
Confident
50-50
Unconfident
Unconfident–
Unconfident– –
Unconfident– – –
Unconfident– – – –

Attachment B

GOVERNMENT ACCOUNTABILITY OFFICE PROTEST DECISIONS

The protest decisions listed below describe or mention a use of the LOCAR process.

Title	*File Number*	*Date*	*Agency*	*Result*
Moore Medical Corp.	B-261758	Oct. 26, 1995	Veterans Affairs	Denied
Resource Applications	B-274943.3	Mar. 5, 1997	EPA	Denied
Advanced Designs Corp.	B-275928	Apr. 21, 1997	Navy	Denied
UNICCO Government Services	B-277658	Nov. 7, 1997	Social Security	Denied
WECO Cleaning Specialists	B-279305	Jun. 3, 1998	Social Security	Denied
Buck Environmental Technologies	B-280520	Oct. 14, 1998	Army	Denied
Duke Engineering & Services	B-284605	May 17, 2000	Energy	Denied
Oregon Iron Works	B-284088.2	Jun. 15, 2000	Navy	Denied
North American Aerodynamics	B-285651	Sep. 15, 2000	Navy	Denied
Digital Imaging Acquisition Networking Assocs.	B-285396.3	Nov. 8, 2000	Treasury	Denied
Colmek Systems Engineering	B-291931.2	Ju. 9, 2003	Navy	Denied
AdapTech General Scientific, LLC	B-293867	Jun. 4, 2004	Navy	Denied

Acronyms

AFFARS	Air Force Federal Acquisition Regulation Supplement
BAA	broad agency announcement
C.F.R.	Code of Federal Regulations
CBD	*Commerce Business Daily*
CICA	Competition in Contracting Act
CLIN	contract line item number
DCAA	Defense Contract Audit Agency
DFARS	Department of Defense Federal Acquisition Regulation Supplement
DoD	Department of Defense (also, DOD)
DOE	Department of Energy
DRFP	draft request for proposals
EPA	Environmental Protection Agency
FAC	Federal Acquisition Circular
FAR	Federal Acquisition Regulation

FedBizOpps	Federal Business Opportunities website (also, fedbizopps)
Fed. Reg.	Federal Register
FFRDC	federally funded research and development center
FR	Federal Register
GAO	Government Accountability Office (formerly, General Accounting Office)
GSA	General Services Administration
GSBCA	General Services Board of Contract Appeals
HCA	head of the contracting activity
ID/IQ	indefinite delivery/indefinite quantity
IFB	invitation for bids
LOCAR	level of confidence assessment rating
NAICS	North American Industry Classification System
NMCARS	Navy Marine Corps Acquisition Regulation Supplement
NASA	National Aeronautics and Space Administration
NFS	NASA FAR Supplement
NRC	Nuclear Regulatory Commission

OFPP	Office of Federal Procurement Policy
OMB	Office of Management and Budget
PRDA	program research and development announcement
RFI	request for information
RFO	request for offers
RFP	request for proposals
RFQ	request for quotations
SBA	Small Business Administration
SIC	standard industrial classification
SOO	statement of objectives
SSA	source selection authority
SSAC	source selection advisory council
SSO	source selection official
TINA	Truth in Negotiations Act
U.S.C.	United States Code
UCLINS	uniform contract line item numbering system

Index

B

C

E

F

M

N

O

P

Q

R

S

T

U

V

W